Praise for *Heart of a Soldier*

"Stunning . . . Soldier of fortune, rugby star, big game hunter, decorated U.S. Army officer, vice president in a major financial firm, patriot, writer, singer, poet, and friend to all who ever knew him, Rick Rescorla was a character out of Hemingway or Kipling. Stewart brings this bona fide hero to life in ways small and larg

—Jim Haner, *Baltimore*

"Excellent . . . Stewart has chosen a subject and rendered it with glass-clear prose that leaves timate understanding of the story and its people. . . . Stewart's description of Rescorla's war experiences in Vietnam—blood, sweat, and terror—is gripping in its heroism as well as its horrors. . . . Stewart gives the reader a monument more enduring than the towers: a man's sacrifice, an act of love that saved thousands of lives and made the dark wickedness of that day a backdrop for the triumph of heroic virtue."

—Christopher E. Baldwin, *National Review*

"Stewart weaves together an almost Forrest Gump–like tale of a man who would touch history and make history."

—Lynn Bronikowski, *Rocky Mountain News*

"James B. Stewart writes with such unblinking honesty about Rescorla that what you are left with is not the portrait of a hero (although if that word has any meaning, Rescorla deserves the title) but that he was one decent guy, a funny thing to conclude about a man whose life was devoted for so long to killing."

—Margo Hammond, *St. Petersburg Times*

"Stewart's painstakingly gathered accounts are crafted into a narrative that reads like fiction, letting the richness of events, personality, and anecdote do their work. . . . A meticulous account."

—Diane M. Bacha, *Milwaukee Journal Sentinel*

"Stunningly detailed . . . movingly rendered."

—Dorothy Rabinowitz, *The Wall Street Journal*

"Stewart writes with enviable precision and careful foreshadowing. . . . His battle scenes are riveting."

—Stephen J. Dubner, *The New York Times Book Review*

"A fast and compelling story . . . of duty, love, and devotion. Through the eyes of Rick Rescorla, Stewart shows the magnitude of the loss of Sept. 11, both in its effect on the nation and on the thousands of people with an immediate connection."

—Ray Locker, Associated Press

Read July 2003 —
an account of two men &
their friendship — and of steady
lines of devotion to duty — shows
heroism as normal & broke action see
day to day in the line of duty — about
page 276 (fescoular) words about
heroic action

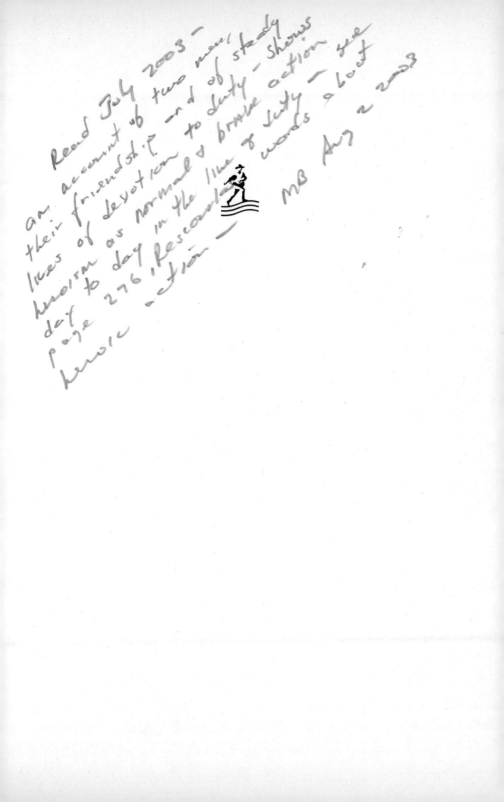

MB Aug 2 2003

ALSO BY JAMES B. STEWART

Blind Eye
Follow the Story
Blood Sport
Den of Thieves
The Prosecutors
The Partners

Second Lieutenant Rick Rescorla in the Vietnamese Central Highlands, 1965.
(Courtesy of Susan Rescorla)

HEART OF
A SOLDIER

James B. Stewart

Epilogue by Susan Rescorla

Simon & Schuster

NEW YORK   LONDON   TORONTO   SYDNEY   SINGAPORE

SIMON & SCHUSTER
Rockefeller Center
1230 Avenue of the Americas
New York, NY 10020

Copyright © 2002 by James B. Stewart
All rights reserved,
including the right of reproduction
in whole or in part in any form.

First Simon & Schuster trade paperback edition 2003

SIMON & SCHUSTER and colophon are registered trademarks
of Simon & Schuster, Inc.

For information regarding special discounts for bulk purchases,
please contact Simon & Schuster Special Sales at 1-800-456-6798
or business@simonandschuster.com

Book design by Ellen R. Sasahara

Manufactured in the United States of America

1   3   5   7   9   10   8   6   4   2

The Library of Congress has cataloged the hardcover edition as follows:
Stewart, James B.
Heart of a soldier : a story of love heroism, and September 11th / James B.
Stewart; epilogue by Susan Rescorla.
p.   cm.
1. Rescorla, Rick, 1939–2001. 2. Police, Private—New York (State)—
New York—Biography. 3. Heroes—New York (State)—New York—
Biography. 4. September 11 Terrorist Attacks, 2001. 5. World Trade
Center (New York, N.Y.) 6. Rescue work—New York (State)—New
York. I. Title.
HV8291.U6 S748   2002   974.7'1044'092—dc21   [B]
2002029427

ISBN 0-7432-4098-7
0-7432-4459-1 (Pbk)

CONTENTS

PROLOGUE

SUSAN GREER HEARD footsteps approaching from behind. She instinctively pulled on the leash to bring her golden retriever, Buddy, closer beside her. It was just after six o'clock on a Saturday morning in July 1998. Susan wasn't used to seeing anyone on these early morning walks, especially on a weekend, when most of her neighbors in suburban Morristown, New Jersey, slept late and lingered over their coffee.

The sky that morning was clear and a soft blue, and already Susan could tell it would be a hot, humid day. She had gotten into the habit of rising early to walk Buddy, and she found that she liked the cooler air, the quiet, and the early morning light. On their walks, she and the dog rarely strayed from Dorado Drive, the street that wound through the complex of Spanish colonial-style town houses where Susan lived. She had moved there five years earlier, after her second marriage ended in divorce.

Susan was blond, attractive, and in good shape for a woman who was fifty-six years old. She jogged regularly, watched her diet, and shopped for stylish clothes—not that anyone would have guessed that from the way she looked that morning. After getting out of bed, Susan had pulled on a loose T-shirt and shorts, barely pausing to brush her hair. She wore no makeup or jewelry. Her mother would have been appalled, but her mother's world of formal lunches, afternoon teas, and antique doll collecting seemed to have vanished.

Susan wondered sometimes what had happened to that world during the years she spent raising children and working to support them. Unlike her mother, who had never held a job in her life, Susan worked as assistant to the president of a bank. She enjoyed foreign films and often went to the Roberts cinema in Chatham, either with women friends or, as was often the case, alone. She had begun venturing into Manhattan on weekends to visit art galleries and antique shops. She visited her daughters but didn't want to intrude on their busy lives. On most Friday evenings, like the night before, she came home from work, had a light supper, settled in with a book, and went to bed early. She didn't like to acknowledge it, but she knew it to be true: she was lonely.

Susan hadn't had a date in the five years since her divorce. She didn't encourage anyone, didn't go anywhere single men congregated, and no one had asked her out. At her age, twice divorced and with three grown children, she knew the odds of meeting an eligible man were so remote that she was better off not thinking about it.

Susan heard the footsteps coming closer. There was something odd about the sound of the steps. Then a jogger passed her. He was tall, a big man, about her age, wearing a knit shirt and tan slacks with the cuffs rolled up. But what really caught her attention was his feet. It wasn't like her to say anything to a stranger, but curiosity overcame her. "What are you doing jogging in your bare feet?" she asked.

The jogger kept running but slowed down. He said that he was writing a play set in Africa. "I need to know what it feels like to run without shoes," he said.

How intriguing, she thought. There weren't many writers in the neighborhood; most of the men commuted to Wall Street or the many corporate headquarters in suburban New Jersey. Susan thought she should leave it at that, but there was something in the man's voice that threw her off balance. Lately she had been thinking she had to take more risks. All her life she'd done the safe thing, the right thing, exactly what was expected of her. She had been told never to talk to strangers.

"Do you live here?" she asked, feeling slightly reckless.

He said he had moved in six months earlier so he could be close to his children and ex-wife.

"That's nice," Susan said. "Sometimes you can be better friends after a divorce."

Buddy was now tugging on his leash, straining to chase after the jogger, and Susan was briefly distracted. She couldn't see if the man had turned around to get a glimpse of her. Then he was out of earshot, picked up his pace, and disappeared around a bend in the road.

She hadn't seen his face. But there was something about his voice, she thought. It sounded so calm, so reassuring, so forthright. And he was single. He had managed to communicate a great deal in just a few sentences. She had a premonition that they would meet again.

Susan found herself at her driveway and turned to go into the house. She looked again to see if the jogger might have turned around, but the street was empty.

PEACHEY AND DRAVOT

Rick Rescorla (*right*) and Daniel J. Hill. In a remote outpost in Africa
they found friendship and adventure. *(Courtesy of Susan Rescorla)*

D ANIEL J. HILL crouched behind the crest of a large hill above
the bridge, his MAT 49, 9 mm submachine gun aimed just past
the stream. His position gave him a clear view of the only paved road
leading south from Elizabethtown, the capital of Katanga province in
the Congo. "They're coming," someone yelled. There was a flurry of
activity along the hilltop, as Hill's fellow soldiers in the Katanga police
force, in reality a paramilitary force fighting for the independence of
Katanga province, checked their Belgian semiautomatic rifles and took
their positions.

Through the shimmering heat, Hill could see the first of the Congolese troops in the distance. They looked tired and disorganized, walking rather than marching, dragging weapons behind them. Obviously the United Nations advisers assigned to the unit hadn't been able to instill much discipline. As the group moved closer, Hill estimated their number at about three hundred to four hundred men, the size of a small battalion. So this was the force the UN and the Congolese government of Patrice Lumumba had ordered south to subdue Katanga and capture its secessionist leader, Moïse Tshombe. Let them come, Hill thought to himself. He was ready, his adrenaline pumping.

Hill, a blond, blue-eyed American, had arrived in the Congo just two months before, in the summer of 1960. He had flown from New York to Berne, Switzerland, then to Cairo, and on to Mombasa, on the Kenyan coast. From there he had traveled by train to Nairobi, then hired a driver to take him to Elizabethtown, in the far southeastern corner of the newly independent Congo. When he arrived, he discovered a faded but still charming city that looked like a corner of the French colonial empire. Palm and banana trees shaded buildings with iron balconies that surrounded a central square. Restaurants served French and Belgian cuisine.

The Congo, granted independence by the Belgians in June 1960, just a year earlier, had rapidly become a hotbed of cold war intrigue and tribal factionalism. Lumumba had requested and accepted Soviet military assistance, leading the United States to conclude that he threatened America's vital interests in central Africa. The CIA launched an assassination plot to poison his toothbrush. An American was still something of an anomaly in Elizabethtown, but Hill didn't attract much attention. There were already plenty of white visitors and residents, including French, Belgians, and Germans. Many of them were connected to the giant Belgian mining concern, Union Minière de Haut Katanga. They had stayed behind when most Belgians fled the rest of the country, after Tshombe declared Katanga's independence and called for international support and recognition. They knew that

Tshombe's independence movement was in reality supported and largely financed by Union Minière, which feared nationalization under Lumumba.

Union Minière had promised Tshombe a fighting force that would make him president for life, and the company had advertised in London, Brussels, and Paris for experienced combat veterans. They were ostensibly being hired to train members of the Katanga civilian police force, the Gendarmerie, but the men who responded and were hired knew they were mercenaries in a war for Katangan independence. They formed a formidable military unit. Many of them were ex-Wehrmacht troops forced to surrender at the end of World War II. The French had offered them a way out of prisoner-of-war camps by recruiting them for the French Foreign Legion, then shipped the German soldiers to Indochina. They fought there until the French defeat in 1954, and then many had been sent to Algeria, where they fought in the brutal Algerian war for independence. They were hardened soldiers, paid directly by Union Minière in U.S. dollars, Swiss francs, or British pounds.

Hill reported to the company headquarters in Elizabethville and said he wanted to join the new Katanga military force. He produced his American passport, his recent discharge as a paratrooper in the U.S. Army, and a certificate showing his completion of the elite Ranger school at Fort Benning, Georgia. As an added bonus, he also spoke German. The recruiting officer immediately escorted Hill to Elizabethville's leading hotel, where he enjoyed a bath, clean sheets, and excellent cuisine. If anyone at Union Minière raised any questions or suspicions about Hill's qualifications, wondering, for example, what an American with Hill's credentials was doing in a remote, strife-torn corner of Africa, no one approached Hill about it. Given the job description, the company rarely asked many questions. Two days later, he was hired and reported for training. In eight weeks, he was an officer in the Katanga Gendarmerie, with the rank of lieutenant.

At age twenty-two Hill was younger than most of his fellow soldiers, who seemed even older than their years. Many of them had been in almost continuous combat since 1939. When Hill saw them naked in the barracks' showers, he was shocked by the visible scars on their bodies. So many had lost an eye that they jokingly called the unit the "one-eyed command." Though they were working for Tshombe, they showed no real loyalty to anyone or any cause, except one another. They were utterly indifferent to the politics of colonial Africa. They were experts in survival, and their mission was to kill before being killed. Hill knew they would kill him in an instant if they suspected betrayal.

For Hill was not what he purported to be, which was an American adventurer looking for mercenary pay. He could allow nothing to reveal the fact that he was actually still working for the U.S. as an undercover agent to monitor military activity in the Congo. Periodically he compiled a detailed written report, then carefully placed it in a designated dead-letter drop. Or he would participate in a so-called live-letter drop. He would place the report in one of his pockets, then follow a prescribed itinerary: to the market, to the post office, to the crowded central square. Somewhere along the route, the report would be skillfully lifted from his pocket by someone whose identity Hill never knew.

Dan Hill had been a U.S. Army Ranger instructor at Fort Benning when his commanding officer had summoned him. The U.S. government had seen the Union Minière ads for mercenary troops and wanted to know more. Hill had already proven himself in undercover operations. Born in Chicago in 1938, Hill had altered a birth certificate so he could leave home and enlist in the army at age fifteen. As a paratrooper in Germany in 1956, he had been infiltrated into Hungary to provide logistical support for the short-lived Hungarian revolution. He had posed as a German, with all traces of his American identity expunged. He had a German passport, spoke German, wore German-made clothing, even German eyeglasses. If captured, he was never to reveal his real nationality. He successfully organized some weapons deliveries and, when the revolution was crushed by the Soviets, made his way out.

In this regard, Hill was hardly alone in the sprawling, resource-rich, but nearly lawless Congo of 1961. The place was teeming with spies and double agents. Many of the Europeans and most of the Americans Hill met he suspected of intelligence connections. In September 1961, United Nations secretary-general Dag Hammarskjöld left Léopold-ville, in the Congo, for a flight to Ndola, just across the border from Katanga in Northern Rhodesia, for a meeting with Tshombe, hoping to broker a truce and an end to Tshombe's secessionist ambitions. Just before the scheduled night landing, witnesses saw an explosion and the plane disappeared from radar screens. The wreckage was found the next day in a forest nine miles from Ndola. There were no survivors. A Rhodesian inquiry ruled the crash an accident, but Hill suspected a bomb, as did many others. But so many factions were arrayed against the growing UN presence in the Congo that it was anyone's guess who might have done it.

With the death of Hammarskjöld, the remaining hopes for a peaceful solution to Katanga's secession were dashed. Hill and his troops hadn't seen any action, but rumors kept circulating in the restaurants and bars of Elizabethville that Lumumba was organizing troops in the north to crush the Tshombe-led independence movement in Katanga. Then reports had arrived that an armed force was moving south on the only paved road into Elizabethville. Hill's commander had ordered him to ambush the troops and defeat them before they could occupy the provincial capital.

Hill had identified the bridge crossing at the Luguga River as a particularly vulnerable point for the advancing troops. It was the only bridge over the river, which was sure to be an impassable torrent at that time of year. Just past the bridge were a series of hills on one side and a deep ravine on the other, formed by a small tributary. If the enemy troops could be confined between the hills and the ravine, they would be easy targets for Hill's forces firing on them from the higher vantage point of the hilltop.

So Hill and his men mined the bridge with tetrotal, a potent explosive. They laced the deep ravine with mines, booby traps, and trip wires. Once the enemy was in the ravine, Hill doubted anyone would come out alive. They also mined several large trees along the road just past the ambush point. He and his men took up positions atop the hill and waited. They were armed with grenades, rifles, bazookas, machine guns, and semiautomatic rifles. Hill ordered that no one was to fire or make any movement until all the Congolese troops had finished crossing the bridge. He didn't want anyone to escape.

The first ranks of the Congolese troops arrived at the bridge and paused, waiting for the others to catch up. But they didn't seem alert or suspicious. Once the battalion had re-formed, they began the crossing. A few men seemed to be Indians or Pakistanis, members of the UN forces, but most were dressed in the olive shirts of the Congolese army. Hill's men watched, motionless. Finally the last group finished the crossing. Hill gave the signal, and a huge explosion rocked the hillside. The bridge shattered and plunged into the river, cutting off any retreat. The trees fell across the road, blocking the troops' forward progress. Then Hill and his men opened fire on the stunned troops below.

The Congolese forces scattered for cover. As Hill had anticipated, most of them ran for the ravine, which was a death trap. Mines and booby traps detonated, sending bodies flying. Seeing the carnage, some soldiers abruptly reversed course but were easily mowed down by grenades and blasts of fugas, a flaming chemical similar to napalm. No one attacked uphill, toward Hill's positions. The rest of the Congolese battalion scattered in panic, managing only a few aimless bursts of gunfire. The entire exchange lasted less than five minutes. On Hill's order, his men vanished, running along a predetermined path to waiting Land Rovers, which roared back to their headquarters. Though badly outnumbered, Hill hadn't lost any men. On their first foray into Katanga, the Congolese had suffered a humiliating defeat.

A week later, Hill was invited to dinner at the copper miners club by his intelligence contact, a Belgian mining engineer working for the

Americans. Hill filled the Belgian in on the ambush and the rout of the Congolese troops. "What were you doing there?" the Belgian asked.

"Commanding it," Hill replied.

Several days later he was again dining with the Belgian, who suggested they take a stroll on the club's grounds. An American materialized out of the darkness.

"Goddammit," said the unidentified American. "What the hell were you doing out there? You don't need to do that good a job," he said, referring to the defeat of the Congolese force. "There have been terrible repercussions. The Congolese will never cross that river again." A United Nations force was going to have to be deployed, the man said. Both the American and British governments were now backing a unified Congo and were pressuring Belgium to stop its support for Union Minière. The threat of Lumumba had been removed, not by poisoned toothpaste, but by a CIA-backed coup led by Joseph Mobutu.

Hill was unapologetic; he was only carrying out the role assigned to him. He pointed out that he was dealing with hard-core, battle-hardened mercenaries who knew exactly what they were doing. Hill argued that if he'd pulled any punches, he would have aroused the suspicion of his men. "If that's the way you feel," he told the American, "then get me the hell out of here."

Even without a new assignment, Hill knew it was time to go. Without at least tacit support from the Americans and Europeans, the Tshombe-led independence movement was doomed. Not long after his dinner at the miners club, Union Minière missed a payroll, failing to pay the mercenary troops. Though payment was promised, it was effectively the end of the Katanga military. His fellow soldiers asked Hill to join them in a daring attack on the Elizabethville and Bukavu banks to seize the money they contended was their due. Then they had a plan to escape over the border into Uganda, where the mercurial dictator Idi Amin, in return for lavish bribes, had promised them the use of an airstrip.

Hill wasn't about to rob a bank with a bunch of ex-Nazis. But he couldn't stay in Katanga. He loaded his few belongings into a tiny four-cylinder Morris Minor automobile that cost him $300 in U.S. currency. Then he set out on the only road to the southeast. The pavement quickly gave way to a dirt path as he headed across the dry landscape of the African bush. Four hours later he reached the border of Northern Rhodesia and showed his passport. After crossing the border, he stopped in the first town he reached of any size. It was Kitwe, a copper-mining town of several thousand people just thirty miles or so from the Katanga border.

★

COMPARED TO THE CONGO, Northern Rhodesia was a haven of British-imposed order and tranquillity. One of the last frontiers of colonial Africa, it was a mostly self-governing territory still loosely tied to the wealthier and more populous Southern Rhodesia. Even as whites were pouring over its border in panic from the Congo, the British Queen Mother had made a state visit to the colony and toured the copper district, including Kitwe. In the capital of Lusaka, she hosted a garden party and unveiled a statue commemorating Cecil Rhodes, the imperialist mining magnate whose British South Africa Company had brought British rule to most of southern Africa, including both Rhodesias. But tensions and unrest were rapidly building between the white-dominated federal government led by Prime Minister Roy Welensky and the two largest factions supporting independence and black majority rule. A British commission concluded late in 1960 that the existing federal government was not viable due to the "strength of African opposition in the Northern Territories," causing shock and dismay among white settlers. At the time there were approximately twenty thousand white residents in Northern Rhodesia and an estimated four million native Africans.

None of this, however, was immediately apparent to Hill as he made his way through the unfamiliar streets of Kitwe, located in the heart of

Northern Rhodesia's copper belt. Kitwe had little of the tropical charm of Elizabethville. As in many African mining towns, its roughly five thousand white settlers lived in tin-roofed, stucco-walled bungalows with wide verandahs in the center of town, while the African mine workers lived in small wattle- or thatch-roofed, mud-walled houses in a segregated adjacent community called N'Kana. A few of the white mine-owning families had become quite wealthy. They lived on large estates outside of town with swimming pools and tennis courts. They favored late-model American cars with enormous tail fins. A newstand incongruously featured an issue of the *Saturday Evening Post* with a Norman Rockwell cover.

Hill made his way into the center of town and discovered what looked like an English pub. He parked, then went in and ordered a beer. It was a Wednesday afternoon, and the place quickly filled up. People seemed excited, in a festive mood. Hill asked what was going on and learned that a big rugby match was being played later that afternoon between the Northern Rhodesia national rugby team and South Africa. Hill had never seen a rugby game, so he joined the throng heading toward the stadium.

Hill was fascinated by the game. It didn't take him long to focus on the Northern Rhodesia player at left wing forward. He dominated the offense with great speed and accuracy. Other players clearly looked to him for leadership. He looked a little over six feet tall, with dark blond, curly hair above his suntanned face. He obviously had great stamina, and his leg muscles under his rugby shorts were lean and taut. He seemed to love every minute of the game. Hill was dazzled by him.

To the crowd's delight, Northern Rhodesia decisively beat the archrival South Africans. Hill followed the revelers back to the pub for a few more beers, and soon after, the rugby team players arrived, still wearing their uniforms. The player he had admired was the center of attention, accepting congratulations and waving to friends and admirers. When he reached the bar, Hill intercepted him. "Hey," he said. "Let me buy you a beer."

The rugby player drew back slightly. "Who the hell are you?" he asked in a soft British accent.

"Daniel J. Hill, late of the U.S. Army Airborne Rangers and Special Forces," Hill replied.

The rugby player paused for a moment. Hill had clearly gotten his attention. "Rick Rescorla," he said, extending his hand.

As they shook hands and looked at each other closely for the first time, Hill felt something profound pass between the two of them. He couldn't say exactly what it was, but it was a feeling he'd never before experienced. The two fell immediately into animated conversation. Rescorla, too, was a military man. He was from Cornwall, the southwestern tip of England whose people are fiercely proud of their Celtic ancestry. That explained his distinctive accent. He'd served in the British army in Cyprus, but after returning to England, he had opted for the colonial police force. The pay was better, and so were opportunities for advancement. Rescorla was now an assistant inspector in the Northern Rhodesia Police Force, which served as both a paramilitary force for the increasingly besieged British colonial administration and more traditional police functions.

Rescorla was fascinated to learn that Hill had been in the middle of the uprising in Katanga. Rescorla and his fellow police officers had heard about the fighting and one weekend had piled into a car and driven to Elizabethville to see for themselves. They took Scotch whiskey, which they traded for weapons and camouflage gear. Elizabethville was now being patrolled by UN troops, which had occupied the province with little opposition once the mercenary force dispersed. Most of the restaurants and shops had closed, and the streets were nearly deserted. Hill's former colleagues had indeed carried out the daring escape they had planned. While in Elizabethville, Rescorla had visited one of the banks they robbed en route to Uganda. A mercenary had stood on the roof with an automatic weapon, holding UN troops at bay before escaping. The incident had quickly passed into local legend.

Hill readily shared his recent exploits with Rescorla. Several beers later, some attractive women joined them and invited Rescorla and the American to a barbecue one was hosting at her family's home. "Come with me," Rescorla insisted. Hill was swept into the festivities. There was a big, friendly crowd, ample food, plenty of beer and gin-and-tonics. It was a beautiful, clear night in tropical Africa. As everyone was leaving, Hill realized he'd had way too much to drink and had nowhere to stay. But then Rescorla materialized, equally drunk. He insisted that Hill return with him to his barracks.

The next morning Hill awoke with a terrific hangover. Rescorla's room was simply furnished, with twin beds, a desk with a shelf lined with books, including Winston Churchill's *History of the English-Speaking Peoples,* a chair for reading, and an adjoining verandah with a small table and two chairs. Rescorla's gun was padlocked to his bed. Communal showers and toilets were down the hall. Rescorla was already awake, and he, too, had a throbbing head.

"I've got the perfect cure for a hangover," Rescorla told him. They would begin with a ten-kilometer run, then a vigorous round of calisthenics, and finally a big breakfast at the officers club. Rescorla would find out just how fit these American military men were. Hill was fit—he'd been a judo champion earlier in his military career—but he barely kept pace with Rescorla, who despite the hangover seemed hardly out of breath. At first Hill's head throbbed and he felt nauseated. But by the time they'd finished, showered, and shaved, Hill conceded that the cure had worked. Now he was famished.

Rescorla led Hill to the officers mess, located in a distinguished-looking white building with French doors opening onto a wide verandah. The main room was the dining room, and next to it was a lounge with a bar. There was also a room called the kitchen, though all the cooking was actually done by servants in an adjacent building and the kitchen served as a butler's pantry. Hill was astounded. He'd never seen anything like this in the American military. There were white tablecloths on the tables. Food was served on elegant china, with silver utensils. Breakfast was a buffet, with a vast array of choices: all kinds of eggs cooked to order, bacon, ham, kidneys, kippers, cereals, milk, and fresh fruit and juices. Black servants dressed in white jackets and Bermuda shorts poured coffee at the table. One man's sole duty was to keep a steady supply of freshly toasted bread propped in a silver toast holder. Hill and Rescorla filled their plates. When they were seated, a waiter brought them Bloody Marys.

This was the life, Hill thought. He'd grown up in a family that never seemed to have enough to eat. No wonder Rescorla had wanted a career in the colonial forces. But when Hill expressed his amazement, Rescorla told him it was nothing compared to the luxury enjoyed by officers in the regular British military.

Hill was in no hurry to move on. He found he liked the British and the easygoing colonial culture and social life. He liked the free-flowing Watney's Red Barrel ale, the gin-and-tonics before supper, and being waited on by white-jacketed servants. And, of course, his new friend. Rescorla insisted that he stay. Hill thought vaguely that he might make contact with his American superiors—a missionary encampment just outside of Kitwe was actually a CIA station, bristling with radio equipment. Surely American intelligence would be interested in his dispatches from Rhodesia, which, while hardly as volatile as the Congo, was facing increasing unrest, white hostility to independence and black majority rule, and occasional Soviet- or Chinese Communist-backed insurgencies. Rescorla had contacts throughout the Rhodesian police force, and he encouraged Hill to join the British force. It needed people with Hill's unusual training and experience. Rescorla felt sure something would materialize.

In the meantime, Hill moved into the barracks. No one questioned his presence there or at the officers mess. He was Rescorla's American friend, and that was enough. Hill could see that though Rescorla was twenty-two years old and an assistant inspector, the other men seemed naturally to defer to him. Because of the spreading political unrest, the group that entered the force with Rescorla had been sent into the field before their training in Lusaka was over. Rescorla was the only one with prior military experience, and the others looked to him for guidance and reassurance. But one of his friends, Marcus Ward, who had shared a room with Rescorla at training camp, discovered that he imitated Rescorla at his peril, joking with Hill that "Rick knew all the tricks and I caught all the flack." The stocks of their rifles were supposed to be kept burnished by rubbing linseed oil into the wood stocks and then hand-buffing them. But Rescorla bought some cheap furniture polish, which more or less achieved the same effect with minimal labor. When Ward tried the same polish on his rifle, he was summoned from the parade ground by their commanding officer, who inspected the rifle stock and reprimanded him by giving him extra parade duty. The men were required to rub their bayonet scabbards with burnt black shoe polish. Rescorla painted his scabbard black and applied a light coat of shoe polish on top of it. Ward copied him but was again caught and reprimanded. As Ward was summoned from the parade ground to be disciplined a second time, he could see a big smile on Rescorla's face.

Regulation uniforms called for khaki Bermuda shorts worn at a length that was exactly one and one-half inches above the knee. But Rescorla wore his at least three inches above the knee, either out of vanity or for greater comfort. Somehow he got away with it. Still, though often irreverent toward his superiors, Rescorla insisted on strict discipline with the men under his command and prided himself on their parade skills and preparedness. His men always used a full salute, not the half-arm–cocked gesture Rescorla had seen used in films of the American military. When the alarm went off signaling an emergency, Rescorla and his unit were always among the first lined up on the parade ground. Most of their action came on weekends, when political demonstrations increasingly spilled into rioting. Thousands of Africans would attend rallies for one political faction or another, with speakers exhorting them to rise up against their white oppressors. Then tankers stocked with the local Chibuku beer would pull up, and people filled plastic bottles and passed them around. The combination of hotheaded political rhetoric and alcohol was often combustive. Rescorla and his colleagues would arrive in riot gear; rocks were thrown, arrests made.

Some of their missions were more serious. The African National Congress (ANC) and United National Independence Party (UNIP), the two major political factions, were beginning to smuggle in weapons and organize their own military units, the ANC backed by the Russians and the UNIP by the Chinese Communists. They had established base camps in the bush outside of Kitwe, and, tipped off to their presence by the Americans stationed at the missionary outpost, Rescorla organized several expeditions to disarm and arrest them. There had been casualties, though not among the British. Indeed, it was obvious that most of the Africans had not yet learned how to use the new weapons confiscated by Rescorla. Many of them believed that the mere sound of the weapon's discharge killed the enemy and, as a result, didn't bother to aim. Still, that would change as they became more experienced.

Except when Rescorla was off on such missions, he and Hill were virtually inseparable. Normally reticent with his fellow British officers, Rescorla told Hill everything about himself, and Hill reciprocated. Rescorla was sensitive to the growing tensions in British rule. He could see it in some of his own men, Africans genuinely torn between their British employers and their own people. And many British settlers, too, were torn between their lifelong loyalty to the Crown, which backed self-determination, and to their fellow colonialists, who fiercely opposed it.

Once a week the officers mess served a formal dinner, with candlelight, wine, and brandy and cigars after dinner. Everyone else had retired for the night, and Rescorla and Hill were sitting on the verandah outside Rescorla's room, finishing off their brandy, when Rescorla asked Hill if he was familiar with the works of Rudyard Kipling.

Hill had already discovered that Rescorla was a prodigious reader. Though lacking a formal education, he had worked his way through the entire sixty volumes of the Harvard Classics, which included such works as *The Wealth of Nations* and the American Constitution and Declaration of Independence. Rescorla laced his comments with quotations from literature, especially Shakespeare. Since he'd joined the army, Hill had discovered that he enjoyed reading, though his taste ran to westerns by Will James, Zane Gray, and Louis L'Amour, and military histories. He had heard of Kipling as the author of *Kim,* which had been made into an animated Disney movie released in 1950. But otherwise he knew little about the famous British author, winner of a Nobel Prize, lionized by the late Victorians but increasingly dismissed as an apologist for British empire.

Rescorla had been mesmerized by Kipling's depiction of valor and sacrifice. In addition to Kipling's best-known works, Rescorla had had read virtually all of Kipling's prodigious output of poetry, verse, short stories, and novels. Rescorla seemed delighted at the prospect of introducing Hill to a writer who had had a profound impact on his life. He insisted Hill join him in his room, where Rescorla turned on the lamp, pulled a worn volume from his shelf of books, settled into his chair, and began reading in a firm baritone.

" 'The beginning of everything was in a railway-train upon the road to Mhow from Ajmir.' " Hill listened with mounting fascination as he was swept into the British Raj, an exotic world not all that different from colonial Rhodesia, where two men—Peachey Carnehan, a "wanderer and vagabond," a veteran of "adventures in which he risked his life for a few days' food," and Daniel Dravot, "a big man with a red beard, and a great swell he is"—proclaim that " 'India isn't big enough for such as us.'

" 'Therefore we are going away to be Kings,' Carnehan says.

" 'Kings in our own right,' mutters Dravot."

The work Rescorla had chosen, "The Man Who Would Be King," is considered one of Kipling's finest stories. Rescorla was an excellent reader, pausing occasionally for dramatic effect, shifting voices and accents for the dialogue. Hill was spellbound, and not just by the excitement of the story. The similarities to his own circumstances were striking.

Peachey and Dravot, of indeterminate but humble origin and adrift on the fringes of the British empire, choose as their prospective kingdom the province of Kafiristan, located in " 'the top right-hand corner of Afghanistan, not more than three hundred miles from Peshawar,' " Dravot explains. " 'They have two and thirty heathen idols there, and we'll be the thirty-third and fourth. It's a mountainous country, the women of those parts are very beautiful.' " The key to their plan is to take with them a case of 450 Snider rifles and use them to organize a fighting force. " 'In any place where they fight a man who knows how to drill men can always be a King,' " Peachey tells the narrator. " 'We shall go to those parts and say to any King we find, "D'you want to vanquish your foes?" and we will show him how to drill men; for that we know better than anything else. Then we will subvert that King and seize his throne and establish a Dy-nasty.' " They sign a contract to rule as equals, to forswear alcohol and women, and to "conduct ourselves with Dignity and Discretion, and if one of us gets into trouble the other will stay by him."

In Afghanistan they do become kings, first Dravot, and then, after the region is subdued by their infantry, Peachey. They are worshiped as gods and direct descendants of Alexander the Great, whose troops passed through in 330 B.C. and whose descendants still inhabit the province. Dravot is beloved by the people; Peachey feared. Someday, Dravot says, when " 'everything was shipshape,' " he would bow on his knees before Queen Victoria and hand over his crown. " 'And she'd say, "Rise up, Sir Daniel Dravot." ' "

It all ends badly. Breaking their contract, and in defiance of local custom, Dravot insists on taking a wife. When the terrified girl is presented for his approval and he asks for a kiss, she bites him, drawing blood. Local tribal leaders are shocked by this evidence that Dravot is as human as they are. His authority collapses. His troops mutiny, and his weapons are turned against them.

They flee but are trapped by the advancing troops in the rugged mountains of Afghanistan. Dravot turns to Peachey. " 'I've brought you to this,' says he. 'Brought you out of your happy life to be killed in Kafiristan, where you was late Commander-in-Chief of the Emperor's forces. Say you forgive me, Peachey.' 'I do,' says Peachey. 'Fully and freely do I forgive you, Dan.' 'Shake hands, Peachey,' says he. "I'm going now.' "

Dravot walks onto a rope bridge precariously spanning a deep ravine. " 'Cut, you beggars,' he shouts; and they cut, and old Dan fell, turning round and round and round, twenty thousand miles, for he took half an hour to fall till he struck the water, and I could see his body caught on a rock with the gold crown close beside."

Peachey is captured, crucified, and left for dead. Horribly disfigured, he makes his way back to India, where he finds the narrator and manages to tell his story. Dismissed as deranged and incoherent, Peachey is taken to an asylum, soon to die. As he is led away he sings,

> The Son of Man goes forth to war,
> A golden crown to gain;
> His blood-red banner streams afar—
> Who follows in His train?

Rescorla reached the end of the story and paused to let its implications sink in.

"You," he said to Hill, "are Peachey."

It went without saying that Rescorla was Dravot.

★

ON SOME EVENINGS Rescorla and Hill drove out into the bush in Rescorla's Land Rover, taking with them food and drink. They built a fire, grilled steaks, and drank beer and whiskey. They chose a site that gave them a breathtaking vista of the Northern Rhodesian landscape. As night fell, they gazed at the stars of the southern hemisphere, looking for the distinctive Southern Cross used by the early navigators around the Cape of Good Hope. Sometimes they heard the sounds of wildlife in the distance—hyenas and the occasional roar of a lion. And they talked for hours sitting by the fire, discussing everything from their love affairs to world politics and philosophy.

Both men had grown up during World War II. After the war, their enmity shifted from the totalitarianism of the Nazis to the totalitarianism of the Soviets, and now they were strong anti-Communists. Rescorla had studied the writings of Marx, visiting the great library of the British Museum where Marx had worked. He could quote passages from *Das Kapital*. He had studied the evolution of Marxism, reading extensively about the Russian Revolution and Stalin's purges. He and Hill both felt that communism was an affront to the human spirit, the latest in a long historical succession of oppressors of freedom and individualism. The Russians were poverty-stricken, which is what Rescorla expected from a system that refused to reward initiative and hard work. Rescorla believed in democracy, individual rights, and self-reliance. He could quote from the Magna Carta, the U.S. Constitution, and the Declaration of Independence. He often told Dan that one should be able to strip a man naked and throw him out with nothing. By the end of the day, the man should be clothed and fed. By the end of the week, he should own a horse. And by the end of a year, he should own a business and have money in the bank. It was a philosophy Hill admired.

After one of these long discussions, Rescorla grew quiet and then turned to Hill. "You know," he said, "I hope you won't find this strange, but I feel like I've known you before."

Hill was amazed, because he realized he'd had the same feeling the afternoon he met Rescorla at the pub. Hill knew that General George Patton, the World War II hero who died in an auto accident in Germany, thought he'd been a soldier in many previous lives. Hill hadn't given Patton's claims much credence, but now he wondered. "I know what you mean," Hill said.

"It's called 'déjà vu,'" Rescorla explained, using a term Hill had never heard. "Maybe we were Celtic warriors, fighting side by side."

"Maybe we were fighting together against the Romans!" Hill said.

Rescorla's face lit up at the prospect.

And maybe, Hill thought, they were both boys who had never quite grown up.

But at that moment, it seemed real. Hill felt it, the déjà vu Rescorla told him about. And he knew Rescorla did, too.

2

WINDS OF WAR

American troops landing on the Normandy Coast, D-Day, 1944. The soldiers stationed in Hayle, England, had given Rescorla his first introduction to America.
(Corbis)

ORN ON THE EVE of World War II, Hill in 1938 and Rescorla in 1939, both were surrounded as infants by preparations for war and then the Allies' struggle to defeat the Nazis and save democracy. The war dominated the news, conversation, and daily life both in Hayle, a Cornish seaport on the southwest coast of England where Rescorla was born, and Chicago, Hill's hometown. In 1943 American GIs arrived in force in Hayle, which served as a staging ground for the Normandy invasion. Hayle was the headquarters for the 175th Combat Regiment of the U.S. Twenty-ninth Infantry Division, many of whose members were from Maryland, Virginia, and the District of Columbia. Hayle also housed the U.S. Army Engineering Unit from Detroit, an all-black unit. Bringing with them heavy machinery, bulldozers, and cranes, and roaring around town and the countryside in their open-air jeeps, they transformed the sleepy port into a noisy beehive of activity.

Nearly everyone in Hayle was fascinated by the Americans who had come to rescue them from the Nazi menace, but four-year-old Cyril Rescorla and his young friends were especially so. Cyril was Rescorla's given name. He told Dan Hill that he had always hated it and began using "Rick" once he joined the British army. His middle name was Richard, and he thought the name Rick conveyed a much more modern, confident, masculine impression. But as a child, he was called Cyril. He and his friends would run down to Foundry Square to watch the Americans pass by in their jeeps. Most of the jeeps had names written on them, American names that sounded exotic and romantic to Rescorla: "Monty," "Oklahoma," "Joe," "Fred." Rescorla kept a notebook in which he dutifully recorded the names. Sometimes GIs would be hanging around the square, and Rescorla worked his way into their midst.

"Got any gum, chum?" he'd ask.

"Got a sister, mister?" was the standard reply.

Sometimes the soldiers handed out treats, such as chocolate-covered cherries, that were scarce in wartime England. Once an American sergeant gave Rescorla and his friends a ride in his jeep. The boys were ecstatic and couldn't stop talking about it.

The men in the engineering unit were the first black people Rescorla and many other people in Hayle had ever seen. There was some racial tension between the unit and the all-white infantry division, and occasionally a fight would break out on weekends outside one of the bars or the dance hall. But the boys were too young to pick up the social and political dynamics. They were thrilled by the presence of the Americans, and the fact that some were black only made them more fascinating. One evening Rescorla and his friends saw a black man who had had his cheek slashed, evidently in a fight. One of Rescorla's friends was impressed by the sight of the man's blood, glistening against his dark skin, exactly the same color as a white person's. The engineering unit also maintained a choir, which gave a performance of gospel music and hymns at the local chapel. The fervent singing made a lasting impression on the residents of Hayle.

As the months went by and D-Day approached, the military preparations grew steadily more intense. Not just jeeps but troop transport trucks and tanks began rumbling through town by the hundreds. The port was used to build large transport ships, called rhino ferries, for moving vehicles and heavy equipment cross the English Channel. At dusk Rescorla and his friends lay on their backs watching the sky as wave after wave of planes headed across the Channel on bombing missions. They all wished they were in a cockpit. At home, Rescorla built models of the airplanes made from balsa wood and decorated his room with photos and drawings of fighter planes. Outside, he and his friends roamed the surroundings of Hayle, enacting mock invasions from the wreck of a French fishing boat that had supposedly been smuggling British agents back to England or staging ambushes of imaginary Germans in the Weir, an undeveloped spit of land within the confines of the harbor. Rescorla and his friends carried pocketknives, which they brandished as weapons against the imaginary Germans. Rescorla taught them a maneuver intended to surprise any attackers, in which they spun around and threw their knives into a tree. Cyril seemed fearless, except for one incident: frightened by the sinister appearance of a gas mask, with its goggle eye openings and strange snout, he balked at putting one on a during an air raid drill at school, and his mother had to be summoned to calm him.

One day in June 1944, all the activity came to a sudden halt. The huge ferries in the harbor had vanished. The troops and all their equipment were gone. Then came news of the Normandy invasion. Nearly everyone in Hayle listened intently to their radios, gathering every night at 9:00 P.M. for the BBC news broadcast. Rescorla told Hill he would never forget the words of Churchill: "This vast operation is undoubtedly the most complicated and difficult that has ever taken place. The ardour and spirit of the troops, as I saw myself, embarking in these last few days was splendid to witness."

But news of Hayle's 175th Regiment was not so encouraging. The unit's soldiers were in the second wave to hit Omaha Beach on D-Day, which meant that they escaped the enormous casualties in the first wave. But a few days later they bore the brunt of fierce fighting in the hedgerows of Normandy, some of it hand-to-hand combat at close quarters, in the pivotal Battle of St. Lô. The American units there sustained heavy casualties. Residents of Hayle were devastated to learn that not one member of the engineers choir survived.

Though Rescorla longed to join the Royal Air Force, his family wasn't directly involved in the war effort. His father, Stephen, whom he called "Ste" as well as "Dad," worked for the local power plant, whose huge brick chimneys dominated Hayle's south quay. Over fifty when the war broke out, he was too old for military service. He was an unassuming man, about five feet six with dark, receding hair. He often took Rescorla fishing on the tidal estuary in his eighteen-foot rowboat, which he kept moored in Hayle harbor, just across the road from the family's modest row house on Penpol Terrace. He also read to him, especially the English adventure comic books, which, in contrast with American comics, were mostly text—titles such as *The Wizard, The Hotspur, The Rover.* They told stories about boy heroes like Cowboy Kid the Footballer and Wilson the Wonder Boy, whose trademark was that he ran barefoot. Many featured stories of the American West. Whenever his father stopped to stoke his pipe, Rescorla grew impatient. "Come on, come on," he begged until the reading resumed.

Rescorla's mother, Winnie, did the shopping and the cooking and kept a neat, tidy house. She was known for her baked goods, and it seemed something was always simmering on the coal-fed stove. She had a cigarette every day after breakfast, then did the shopping in town and, with her best friend, stopped for coffee at Curnow's Café. It was a daily ritual. Rescorla's sister, Annie, whom he called "Sis," worked as a housekeeper at the White Hart hotel. There was a big difference in their ages; she was nineteen years older, though she continued to live at home. All of them seemed to dote on young Cyril. He showed a taste for adventure at a young age and, when he was four, gave them a scare that was reported in the *Cornishman* of March 31, 1943:

> In the dock opposite Penpol Terrace, some children were playing along the water's edge, and without any of them noticing it, one youngster, Cyril Rescorla, fell in. Ronnie Williams was the first to notice the boy floating in the water, and ran to the spot and succeeded in pulling him out.

Unlike other members of his family, perfectly content in Hayle, Rescorla dreamed of foreign places and adventure, fantasies fueled by weekly trips to the Palace cinema. On most Saturdays, his mother gave him a shilling, the cost of admission for the cheaper seats, but other times he and a friend climbed the back stairs and sneaked in through the emergency exit. Almost all the movies were American, many of them westerns or action-filled adventures about World War II. He loved the actors Burt Lancaster, Randolph Scott, and Audie Murphy, who starred in movies like *Gunsmoke, Destry,* and *To Hell and Back,* in which Murphy, the most decorated American soldier in World War II, played himself. Colin Philp, one of the friends who often accompanied Rescorla to the movies, would sometimes see the glow of excitement on Rescorla's face when the cavalry came to the rescue or the Yankees rolled over a German position. The movies only reinforced the heroic, romantic images of Americans Rescorla had forged during the war. In his view, Americans were men of honor, principle, and determination who made something of themselves.

Rescorla and his friends were riveted in 1946 when they learned that postwar British heavyweight boxing sensation Bruce Woodcock would be contending for the title of heavyweight champion of the world in New York City on May 17. Woodcock, undefeated in forty fights, winner of the British title in six rounds, was heavily favored against an American, Tami Mauriello, a former light heavyweight who had failed in two previous title bids. The British press viewed Woodcock's success as a metaphor for Britain's hoped-for return to its rightful place in the postwar world, and local sentiment in Hayle was overwhelming for Woodcock. Among the local boys, Rescorla was Mauriello's lone supporter. He insisted that Mauriello would win simply because he was an American.

When the day of the match came, he and his friends gathered around the radio for the blow-by-blow coverage. Woodcock seemed to have Mauriello at bay during the first four rounds as he punched methodically and Mauriello threw a few powerful but wild right swings. The Hayle boys were cheering Woodcock wildly, eager for what seemed an inevitable victory. Then, in the fifth round, Mauriello exploded with another of his wild right swings, and this one connected. Woodcock was knocked out. "Tami won!" Rescorla shouted in delight. "Tami won!" His friends were dejected. And they weren't going to let Rescorla forget it.

At some point, most Cornish men acquire a nickname, and after the fight, everyone called Cyril "Tammy." Rescorla liked the name because of its association with an American prizefighter, and when he dispensed with Cyril once he joined the army, he thought of keeping it. He settled on Rick instead, since it was his given middle name. But not in Hayle: there he would always be known as "Tammy."

★

DAN JOSEPH HILL'S first memory, at age three, was the Japanese bombing of Pearl Harbor. He was living with his parents and two sisters in Oak Park, Illinois, where his father, Daniel John Hill, worked for the railroad. His job made him exempt from the draft, but he immediately volunteered for the infantry and left almost immediately for England as part of the Seventy-ninth Infantry Division. Dan didn't really notice his father's absence, because he traveled as part of his job and was rarely at home anyway. On Christmas Day 1942, with his father abroad, Dan's mother, Roberta, gave birth to another daughter. Dan was furious that she wasn't a boy.

The Hill family lived in an apartment upstairs from the Geyers, a family of German immigrants. The father was a carpenter who had fought for the kaiser in World War I, and the family spoke German, which was where Dan first picked up the language. He also spoke it with his maternal grandmother, who was German. The Geyers had three sons, and the two oldest enlisted in the U.S. Marines. Dan watched in awe as they came up the steps to his apartment, wearing their dress-blue marine uniforms. They brought him a rocking horse. After that, it was hard to get him off of it.

A couple of years later, Dan became obsessed with the comic hero Superman, and his mother made him a red cape and sewed an "S" onto a blue sweatshirt. He would wear the cape and jump out of their second-story windows, somehow escaping injury. One of Dan's cousins was a fighter pilot, and he sent the boy an actual air force parachute. Dan got into the harness, climbed on the roof, and waited for his mother to come home. When she did, he leaped off the roof. The parachute barely deployed but opened just enough to break his fall. For the rest of his life, he wanted to jump.

Dan would spend hours downstairs with John Geyer, the youngest of the sons, watching and helping him build models of fighter planes. John's father had mounted a huge map of the world, and he had small flags on it to identify the locations of his two sons and Dan's father. Usually the radio would be on, tuned to the latest news of the war.

In 1943, Dan's father came home for a brief visit before returning to England. There was beginning to be talk of an American-led invasion of the continent, and Dan senior wanted to be part of it. His father took him by the shoulders and looked into his eyes. "You're the man of the house now," he said.

That meant Dan had to go to work. His father's pay came to $100 a month—$25 in base pay plus $75 a month for family support—which barely paid the rent, let alone food and clothing for a family of five. The Hills left the Oak Park apartment and the Geyers and moved to something less expensive in Chicago. Dan went to work for the milkman, who picked up the young boy each morning at 1:30 and drove him to the dairy in his milk truck. They loaded the truck, then drove to the icehouse and packed it in. Dan ran from the truck to the various houses and apartments. He could carry eight quarts of milk in a single trip. When they finished, the milkman took Dan to a diner for breakfast. The first time, he was so excited to be eating out that he ordered everything on the menu. He was at school by 8:00 A.M. In addition to his breakfast, Dan earned $3 a day.

Dan's mother had enrolled him in the second grade at Our Lady of Perpetual Help, a parochial school with a reputation for higher academic and disciplinary standards than the Chicago public schools. Dan had trouble understanding why, but he constantly ran afoul of the nuns trying to teach him. One day his teacher, Sister Francis Marianne, asked him to spell the word *I,* a seemingly simple task. "E-y-e," Dan replied.

"Spell it again," the nun insisted.

"E-y-e," Dan replied.

His teacher took a metal ruler and hit him on the head. "Again."

The exchange continued in this vein, Dan stubbornly spelling "eye," the teacher demanding that he spell the single-letter pronoun. The more he persisted, the more she struck him.

That night Dan's mother saw his scalp. He was enrolled in public school the next day.

Children in the parochial school had come mostly from Italian immigrant families, but the public school was more racially and ethnically diverse. The neighborhood had a growing black population as well as a mix of Eastern European immigrants. There was a movie theater in the neighborhood, and Dan went as often as he could afford to. He drank in the newsreels about the war effort. He loved westerns and war movies, like *Back to Bataan,* starring John Wayne. Hill would always re-member the scene where the Japanese hung an American school-teacher who was wrapped in the American flag.

Even with Dan's milk money, the family budget was stretched thin. Dan was always on the lookout for ways to make extra money. He'd gotten to know a woman who lived on the block behind their apart-ment named Juju. Juju was often sitting out on the steps, smoking, when Dan passed by, and she seemed to enjoy talking to him. She was about thirty years old, a strawberry blonde with a figure like Betty Grable's. Young Dan thought he was in love. Juju was good-looking, and so were other women he met at her house. Though still in the third grade, Dan figured out pretty quickly that the men he saw going in and out were Juju's customers. Juju was a madam, and she didn't hide it from Dan. On the contrary, she offered him twenty-five cents a head for every man he steered to her place.

Their neighborhood wasn't all that far from the Great Lakes Naval Base, and Dan quickly learned that sailors were easy targets. He not only introduced them to Juju and her girls, but also supplied them with whiskey from the liquor store down the street, earning a profit on the markup.

Juju told Dan a lot about life. She lived pretty well, from his point of view, and gave him a taste of small luxuries like boiled shrimp. One day she took him into her salon and pulled a nickel-plated handgun from her drawer. In her business, you never knew when you might need something like that, Juju explained. It was hard for Dan to believe that something so small and shiny could kill a man. He took it out into the backyard, pointed at a garbage can, and pulled the trigger. It went off with a loud crack, and Dan jumped back from the recoil. But he'd shot a gun!

In late 1944, Dan's mother gave birth to another girl. This time he was less angry that it was a girl, but he was more puzzled by the birth. He knew from Juju about babies and their gestation period, and it seemed to him that his father had been gone a long time. Indeed, his father had been wounded in France after landing in Normandy on D-Day and had been sent to a British hospital. For a while they didn't know if they'd ever see him again. But he had recovered and fought his way with General Patton's Third Army all the way to the Elbe. He stayed in Germany during the occupation, then, a few months after the German surrender, Dan learned he was coming home.

Dan was beside himself with excitement, yet it was not the glorious homecoming he'd looked forward to. He brought Dan a captured German helmet and a Nazi flag, but practically the first thing he told the boy was that he never wanted to hear him speak German again. Dan watched closely to see how his father reacted to his new daughter, now just over a year old, whom he'd never seen. But he seemed delighted. Nothing suggested to Dan that he might not be her father.

Much to Dan's disappointment, his father didn't want to talk about his combat experiences. Gradually, from things his father told him and things he overheard, Dan learned that his father's stint in Europe hadn't ended heroically with the Allied victory. While in Frankfurt, Dan's father had been arrested by military police and charged with fraternizing with the enemy. He drove a rations truck, and his crime, as he explained it, was giving away food meant for the Allied troops to orphaned Germans. Then he was accused of killing German prisoners of war and court-martialed. The day before the incident, he and other American soldiers had entered a concentration camp and taken a group of SS guards as prisoners. Although the full horror of the Holocaust wasn't yet known, what Dan's father found at the camp had horrified him. Although he was charged with transporting the guards to an Allied prisoner-of-war camp, he shot them instead. The young Dan never knew the exact circumstances, but at his father's military trial, the verdict was "not guilty." He was honorably discharged. Before returning to Chicago, he was sent to a military hospital to be treated for what was diplomatically described as "combat fatigue."

Dan felt his father never quite got over it. He would explode at the slightest provocation, and he was always looking for a fight. In the summer of 1952, he put his family into their 1946 Plymouth sedan and drove them across Route 66 to Las Vegas, where he found low-paying work at the Nevada Test Site. The family lived in drab government housing and still struggled to make ends meet. No one realized the hazards at the time, but Dan's father was exposed for long periods to low-level atomic radiation. After finishing work, Dan's father would challenge other men to fights, then take bets on the outcome. Dan senior never lost a fight. On those nights, he spent generously, and there was plenty of food and drink. The only time Dan felt his stomach was full was after his father had rustled up a fight.

★

AS RESCORLA GREW OLDER, he became increasingly impatient with the uneventful domesticity and routine of life in Hayle. His parents lived modestly on Stephen's salary from the power plant and later on his government pension. They never complained about their standard of living and, as far as Rescorla could tell, never aspired to anything better. They seemed content to stay home. Rescorla couldn't understand why they never wanted to go anywhere, even on vacation. They didn't attend church but sent Cyril to Sunday school at St. Elwyn's, the Anglican parish church. But that, too, he found stultifying. One day he announced, "I ain't goin' no more," and they didn't insist.

Rescorla was always respectful of his parents and loved them, but he confided in Hill that he felt estranged from his family from an early age and found his father to be distant. Everyone was so much older than him, even his sister. And despite the reading and the fishing trips with his father, which he loved, he craved more attention and affection. He spent most of his free time roaming the town and its outskirts with other boys; his father never played sports with him or took him on outings like other fathers Rescorla knew.

The Rescorlas may have been content to live provincial, circumscribed lives, but by the standards of Hayle, this wasn't unusual. The Cornish are fiercely proud of their independence and Celtic heritage;

Cornwall has its own dialect and distinct accent. Cornishmen love to sing, and "Trelawny" is Cornwall's unofficial national anthem. There was an active Cornish independence movement, as many people felt little kinship with the English or interest in mingling with them. Many viewed London with suspicion and felt out of place there. Few had any cause to go abroad.

Hayle was also a decidedly working-class village, divided between workers in the copper-smelting plant and the iron foundry, both industries in a prolonged state of decline. There was a fierce rivalry between the two sides of town, with boys from one side often picking fights with the others. In these brawls, Rescorla fought with the iron foundry boys, many of them his neighbors, even though as a power plant employee, Stephen Rescorla and his family occupied a social rung a little above the foundry workers. But compared with many English villages, class distinctions were less significant, since Hayle was so homogeneously working class. There was no local gentry to speak of, ownership of the industries long ago having passed into the hands of absentee owners and public corporations managed from London. Still, Rescorla recalled an incident when Lorna Buchanan, wife of the factory manager, had walked by as he was helping his mother in the garden. She had smiled and nodded, and he had greeted her and begun a brief conversation. As soon as she left, his mother had rushed over. "Don't you know that was Mrs. Buchanan? You mustn't speak to her!"

No one in Rescorla's family had ever attended college or set much store in formal education. It wouldn't have occurred to them. But they did feel that Cyril was a precocious, intelligent child, and they boasted about him to friends and neighbors. He had an avid interest in reading, an active imagination, and great curiosity. At age eleven, he took a standardized, mandatory test of verbal and logical reasoning, and as a result of his high scores, he was enrolled in Penzance County Grammar School in Penzance, about five miles from Hayle. Rescorla, his friend Mervyn Sullivan, and a handful of boys also from Hayle traveled to Penzance each morning on the train.

Though Sullivan and some of the others were older than Rescorla, he quickly donned the mantle of leader of the Hayle contingent. Perhaps it was because he was unusually tall and strong for his age, with broad shoulders and a thick shock of curly brown hair. His hair was so thick that he had trouble wearing the regulation school cap along with his red blazer, gray slacks, and red-and-yellow tie. At the age of eleven, he nearly died from a burst appendix, but the doctors said his strength, stamina, and sheer determination carried him through. Increasingly, these qualities surfaced at home and in school. If he and his schoolmates were in danger of missing the train to Penzance, Rescorla gave the order to start running. But no one ever ran unless he gave the command. On rare occasions they were late, and the headmaster marked down their names at morning assembly and summoned them to his office. The first time this happened, Rescorla entered the headmaster's office while the others waited nervously. When Rescorla emerged, he was smiling broadly. "It's all right, lads," he said expansively. "It's all taken care of." They never knew just what it was that Rescorla said, but it always seemed to work. Other boys were caned in full view of their classmates, but not Rescorla.

Rescorla's academic work left little impression. Despite his later love of reading, he showed only dutiful interest in the required works of literature: Swift's *Gulliver's Travels,* Chaucer's prologue to the *Canterbury Tales,* and Shakespeare's *Romeo and Juliet.* Neither Kipling nor Conrad was part of the curriculum; both had fallen from favor in postwar Britain, where notions of empire seemed anachronistic. He made even less of an impression as a musician. His class was supposed to have one music lesson per week. The music teacher handed them recorders, still damp from the previous class, with instructions to wipe them off before using them. "If anyone makes a sound on one of these before I say to begin playing, that will be the end of it," he sternly ordered. Someone promptly blew a loud note. The instructor angrily collected the recorders, and they were never seen again. At choir auditions, the teacher played a middle C on the piano and instructed the students to sing a scale. "Do, re, mi," a friend of Rescorla's began.

"Stop!" yelled the teacher. "Don't ever sing again."

Rescorla apparently met a similar fate, since he too failed the audition.

Rescorla left more of an impression on the playing fields than he did in the classroom. He grew to be six feet one, with a powerful, lean physique, blue eyes, and the thick curly hair he'd had since childhood. He was a magnet for girls but showed little or no interest. His work at the post office and sports left little or no time for his academic work, let alone dating. He excelled at sports. He played cricket, ran track, threw the discus and the shot put. He set a shot put record at Penzance Grammar School that was never surpassed. Rescorla also excelled at Cornish wrestling, the unofficial Cornish national sport and a Celtic tradition said to date from 1800 B.C. The sport is performed outdoors in bare feet while wearing canvas jackets, and the goal is to lift one's opponent, then hurl him to the ground, pinning his shoulders and buttocks.

Rescorla's Cornish wrestling matches, usually held in the summer, were good training for rugby. Recorla starred on the rugby fields, first at school and in the Hayle Junior Rugby Football Club, and then for the Hayle Colts. His teammates assumed that he'd eventually turn professional. Success at rugby is less a function of sheer mass and strength than is the case with American football, but it still takes great stamina, speed, agility, and aggressive determination. Rescorla was naturally athletic and worked hard to keep himself fit, but it was his determination that most impressed and inspired his teammates. He simply could not lose. Though he was scrupulous about the rules, he was so aggressive and seemingly fearless that other boys at grammar school begged to be on his team so they wouldn't get hurt playing against him. Once his school team was playing a team from a prestigious public school, the equivalent of a private American prep school. When Rescorla felled the team's star forward, he got up and yelled in a noticeably upper-class accent, "You bloody great oaf!"

"Can you believe that?" an incredulous Rescorla later repeated to his teammates. He imitated the accent: "He called me a bloody great oaf!" He was proud that he had gotten the better of a public school boy.

Mervyn Sullivan played on the Colts team with Rescorla. In one match, the opposing team had kicked the ball over the halfway line, putting them on the offensive. Rescorla told him, "Get the ball and kill it dead." Sullivan ran after it and threw himself on the ball. That meant the ball was dead, but Rescorla didn't like to take any chances. He raced over and kicked the ball deep out of play but managed to kick Sullivan in the head at the same time. Sullivan passed out.

When he gained consciousness, he was in the clubhouse, where a doctor was stitching up his head. Rescorla was sitting at his side, still flushed with excitement from the game. "We won!" he exclaimed. Still somewhat dazed, Sullivan just looked at him. "We won! Come and have a pint."

Sullivan declined. "I think I'll go home," he said.

"What's the matter with you?" Rescorla persisted. "Are you alive or dead?"

Sullivan struggled up and went with Rescorla to the pub.

It was on such occasions that Rescorla was able to indulge his love of singing, whatever the musical frustrations at school. Postrugby sessions at the pub almost always ended in rounds of lusty singing of traditional British fight songs and bawdy ballads, as well as Cornish favorites like "Trelawny" and "The White Rose."

Rescorla often challenged bullies and came to the defense of smaller, weaker boys. After he vanquished several older boys, his reputation as a fighter spread, and other boys backed down. At a rugby match in Redruth, the Colts were playing a team that boasted the Cornish wrestling champion, who also happened to be a bully who had been taunting one of the Colts' smaller, younger players. At the next line-out, where the players from opposing teams face each other before beginning play, Rescorla tapped him on the shoulder, beckoning him to come out and settle the score. Terry Mungles, one of Rescorla's teammates, recognized the look on Rescorla's face. It was the gaze of intense concentration and determination that meant nothing was going to stand in his way. The wrestling champion backed down, and the taunting stopped.

When Rescorla was sixteen, he took the battery of British examinations called the O levels, standardized tests in a range of subjects. Students who do well may choose several topics to study in greater depth for the following two years and then take the A levels, which qualify them for university study. Rescorla took the O levels in eight subjects and passed all eight. But moving on to the A levels in anticipation of university study was not an option for Rescorla, whose parents lacked the financial means and were more concerned about his getting a job. Rescorla was apprenticed to the British Post Office as an engineer and attended a local technical college one day a week.

For someone like Rescorla, who craved adventure and displayed a lifelong disinterest in anything technical or mechanical, work as a postal engineer trainee must have been stupefyingly dull. The life Rescorla's apprenticeship was preparing him for was little different from the one his father already led, and the prospect of a lifetime as a British civil servant filled him with dread. In any event, Rescorla had no intention of continuing his apprenticeship.

As soon as he turned seventeen and a half he announced to his family that he was leaving for London to join the army. They weren't surprised; at the time, everyone had to perform some form of national service, and Rescorla had been talking about becoming a soldier all his life. But they thought he'd try for the Royal Air Force. At age fourteen, Rescorla and Sullivan had eagerly joined the Royal Air Training Corps, a youth training program, and gone to training camps twice a year, where they were taken for a few flights in old military aircraft. The Hayle contingent also did target practice at the dunes near the harbor. Rescorla was an excellent marksman and competed in tournaments in other towns. Yet he could be reckless, sometimes deliberately firing over the dunes toward the sea, where he might have hit a passing boat. But the army had immediate openings. As Rescorla later told Hill, "There was a world out there to be seen and conquered." He intended to "climb the ladder of achievement," which he could never hope to do in Hayle.

In autumn of 1957, Rescorla packed up his few belongings. A cousin, Anthony Bawden, came by to see him off at the train station. Rescorla embraced his parents and sister. "No tears," he said as he left. "I don't want none of that."

★

BY THE TIME DAN HILL WAS FIFTEEN, he had developed into a handsome young man with piercing blue eyes, tan from working outdoors under the Nevada desert sun. He was just under six feet tall, a little shorter and slighter of build than Rescorla but just as tough. Unlike Rescorla, he had never had time for sports at school, but he had developed a powerful chest and shoulders from the heavy lifting he did at a lumberyard and from his own construction business, which was bringing in nearly $150 a week, far more than his father made. He had bought a truck and tools and was pouring cement sidewalks and driveways, all while attending high school. In late September 1954, he returned home one day to see a 1952 Kaiser automobile in the driveway. He knew his mother had been eyeing the car, which had been for sale in the neighborhood. He knew they didn't have the money for it. When he asked, he learned that his mother had traded his truck and tools, the core of his construction business, for the used car. Dan was apoplectic, and, as he readily acknowledged, he was "rude and disrespectful." He also announced he was leaving home and not coming back. He would support himself.

His mother called his father, and as he was leaving with a few of his things, his father came storming up the front steps. He tried to block Dan, and Dan instinctively pushed him, knocking him back down the steps. Father and son plunged into a fierce battle, and Dan ended up with two broken ribs. His mother called the police, and they broke up the fight. Dan stormed off, vowing never to speak to his father again.

Three weeks later, Dan went to a grocery store to cash a check. As he got out of his car, he saw his mother and father coming out. His father spotted him and came rushing over before he could get away. "Danny," he said, "I'm so damn sorry. I'm so sorry." He paused and wiped the tears from his eyes. "You became a man and I never realized it."

Hill forgave his father, but he was not coming back. By then, Dan was already headed for the army, even though the minimum age to enlist was eighteen. His sister Donna was two years older than he was. He got a copy of her birth certificate, and it was easy enough to alter the few letters necessary to change "Donna" into "Daniel." Ever since he'd seen the Geyer brothers in their marine blues, Dan knew he would join the military. He longed to be a paratrooper so he could finally jump out of planes. He was steeped in the patriotism of World War II, the Korean War, and the fight against communism. He wanted to fight and win the next world war and come back a hero. It didn't bother him that he hadn't graduated from high school and was only fifteen years old. He'd seen a newsreel about an association of "boy soldiers," all of whom had lied about their ages to get into the military. One had fought in Korea at the age of thirteen and risen to the rank of captain.

The day he left to report for duty in Los Angeles, Dan went to say good-bye to his parents. His mother cried and hugged him, and his father gave him a pack of Lucky Strikes and three dollar bills. It was all the cash he had. His sister, Donna, hugged him, and he gave her $50. "Don't say anything, and use it to buy them some groceries," he said. He knew they were struggling without his income.

Dan was assigned to basic training at Fort Ord near Monterey, California. He was handed his uniform and clothing, afterward spreading them out on his bunk in amazement. He had six pairs of underwear and socks and two pairs of shoes. He'd never had two pairs of shoes at once and so many changes of underwear. His bunk had clean sheets, both top and bottom. He'd never slept with more than one sheet. On Sunday morning, they had all the ham and eggs they could eat.

About halfway through his basic training, shrimp was on the Sunday dinner menu. Dan hadn't tasted shrimp since Juju had shared the delicacy with him all those years ago. Because of the weekend, only about 40 of the 220 men in the barracks were around, so there was more than enough shrimp to go around. "You can have as much as you want," the mess sergeant said, and when he saw Hill's face light up, he ordered, "Get me a gallon for Hill!"

Hill had only one thought: This is the greatest goddamned place God ever made.

★

A BATTERY OF MILITARY TESTS showed Rescorla to be of high intelligence, though he displayed "unconventional thought patterns." As a result, he was assigned to an army intelligence unit and posted to Nicosia, the Mediterranean capital of Cyprus, then a British protectorate and subject to British military rule. Like the Congo, Cyprus was another unlikely outpost of cold war intrigue, caught up in the crosscurrents of the Greek civil war, split between Greek Cypriots and Turkish nationalists. Britain had annexed Cyprus as a colony during the First World War, when Turkey entered the conflict on the side of Germany and Austria-Hungary. It avoided Nazi occupation during World War II, but after the war there was a growing movement among the majority Greek population for union with Greece, as well as a strong nationalist Communist-backed insurgency. Local hostility was intense toward the occupying British forces, which conducted antiterrorist sweeps and were housed in heavily fortified camps.

In the British military, Rescorla finally ran squarely into the class system that still dominated most British institutions. He was under the command of an officer corps consisting mainly of public school and university graduates, many of them from upper-class English families. He later confided that for the first time, he became acutely aware of his own Cornish accent and working-class patterns of speech, which embarrassed him. He began systematically to change his accent and speech patterns, with considerable success. He had always been a skilled mimic. But he realized he would need to do far more if he were ever to advance in the British military. He needed more education, and even then his humble origins might always hold him back. Still, he was convinced that education was the key to advancement. As he later lectured to Hill, "Never stop studying, learning, improving yourself. You should study and learn something new until the day you die of old age."

The reality of intelligence work in the harsh environment of Cyprus was also considerably less inspiring than Rescorla had imagined. He later confided in Hill that aspects of his work had disturbed him, such as the interrogation of prisoners. Rescorla watched as suspects were seated under intense lights, then systematically beaten in the head with a sock filled with sand. The rhythmic thumps of the sock reduced the men to sobbing, incoherent supplicants, begging for mercy, willing to say anything. Surely there were better, more humane and reliable ways to get information, Rescorla thought. He asked Hill what the Americans did and seemed fascinated by the use of drugs, such as Pentothal, to extract confessions.

On leaves, Rescorla returned home to Hayle. On one of his visits he proudly showed his cousin Anthony a six-inch knife in a leather sheath. "I took this off a bloody Cypriot," he reported, "and I thought I'd bring it home." Otherwise he was deliberately vague about the nature of his work, which seemed to consist of secret nighttime raids on suspected Communist cells. He hinted that he had killed people. "Anthony," he said, "I usually go out and take them out, me and my boys."

★

BY THE TIME Rescorla was in Cyprus, Hill was also undertaking top secret missions as a Special Forces paratrooper. After finishing his basic training at Fort Ord, he'd applied for an airborne battalion and gone to Fort Campbell, Kentucky, for jump school. Having dreamed since childhood of jumping from planes, Hill took to it as easily as other people dive into swimming pools. Despite the army's intense psychological conditioning, not everyone managed as well. Of the entering group of 220 men, 120 made it to graduation.

Hill was stationed in southern Germany, at Augsburg, near the magnificent scenery of the Alps. There, he polished his German language skills and was sent on his secret mission into Hungary. Two years later, in 1958, Syrian troops toppled the democratic government of Lebanon and installed a puppet regime, which alarmed the United States and brought the condemnation of the United Nations. In April, a commercial flight bound for Beirut was diverted by U.S. fighter planes. So as not to arouse the suspicion of air controllers at the Beirut airport, its place in the flight plan was taken by a U.S. military transport filled with a platoon of paratroopers from the Eleventh Airborne Division, Hill among them.

The plane passed over the airport, then turned and circled back. At about 2:30 A.M., under cover of darkness, Hill jumped. He and his platoon members carried infrared signals, beacons, all the tools necessary to establish a temporary landing zone. But they proved unnecessary. Hill and his men stormed the air traffic control tower, which surrendered without any resistance. They changed the broadcast frequency and guided in a task force of the 101st Airborne Battle Group. The American forces came pouring off the planes and fanned out through the city. By dawn, all critical points were under American control. The Syrians and their Lebanese surrogates fled.

Lebanon's democratic government was reinstalled, but the American troops stayed on for six months. Hill was fascinated by Beirut, then a beautiful city considered the Paris of the Middle East. It was a major banking center, a center of learning, a city of culture, cafés, and palm-lined boulevards. Before dropping into the airport, Hill and his comrades had taken a crash army course in Arabic, and with his natural facility for languages, he was soon conversing with local people he encountered as he explored the city.

Hill had also been reading a paperback English version of the Koran to familiarize himself with the dominant religion of the people he'd be meeting. It was his first encounter with Islam. Though raised a Catholic, Hill hadn't attended church since before he joined the army, and somewhat to his surprise, he found himself intrigued by some of the teachings of Mohammed. From early morning until dusk he heard the calls to prayer of the muezzin, and he wondered what was going on behind the graceful minarets of the many mosques he encountered on his trips around the city.

Finally, Hill decided to see for himself. He went to the closest mosque and introduced himself as an American soldier. The imam seemed delighted to meet him. He spoke English and was a professor at the renowned American University in Beirut. Hill began going to the mosque on a regular basis, and the imam invited him to his home. Hill, the imam, and other men would settle in for long afternoons of conversation and drinking tea. The imam's wife would serve them, quietly carrying in a tray, her head and face veiled. Hill never saw the imam's children. The imam gave Hill a better English translation of the Koran, as well as a book of commentary. Hill read them and enjoyed the ensuing discussions with such learned Muslims. The imam stressed that Islam was a tolerant faith, one that embraced Jesus as a great prophet and that welcomed Christians, Jews, and even Buddhists into its beliefs. "They are all prophets," the imam said of the great leaders of other faiths. "All that matters is that you follow the prophets."

In September 1958, the Americans left Beirut and Hill returned with his unit to Germany. One day, on a whim, he consulted a gypsy fortune-teller. "Daniel Hill will not live to be thirty," she solemnly intoned. Hill wasn't sure how seriously to take the message, but if his life was going to be short, he intended to make the most of it.

When his tour in Germany ended, Hill was selected for Ranger school at Fort Benning, which included an intensive program of physical conditioning and training in hand-to-hand combat, survival skills, ambushes, raids, and patrols. Then he spent several weeks in Florida swamps, learning amphibious and jungle operations, followed by a stint at a northern Georgia mountain camp, learning mountain climbing and special operations in rugged terrain and participating in survival exercises. Hill excelled so much at what many consider the army's toughest training program that he was asked to return to Fort Benning as a Ranger instructor. Eight months later, his commander asked him to infiltrate the Katanga insurrection in the Congo.

★

RESCORLA HAD INITIALLY SIGNED on for a three-year tour of duty in Cyprus. When it ended, he had no intention of returning to Hayle. Toward the end of his tour, he sought out Terry Mungles, a friend from Hayle who was also stationed in Cyprus. Mungles was resting in his tent one afternoon when Rescorla threw back the flap. "Mungles, what are you doing here?" he asked, wearing his khaki sergeant's uniform and a mischievous smile. The two talked, and Rescorla asked Mungles what his plans were when he left the army.

"I'm going back to Hayle to get a job," Mungles replied. He was eager to finish his military service and return home.

"No, you're not going back to Hayle," Rescorla insisted. "You're coming with me."

"Where?" Mungles asked.

"Africa," Rescorla said, a gleam in his eye. "They're crying out for police in Rhodesia and South Africa."

3

HEART OF A LION

Lion trophy with members of the Northern Rhodesia police force.
(Trustees of the Imperial War Museum, London)

THOUGH KITWE was a remote corner of the British empire, Rescorla had quickly created a comfortable life for himself. He occasionally encountered a member of the titled nobility, but class distinctions were minimal, at least among the white residents. Like officers in the British Army, Rescorla had a batman, a young African man who functioned as his valet, washing and pressing his uniforms, polishing his boots, serving tea in his quarters. Apart from the periodic riot and military mission into the bush, Rescorla's duties as a member of the police force mostly consisted of keeping in shape and playing rugby. He had plenty of time to read. And he was having a discreet romantic relationship with one of the Englishwomen assigned to the police force. His colleagues didn't know much about it, though they noticed Rescorla pulled back as it threatened to become too serious. By the time Hill arrived on the scene, it seemed to be over. Rescorla told Hill that the woman had fallen in love with him, but he had no intention of getting bogged down in any romantic entanglements at this stage of his life. Dravot's downfall was too much on his mind.

Hill could identify with Rescorla's attitude, since he shared it. Nonetheless, he had ended up married. While he was at Fort Benning, he had met an attractive secretary who was a few years older than he. Patricia Amandelora had been married briefly and divorced and indicated that she couldn't have children, which Dan liked, since he didn't want to leave children behind should he die young, as the fortune-teller had predicted. Patricia said she understood that Dan's military career was dangerous and that he might be gone for extended periods. Still, he resisted getting married. But then he realized that she would be eligible for life insurance benefits if he were killed. So Dan took her to see his parents in Las Vegas, and they were married there, in the Little Chapel of the Flowers. The ceremony cost a total of $15. A month later, Patricia told him she was pregnant. At first he couldn't believe it. But a daughter, Gigi, was born nine months later. Marriage and fatherhood hadn't changed Hill's military ambitions. When he was assigned to a secret mission of indefinite duration in Africa, he took his wife and child to New Jersey to live with Patricia's parents. He and Patricia said good-bye at the airport in New York, and she never complained about being left behind with a baby. That had been part of their understanding.

Now both Hill and Rescorla were far from New Jersey and Cornwall, and adventure beckoned. The two friends were finishing breakfast one morning, when a sergeant came up to their table. "There's a villager outside," he said. "It's hard to understand what he's saying. He seems to be upset about a lion."

"Let's take a look," Rescorla said, and got up from the table. Hill followed him outside.

A man was in front of the building, trembling with excitement. Several native residents had gathered around him, trying to translate. But his speech was incoherent.

"Calm down," Rescorla told him. He let the man take a few breaths, then gently urged him to speak slowly. Gradually his story emerged.

The man was from a neighboring village, about five miles from Kitwe. Most of its residents were subsistence farmers. A female lion had taken to preying on the villagers' livestock, which threatened their livelihoods. Already, several goats and a cow had been slaughtered.

Rescorla told him to wait there, then went to the general store. He came back with a massive .577 double-barreled rifle. Then he and the villager got into Rescorla's open Land Rover and drove off in a cloud of dust. Hill would have liked to go along, but Rescorla told him to stay behind.

When Rescorla got to the village, he bought one of the villagers' goats, then drove to a small clearing near one of the farms where the lion had struck. He drove a stake in the center of the clearing and tied the goat to it. Then he and the man from the village built a blind on the edge of the clearing, using branches and grass as camouflage. By then it was late afternoon. Rescorla loaded the rifle and settled in to wait.

Rescorla didn't expect anything to happen before dark, but dusk was just beginning to fall when the villager signaled that he heard something. Then Rescorla heard it, too—the breaking of branches and other signs of a heavy tread. Suddenly the lion appeared on the edge of the clearing, a magnificent sight even in the fading twilight.

The plan was to remain in the blind until the lion attacked the goat and then fire while it was preoccupied with its prey. The .577 had only two shots and was cumbersome to reload. But Rescorla was overcome with excitement at the sight of the lion and, his adrenaline surging, he leaped out of the blind into the clearing. The lion immediately shifted its attention from the goat, now bleating wildly, to Rescorla. It dropped into a crouch. Then, as Rescorla took aim, it sprang toward him in a single powerful leap. The gun exploded.

The lion fell dead at Rescorla's feet.

Hill and the others at the barracks were eagerly awaiting Rescorla's return. At about 8:00 P.M., the Land Rover pulled up, and in the open rear of the vehicle was the body of the lion. People from the neighborhood came running to gawk. It looked huge, sprawling over the sides of the vehicle. It turned out to weigh 350 pounds. Before disposing of the carcass, Rescorla had his batman carefully remove and save its teeth and claws. The next day, he returned to the village and handed them out to the villagers, who believed they protected the bearer and brought good luck. The people seemed in awe of Rescorla and expressed their gratitude with offerings of fruits and vegetables from their small plots. For himself, Rescorla had two of the lion's teeth and the shell from the bullet that killed her strung into a necklace, which was blessed by the village's witch doctor. Rescorla began wearing it as a good-luck charm.

"They say it gives you the heart of a lion," he told Hill.

★

AFTER THEY READ "The Man Who Would Be King," Hill had been using his spare time in Kitwe to explore more works of literature. Rescorla encouraged him to help himself to the small library he had assembled in the barracks. Hill had read more of Kipling's works recommended by Rescorla: the novel *Soldiers Three* and the poem "Gunga Din." Hill was particularly captivated by the poem "If," which Woodrow Wilson had often cited as his favorite literary work, especially the stanza that ends:

> *If you can force your heart and nerve and sinew*
> *To serve your turn long after they are gone,*
> *And so to hold on when there is nothing in you*
> *Except the Will which says to them: "Hold on!"*

Hill and Rescorla often discussed these works in their long conversations. Like Rescorla, Hill responded strongly to Kipling's themes of courage in the face of impossible odds, integrity, individualism, and personal advancement. At the same time, they shared Kipling's skepticism about the future of colonialism. Kipling may have embodied the spirit of the British empire at its height, but in story after story, including "The Man Who Would Be King," he prophesied its doom.

Kipling was by no means the only author they read and discussed. Hill was amazed that Rescorla could quote from memory stretches of Marx's *Das Kapital* and, in formulating his anti-Communist views, had read nearly all of Marx's works. Hill also browsed through volumes of Rescorla's Harvard Classics and Churchill's *History of the English-Speaking Peoples,* which had also been an inspiration to Rescorla.

But the idyllic days of reading, exercising, eating well, and drinking brandy-and-sodas at the officers mess couldn't last indefinitely. Rescorla's efforts on Hill's behalf didn't turn up any openings in Northern Rhodesia, but they did in wealthier and more populated Southern Rhodesia, which was facing stronger white opposition to a militant independence movement. In October, little more than a month after meeting Rescorla in the pub, Hill packed his few belongings into his tiny car and headed south for Salisbury, the capital. He entered the Rhodesian army as a private in an infantry brigade but was quickly enrolled in an officer training program.

Hill stayed in close contact with Rescorla through a steady stream of lengthy letters and an occasional phone call. One night Rescorla called. "I've got something I want to talk to you about, in person," he said.

"Come on down," Hill said, eager to see his friend again. But he wondered what it was that Rescorla didn't want to discuss on the phone.

Rescorla arrived in his Land Rover, dusty from the long trip from Kitwe. After cleaning up, he and Hill drove into Salisbury for dinner. They had a few drinks, and finally Hill said, "What's the big deal you want to talk about?"

Rescorla lowered his voice. "It look like British troops might be coming in," he said. The news was potentially explosive in both Northern and Southern Rhodesia, which were scheduled to gain their independence as separate nations in 1964. Despite proposed constitutions that would supposedly guarantee property interests and white minority rights, the white colonialists were becoming increasingly restive at the prospect of black majority rule, especially after the turmoil and bloodshed they'd witnessed in the Congo. In Northern Rhodesia, Roy Welensky was talking of seceding from the commonwealth and setting up a white-controlled government. The arrival of British troops might mean civil war, with British regulars and black nationalists pitted against Northern Rhodesia's white-dominated police and military forces.

"Yeah," Hill replied. "It's the same down here." Indeed, the even more militant white prime minister of Southern Rhodesia, Ian Smith, had already notified the army that all soldiers would have to swear allegiance to the government of Rhodesia and be prepared to fight any foreign power on its behalf, including Great Britain. Anyone unwilling to sign such a statement would be discharged.

"What do you think?" Rescorla asked. Hill had noticed that Rescorla often expressed himself by asking questions.

"I don't want to go to war against the British," Hill said emphatically, no matter what the pay, the perks, the possibility for adventure, or the U.S. Army's eagerness for inside intelligence. "They're our people," he said, noting that his family was half English. "I don't want to fight against members of my own family. Half of them are our friends we've met down here. These are Winston Churchill's troops!"

"I know what you mean," Rescorla said. "Some of those men could be from Cornwall."

They paused thoughtfully. With its natural resources and climate, southern Africa seemed to offer such potential. They foresaw chaos once the British were gone, but armed insurrection and white minority rule weren't the answers.

"I'm taking the discharge and getting the hell out of here," Hill finally said.

Rescorla nodded in agreement. "What are we going to do next?" He said he couldn't see going back to Britain, where, after having grown accustomed to being an officer in the colonial forces, he'd be reduced to the rank of an enlisted man in the British Army.

Hill had already been giving the question some thought. "Look," he said, "we both want to fight Communists, and keep them from world domination. There's only one place to do that. If anybody stands a chance of holding them back and defeating them, it's the U.S. We have the industry, the money, the population, and the power in the world to hold them off." With the Cold War in full tilt and Communist threats brewing in Cuba, Latin America, and Indochina, Hill predicted the U.S. military would have to expand rapidly. Hill knew the army welcomed foreigners who hoped to become U.S. citizens.

"We can go to the States, enlist in the army, enroll in Officer Candidate School. It will be a snap for us because of our background. We'll have all the men, money, equipment, and materials that we need.

"Meet me in the States," Hill continued. "When you get to New York, call me. I'll come pick you up and put you up in our house."

"How will I get in touch with you?" Rescorla asked.

Hill scribbled his phone number on a piece of paper and handed it to him. Rescorla hadn't yet committed himself, but Hill knew he'd show up. He could see the familiar gleam in Rescorla's eye that meant he had kindled his spirit of adventure.

Like Peachey and Dravot, they would set off for a new land where they could make something of themselves. And if one of them got into trouble, "the other will stand by him," Hill reminded him.

4

AMERICAN DREAM

Susan Greer on a beach in Portugal.
(Courtesy of Susan Rescorla)

SUSAN GREER glanced nervously across the elegant dining room of a restaurant in Lisbon, Portugal. At first she had thought it was her imagination. Then she thought she would ignore it. But she had felt a little flutter of excitement. Now she was sure: the strikingly handsome man in the dark suit was staring in her direction.

She brushed her light frosted hair aside and leaned across the table to confide this realization to her friend. This was their first evening in Portugal, but Susan had grown accustomed that year to the attentions of European men. She was twenty years old, five feet one, slender, and spoke fluent French in addition to Spanish, which she'd been studying at the University of Madrid. She'd graduated the year before from Endicott College, an all-women's two-year college outside Boston that, while academically sound, catered to the well-bred daughters of affluent families preparing primarily for marriage. Susan fit the Endicott stereotype: her father was a successful gynecologist and general practitioner in New Jersey, and her grandfather had been an executive in New York with Texaco. Her ancestor had fought in the American Revolution and was a direct descendant of Sir Francis Drake. The family lived in an eighteenth-century stone-and-brick mansion with massive white pillars, once occupied by George Washington.

Many of her classmates had gone from May graduations to June weddings, but something in Susan resisted. Not that she minded the prospect of marriage. It was 1962, and young girls of Susan's generation had been encouraged since birth to view marriage and motherhood as a woman's highest calling. The Kennedys were in the White House, and though Susan's parents were staunch Republicans, the Kennedy vision of Camelot was her dream, too. Susan longed to emulate Jacqueline Kennedy, her beautiful manners and soft-spoken elegance, her stylish clothing and hairstyles. Still, despite her traditional upbringing, Susan felt there was something of a free spirit buried inside her. She was strongly drawn to the arts, and on trips to Manhattan she'd had glimpses of a bohemian world far from the orderly, comfortable life of suburban Glen Ridge, New Jersey. She'd also been reading avidly, especially the novels of Ernest Hemingway. She was captivated by the stories of American expatriates leading glamorous lives of romance and intrigue in Europe.

So Susan had come to Europe to study art history, choosing Madrid because, after years of Latin and French, she wanted to learn a new language. It was also a setting of one of her favorite Hemingway novels, *The Sun Also Rises*. Generalissimo Franco, the only surviving fascist dictator, still ruled with an iron hand, and his black-shirted police were still everywhere in evidence. The civil war was twenty years in the past, but Spain had yet to join postwar Europe and remained poor, with little economic development. Susan enrolled in classes at the University of Madrid and, at her parents' insistence, lived in a convent, the Collegio Santa Teresa, with strict curfews and standards of decorum enforced by the resident nuns. Susan's room was nearly bare, furnished with a simple single bed and washbasin. Susan was struck by the contrast between the austere, ascetic life of the nuns and the splendor of the Spanish baroque churches, the sumptuous trappings of the Jesuit order, and the magnificent religious paintings and sculptures of the Prado museum, where she spent many hours of study and contemplation. Susan and her family were Episcopalian, and Spanish Catholicism was new and exotic.

None of this had kept Susan confined to the convent, however. She was eager to explore, taking trolley cars to random destinations, then walking for hours. She soon became close friends with Marilyn Rollins, another young American woman residing at the convent. Marilyn was a striking blonde, the daughter of an Italian family that lived in Brooklyn. The two friends took weekend trips whenever possible, traveling by train to Toledo, Granada, Avila. When they tired of a steady diet of olive oil, they went to a restaurant they found on the outskirts of the city, not far from a U.S. military base, that served hamburgers. Once they stayed out after the 11:00 P.M. curfew, and when they returned to the convent, they found the massive wrought iron gate closed and locked. Some athletic young men from the University of Nebraska, also studying in Madrid, hoisted them over the fence, and they thought they had made it to their rooms undetected. But the next morning they were summoned by the Mother Superior, who lectured them sternly in Spanish that the incident was never to be repeated.

Marilyn had declined Susan's suggestion of a week-long holiday in Portugal, but toward the end of the summer term, Susan persuaded another friend to join her on the trip. They had taken an overnight train from Madrid, arriving in Lisbon tired, hot, and lacking any hotel reservations. But Susan was immediately captivated by the city, whose turn-of-the-century architecture and broad avenues had been untouched by either World War II or the Spanish Civil War. They had quickly found an inexpensive hotel room and, after sundown, made their way to a charming restaurant recommended by the hotel.

Out of the corner of her eye, Susan could see the handsome man rising from his seat. Maybe she shouldn't have risked a glimpse in his direction. It had probably only encouraged him. Still, she was flattered. Usually, attractive men pursued Marilyn, occasionally urging her to bring her demure friend "Suzita" along as her *dueña,* or chaperone. And as he approached the table, Susan looked again. Her first impression had been right: he was undeniably handsome.

"Bon soir, mesdemoiselles," he began, looking directly at Susan. He had addressed her in French! Susan thought that was incredibly charming and romantic. She offered him her hand, and he bowed gracefully and kissed it. She felt a bit dizzy. Maybe it was the lack of sleep from the train or the Portuguese wine she and her friend had been sipping.

He introduced himself as Enrique Godhino and said he had an apartment in Lisbon, where he owned an antique furniture shop. Susan estimated he was about thirty. He had dark eyes and hair and looked dashing in his white shirt and suit. Replying in French as well, Susan explained that they were Americans studying in Madrid. They had decided on the spur of the moment to spend a holiday in Portugal, and this was their first evening in the country. Enrique asked her if she and her friend would join him the next night for dinner and dancing at the casino in Estoril, the resort town on a beach just outside of Lisbon. He had a friend, he said, an attorney, who would love to meet Susan's friend.

Susan and her friend conferred briefly. This was exactly the sort of thing she'd been warned about and that the nuns would severely disapprove of. Susan knew that she should politely but firmly decline and then studiously ignore the man for the remainder of the evening. Yet Susan could sense a bohemian impulse. She felt a little reckless. And he was so handsome and charming. What could be the harm in an evening of dinner and dancing, with her girlfriend as chaperone? Throwing caution to the winds, the two young women agreed to meet him at their hotel the next night.

Even though she was a student roaming through Europe, Susan had brought the clothes for just such an occasion. She had packed high heels and a chiffon cocktail dress with a short skirt and a handwoven bodice. The casino was Estoril's most elegant night spot, situated right on the beach with views of the Atlantic Ocean. It offered gambling, live entertainment featuring Europe's best-known performers, and dancing into the early hours of the morning. Like the Spaniards, the Portuguese usually dined about 10:00 P.M. and thought nothing of staying out until two in the morning.

Over drinks and dinner, Susan asked Enrique about his family and learned that he was actually a count, the descendant of an aristocratic Portuguese family that owned a large estate in northern Portugal. Susan had never met a European aristocrat before. Soon she and Enrique were deep in conversation, always in French, increasingly oblivious to her friend and the lawyer. When Enrique took Susan to the dance floor, he proved to be a polished dancer, whirling her confidently through the steps. Susan was an accomplished dancer herself, having studied ballroom dancing while growing up in New Jersey, and she quickly adjusted to the tricky Latin rhythms. She and Enrique made a striking couple. To Susan it seemed almost indescribably glamorous, and by the end of the evening, she realized she was smitten.

The next night the count took Susan to the rooftop garden of Lisbon's leading hotel, the Mundial, where they had dinner and gazed out over the lights of the city toward the ocean in the distance. Then he drove her to Cascais, a picturesque fishing village on the coast just north of Estoril. From there they explored other villages and sights, such as the hilltop town of Pena. Inevitably, the idyllic week neared an end, and Susan had to return to Madrid. Enrique told her he loved her. She couldn't believe it had all happened so fast, but she had been swept off her feet. She, too, felt she was in love. She promised to see him again and said she would return in a few weeks, as soon as the term ended.

Back at the convent, Susan couldn't wait to tell her friend Marilyn.

Portugal, she said, was a beautiful, magical country, like none she'd ever seen. Only one day after her return, she received a telegram from Enrique, reiterating his love. Then he phoned. She received a telegram or phone call nearly every day. When she asked for a photograph of him so she could better picture him and show her friends what he looked like, Enrique readily obliged.

The photo arrived, and Susan carefully opened the envelope. How handsome he was! He was smiling, wearing a beautiful casual shirt, open at the neck, and slacks. He was seated in one of the handsome chairs he sold at his shop. Then Susan noticed something she was sure she had never seen when they were together. On the fourth finger of his right hand was a simple gold band.

Susan looked again. It was unmistakably a wedding ring. She was stunned. He'd said nothing about having had a wife or being divorced or widowed. She had to consider the painful possibility that he was still married. When he called her the next day, she confronted him with the evidence of the ring, and he acknowledged that he was indeed married. But he couldn't understand why she was so upset. He said that he and his wife were separated and never saw each other, but that the church made it impossible to for him to divorce. He insisted that he loved only Susan.

It had been daring enough for Susan to embark on an impetuous romance with a Portuguese count she barely knew. But to have an affair with a married man was unthinkable. Susan said she never wanted to see him again and slammed down the phone. Then she burst into tears. She felt angry, hurt, and betrayed. She had been happily ensconced in a fairy tale, and suddenly it had turned out to be an illusion.

★

SUSAN'S FRIEND Marilyn tried to console her. As they often did in the evenings, she and Susan walked to the Plaza Mayor, the cobblestone square where Susan and her friends had spent hours sitting in the sidewalk cafés or in the many wine bars near the square, eating tapas, drinking sangria, and listening to Spanish music and strolling musicians. Just a few weeks before, they had enjoyed a fully staged open-air performance of *Carmen* there. She enjoyed watching the male students from the university known as Las Tunas. They gathered there, wearing colorful tunics and capes, then roamed from one bar or café to another, drinking and singing late into the night. They capes were decorated with colorful ribbons, supposedly one for each woman they had conquered. There were plenty of ribbons on display. That had once seemed charming and amusing, but now Susan felt she had been reduced to little more than a conquest, another ribbon on the cape of a married man.

Perhaps travel would help. She and Marilyn boarded a plane for Rome, then hired a car and driver to take them south along the cliffs and panoramic views of the Amalfi coast. They went by boat to the island of Capri, then to Sorrento, Naples, Florence, Venice, and finally back to Rome. They toured Roman ruins, sought out museums, cathedrals, and Renaissance art treasures, and enjoyed the beautiful landscapes and local cuisine, especially the fresh seafood along the Mediterranean coast. While they were sitting on a terrace in Capri, they overhead a radio report that Marilyn Monroe had committed suicide. They were stunned. She was beautiful, young, a movie star. They didn't understand how such bad things could happen to people.

While in Florence, Susan confided to Marilyn that she wasn't feeling well. As the trip proceeded, she began to tire easily, lose her appetite, and then vomit after almost every meal. She grew weak, her skin became pale and waxy, and she developed a faint but unpleasant odor that persisted no matter how often she bathed. Marilyn cared for her, staying by her side, mopping her brow, cleaning up after her.

By the time they reached Rome, Susan could barely leave the hotel. Marilyn called the American Hospital, and they were referred to a doctor who boasted that he had recently treated Elizabeth Taylor. The doctor was charming and flirtatious but didn't inspire professional confidence. Susan felt he was more interested in examining Marilyn than her, and in any event, he dismissed her symptoms as a likely case of food poisoning that would soon pass. But Susan's condition only seemed to worsen, so Marilyn finally called Susan's father in New Jersey. Dr. Greer was immediately alarmed, and from Marilyn's description of Susan's symptoms, he thought he knew the diagnosis. He ordered them to cut their trip short and get the earliest available flight from Rome to New York.

Susan, who ordinarily wouldn't have dreamed of flying in anything but a dress and high heels, boarded the plane in rubber flip-flop sandals. She was so weak when they arrived at Idlewild Airport in New York that Marilyn had to hold her up and help her walk off the plane. Susan got as far as the terminal, where she saw her father waiting with a wheelchair.

"Dr. Greer, Susan isn't feeling very well," Marilyn said anxiously, stating the obvious. Susan's skin had turned a pale yellow.

Melvin immediately bent over to smell Susan's skin, which confirmed his suspicious. "Couldn't you smell the bile?" he asked. But Marilyn had gotten used to the odd odor and hadn't thought to mention it. Then Susan collapsed into the wheelchair.

The next thing she knew, she was in East Orange General Hospital, suffering from an advanced case of infectious hepatitis, possibly contracted from tainted shellfish. In a sense, it was lucky she had been misdiagnosed in Rome, since she would never have been allowed to board a plane were it known she had such a contagious disease. She was kept in isolation, with no visitors allowed. She was barely conscious.

★

SOME OF SUSAN'S earliest memories were of her father setting out for his rounds at the hospital. Melvin Greer returned every day for lunch, then spent afternoons seeing patients who came to his office, which was attached to their large pre–Revolutionary War house. He also made house calls, for the then handsome sum of $3 a visit. Though her father was an obstetrician, doctors who specialized in difficult deliveries and pregnancies had delivered Susan herself at St. Vincent's Hospital in Manhattan. Her mother, Marian Sartorius Greer, had had five miscarriages, including the devastating loss of a male fetus when she was eight months pregnant. Marian's water had broken while she was at home, and Susan's father had rushed her through the Lincoln Tunnel to Manhattan. An ambulance from St. Vincent's was waiting at the end of the tunnel to collect her. The city was experiencing a power blackout, and none of the streetlights or traffic signals were working. Fortunately, St. Vincent's had a generator and was functioning on emergency power. Susan was born on March 26, 1942.

Susan heard the stories of her birth and her mother's miscarriages on a few occasions when she said she wished she had a brother or a sister. She was destined to be an only child, doted on by parents who considered her birth a near miracle. At home she was surrounded by adults, her parents and her grandparents, Melvin and Martha Greer and Betty Rose, who did the housekeeping, cooked some of the meals, and looked after Susan, whom she always called "Baby."

Shortly after she was born, Melvin Greer joined the U.S. Army Medical Corps and was dispatched to the Persian Gulf command, based in Teheran. He helped set up a hospital to treat the wounded from the front in Afghanistan. Later in the war he accompanied American forces into Iraq and Egypt. During the three years he was overseas, Susan's grandparents closed up the house in New Jersey and went to their summer home on the eastern shore of Maryland, on the Chesapeake Bay. It was a large nineteenth-century farmhouse with five bedrooms and wraparound porches that afforded commanding views of the bay. There were orchards, vineyards, chickens, and ducks. A large garden grew popcorn, peanuts, and melons. A local man, Tom Mills, oversaw the estate. There was a dock where her grandfather kept a rowboat and Susan's father moored his cabin cruiser, which slept four passengers. When they needed to go to town, a ferry took them across the bay to the town of Oxford, or they drove to nearby Easton or St. Michael's. Susan was too young to remember her absent father. The war had no effect on the passing seasons, the tilling of the fields, or the languid summer days spent drinking homemade lemonade on the porch. Susan loved it there. Then the war ended, and Susan's father came home. He said virtually nothing about his war experience. They returned to New Jersey, where he resumed his medical practice. But every summer, Susan and her mother and grandparents retreated to the eastern shore.

When Susan's father graduated from medical school and married Susan's mother, he was still a medical resident, and there was plenty of room in the house in Glen Ridge. His parents visited Palm Beach during the winter and traveled so often—to Europe, the Caribbean, and Central and South America—that most of the time they had the house to themselves. A new wing was built to house his medical offices.

Soon life settled into a comfortable pattern. Lunch was a formal affair, often served by Betty Rose in the dining room on fine china. Susan's mother never cooked or went into a grocery store. Susan's father and grandfather always wore a suit and tie, and her mother and grandmother wore dresses or suits. Susan, on arriving home from school each day, was expected to listen attentively and participate in the conversation, even though it was dominated by the men and often turned to the stock market and politics. Sometimes her grandfather interrupted lunch to take calls from his brokers. Her father's sister and Susan's cousins, who also spent summers with them in Maryland, often joined them.

As Susan was growing up, her mother made sure she was exposed to practically every cultural offering in New York City and showered her with lessons. They went to the old Metropolitan Opera on 38th Street, to the ballet, to Broadway shows, and to art museums. Susan studied piano, horseback riding, painting, sailing, and ballroom dancing, which later proved so useful in Lisbon. Susan's mother was an avid collector of antique dolls and belonged to an international guild of doll collectors. She often traveled to Manhattan for meetings and sometimes held elegant teas in their home for fellow doll collectors. Susan loved her mother's collection, which had over three thousand specimens. Many were antiques, with china heads; her father bought others while he was in the Middle East, and her grandparents also brought home dolls from their wide-ranging travels. Marian Greer was in demand as a lecturer and spoke widely on the subject of dolls as reflections of geography and culture.

Susan attended the Watsessing School in Bloomfield. One of her best friends was Anne Robinson, who at age five fell down a set of stairs and cracked her head. Susan's father stitched up the wound, and the two families became close, with Anne calling Susan's parents Uncle Mel and Aunt Marian and Susan similarly referring to Anne's parents as Uncle Tom and Aunt Mary. Susan's parents and her friends spent many weekends and summers in a waterfront house the Greers purchased on the north fork of Long Island, with a view of the sound and Shelter Island. Another childhood friend was Terry Caprio, whose family invited Susan to join them in Bermuda for Easter vacation in 1958, when Susan was sixteen. It was her first foreign trip.

The next year, when she was seventeen, her parents decided that it was time for Susan to see Europe. They spent six weeks, beginning in London, and visited ten countries, staying in the finest hotels and dining in leading restaurants. Susan fell in love with Paris and concluded that some mistake had been made at her birth: she should have been born in Paris. In Nice, they met Terry Caprio and her family and traveled together to Monte Carlo. Susan loved the experience, and it whetted her appetite for more foreign travel.

At home, Susan had few responsibilities. Betty did the cleaning, washing, and ironing. Her parents showered her with gifts and beautiful clothes. Her mother bought her a Chanel suit on Madison Avenue in Manhattan. Her father gave her a full-length beaver coat. And at age seventeen, he presented her with a 1958 gold-colored Packard car. Susan knew that she lived differently from most people and that her parents were financially comfortable, but she didn't give it much thought.

Susan attended Glen Ridge High School, where most students

came from affluent families and 95 percent went on to college. At age fifteen, she had her first date with a classmate, Robert Miele. Robert came from a large, first-generation Italian family, and his father had started a successful insurance business in Bloomfield. Robert's father had prospered in the United States, was prominent in New Jersey Republican politics, and had even run for Congress. Robert was six feet two and played baseball. He was handsome, articulate, popular, and a good student. Susan was impressed that he spoke fluent Italian and Spanish. Unlike most of the boys in her class, he was interested in art and photography and was an amateur photographer and wrote poetry. From their first date, Susan had thought seriously that she might marry him. When they were seniors, he asked Susan to the prom, and she invited him to accompany her and her parents on a three-week vacation in Jamaica. Robert loved Susan's parents, and they were always outwardly gracious and welcoming toward him. But Susan knew their feelings toward him were more ambiguous and that they hoped his relationship with Susan didn't become too serious. They were wary of the fact that he was Italian and Catholic, from a large family that was so culturally different from the reserved, dignified Greers.

Susan and Robert graduated from high school in 1960. In the yearbook, Susan wrote that she "wanted to travel all around the world before I die." Robert was voted Most Handsome and Best Dancer. Though they were still dating, Susan and Robert headed in opposite directions, Susan to Boston and Endicott College, Robert to Philadelphia, where he enrolled at Villanova. Under Susan's picture in the Endicott yearbook, the editors wrote, "She walks in grace." By 1962, when Susan graduated from the two-year college, she felt her interest in Robert was cooling somewhat. He still had two years of college, and she wanted to see more of the world before she even thought about settling down. Her parents seemed happy to finance further study in Spain and were reassured that she would be living in a convent. Of course, had they known how ill she would become, she was sure they never would have allowed her to go.

★

IN THE HOSPITAL, Susan suffered for a week from high fever and hallucinations. Only her parents were allowed to visit, and then they were required to wear surgical masks, gloves, and white robes. All of Susan's clothing was destroyed. But her photographs, including the portrait of Enrique, the Portuguese count, were spared. Gradually, the regimen of rest and fluids began to work. Her fever subsided and she felt a slight appetite. Her parents visited every day.

Toward the end of her stay, she was released from isolation. One afternoon, she awoke from a nap, opened her eyes, and saw Robert standing in the doorway. Perhaps it was the heartbreaking relationship with Enrique, or her recent near-death experience, or both, but suddenly he seemed like the answer to her prayers. She hadn't seen him since leaving for Spain, and he seemed more handsome than ever. Perhaps she had been foolish to take him for granted.

After a month in the hospital, Susan returned to her parents' home, though she remained mostly bedridden for another month and spent six months convalescing. Robert courted her assiduously, dropping by nearly every day. Susan's parents were grateful to Marilyn, whom they felt had saved their daughter's life. To thank her, they gave her season tickets to the Metropolitan Opera. Preoccupied with her own recovery and her blossoming relationship with Robert, Susan paid little attention to politics or foreign affairs. But then, in November, President Kennedy was assassinated, shattering the image of Camelot Susan had cherished. She called her friend Marilyn, and they shared their grief. It was heartbreaking that Jackie would have to leave the White House, alone with two children. Susan couldn't help but feel that an era had ended.

In December, Robert asked Melvin for permission to marry Susan. Melvin was reluctant, but he granted it. He and Susan's mother were especially upset that Robert's religion required that the wedding be held in a Catholic church rather than in their Episcopal parish. But they swallowed their reservations and told Susan that they only wanted her to be happy. Afterward, Susan came downstairs and her parents left her alone with Robert in the living room. He proposed to her on bended knee, offering her a small box wrapped in white ribbon. Inside the box was a 2.5-carat solitaire diamond. Susan thought it the most magnificent diamond she'd ever seen. She accepted without hesitation.

Now that she was feeling so much better, with her future secure, Susan plunged with zest into her last few months as a young single woman. She got a job in public relations for an advertising agency in Montclair, New Jersey. She joined a ski club. At one point she had second thoughts about the marriage and returned the ring when Robert mentioned that he might want to postpone the wedding so he could spend the summer traveling through Europe with his friends. But by March, they had compromised: they would have the June wedding Susan had always wanted, and then they would spend the entire summer on a European honeymoon.

*

JUNE 28, 1964, was a beautiful, clear, early-summer day. Susan slept late, went downstairs, where Betty served breakfast, and then bathed. She wrapped herself in a soft robe and went outside into the garden of the beautiful old house where she'd spent her entire life. She sat in a lounge chair on the terrace and put her head back so the sun could dry her hair. She felt calm, at peace, and very happy.

Later that afternoon, Susan got out the picture of the Portuguese count. She had never quite stopped thinking of him. Even now, she couldn't bring herself to throw it away. Still, she didn't want Robert to see it. She carefully removed the photo and placed it in a box with a lock and key. Then her five bridesmaids came to the house. Anne Robinson was maid of honor. They wore matching silk organza gowns layered in three shades of pink. Susan had had her wedding dress custom-made in New York. It was made of ecru silk with a high neckline and long train, which Susan thought was very European. On her head she wore a white satin pillbox hat like the ones worn by Jacqueline Kennedy. Attached to it was a lace cathedral train, a magnificent hand-made mantilla that Susan had brought with her from Spain.

The wedding ceremony began at 4:00 P.M. at Holy Name Catholic Church. Susan's mother wore a full-length mint green gown and a huge, wide-brimmed hat wrapped in matching tulle. Her father, a life-long smoker, was suffering from the early stages of emphysema, but he was able to walk her down the aisle. The men wore black tie and tails, which perfectly set off Robert's dark hair and tan.

The reception was a lavish catered affair for three hundred guests at Mayfair Farms in West Orange, New Jersey. A sit-down dinner was accompanied by dancing to a live orchestra, and Piper-Heidsieck champagne flowed throughout the evening. Susan whirled through her ballroom steps with one man after another, until the whole evening began to blur. She felt like a princess, and this was the storybook ending that everything in her life thus far had prepared her for. She fully expected to live happily ever after.

The next day, she and Robert boarded a flight for Amsterdam and began a three-month trip through Holland, Belgium, Germany, France, Italy, and Austria.

5

HARD CORPS

Rescorla at Officer Candidate School, Fort Benning, Georgia.
(Courtesy of Susan Rescorla)

ONE DAY IN JULY 1963, the phone rang at the house in Roselle, New Jersey, where Dan Hill and his family were living in an apartment upstairs from his in-laws. Hill had taken on some construction work to make extra money before rejoining the military, and he had just gotten home from the job. "It's Rescorla," his friend said. "I'm in Times Square!"

Rescorla had stayed only briefly in Hayle before following through on Hill's suggestion to join him in America. He'd already been to see the military recruiting officer in Times Square and had been staying for three days at the YMCA on 34th Street.

"Why didn't you call me sooner?" Hill asked.

Rescorla said he wanted to wander around New York for a few days, getting a feel for the place. He was dazzled by the crowds, the lights, the energy. He was captivated by a strange man he'd met who drifted along Central Park South dressed as a Viking, complete with fur tunic and a helmet with horns. "It's incredible," Rescorla excitedly told Hill. "In America you can be anything you want—even a Viking!"

Rescorla spent several days with Hill and his family before reporting to Fort Dix, New Jersey, for basic training. Hill joined him there a few months later, after finishing his construction project. Though they started in basic training—Rescorla because he was new to the U.S. Army and Hill because he'd been officially detached from service for more than ninety days—they had more experience than most of their instructors. They were quickly made acting sergeants and drill instructors. On weekends, they joined Hill's wife and two children in Roselle. Hill's family loved Rescorla, especially his mother-in-law, who was an excellent cook. She even learned to make Cornish pasties for him and served him prodigious quantities of the Italian dishes that were her specialty.

That summer Rescorla, Hill and his wife, and one of her friends visited the New York World's Fair, where they discovered a British pub that served Watney's Red Barrel ale. The women had to drag them out or they would have spent the day there. They saw Michelangelo's *Pietà*, on loan from the Vatican. Hill had never been to an art museum, and he was stunned by the power of Michelangelo's work. He vowed that someday he, too, would learn to carve. That night, the two couples danced to the music of Guy Lombardo.

Hill and Rescorla also studied and discussed military history, both at Fort Dix and in their free time. As often as they could, they traveled to battlefields and historic sights in the area, such as Valley Forge and

Jockey Hollow. Rescorla was impressed by the reproductions of shacks that Washington's troops had used as shelter during the harsh winter of 1775. "Such heroism and fortitude," Rescorla observed. "Those men lost nearly every battle and yet they won the war." The American Revolution fascinated Rescorla, as did the values of freedom, religious tolerance, and individualism enshrined in the United States Constitution. But he thought it a tragedy that Britain and American hadn't become one great English-speaking nation. "It's a damn shame that crazy bastard King George the Third didn't recognize what good Englishmen they were," Rescorla said of the American colonists.

One Saturday afternoon they were picnicking in Warinanco Park in Roselle, discussing George Washington. They were speculating about the nature of leadership and where it came from. Was it genetic, or was it instilled by the parents? Hill's son, named Daniel P. Hill in the family tradition, had been born earlier that year. Hill was surprised that his wife was able to have another child and he promptly had a vasectomy. But he was pleased the baby was a boy, especially given the gypsy fortune-teller's warning. "If something happens to me," he told Patricia, "you'll always have Danny to take care of you."

Danny was playing in the background, and Rescorla gestured toward Hill's son. "Look at him," Rescorla said. "He's got his whole life ahead of him. I wonder what he'll turn out like."

"I don't know," Hill replied. "I worry about my ability as a father." He wondered if he was doing the right thing pursuing a life of adventure that would take him from home for long periods.

Rescorla reassured him, saying that the very fact he was worrying about it showed that he loved his son. He recited:

> *If all men count with you, but none too much;*
> *If you can fill the unforgiving minute*
> *With sixty seconds' worth of distance run,*
> *Yours is the Earth and everything that's in it,*
> *And—which is more—you'll be a Man, my son!*

It was "If," the poem they had read in Africa. "Raise your son to be like that," Rescorla said. Hill said he would go to the library and get a copy, but the next evening, back at Fort Dix, Rescorla showed up at his barracks. He handed Hill a piece of paper on which he'd carefully typed the verses of the poem. Hill folded it and put it in his wallet.

One weekend they went to a drive-in theater to see *Zulu*, starring Michael Caine. Based on an actual battle in the province of Natal, South Africa, in 1879, *Zulu* tells the story of a beleaguered garrison of 140 Welsh infantrymen attacked by 4,000 armed Zulu tribesmen. Hill and Rescorla sat in the front seat. Patricia and the children, quickly bored, went to sleep in the back. But Dan and Rick were riveted. They felt like leaping out of the car to join the garrison onscreen. As the Zulus attacked, the British soldiers broke into song, the old military anthem "Men of Harlech," also known as "Welshmen Never Yield." Rescorla had learned the song in Hayle, substituting "Men of Cornwall" for "Men of Harlech," and for weeks after they saw the movie, he sang it at every opportunity.

In November 1963, Hill was training new recruits at the mortar range when he received the order to return immediately to the barracks. On arriving, he learned that they had been placed on highest alert. That night he and Rescorla listened to Walter Cronkite as he delivered the news that the president had been shot and killed in Dallas. Hill had voted for Kennedy; his father had been an ardent supporter of FDR, and the family was staunchly Democratic. Rescorla was even more stunned and upset than Hill. No English king had been killed since Charles I was beheaded in the early seventeenth century. How could this have happened? They and their colleagues were full of conjecture, speculating, as were many others, that Lee Harvey Oswald was a Soviet or Cuban agent. If so, they feared that another world war was imminent. But the alert was lifted two days later, and life at the base resumed its routine.

A few weeks later, not long before Christmas, Rescorla was granted a week's leave to visit his father in Hayle. Rescorla told Hill that he'd gotten a telegram: his father was gravely ill and might not survive. He urgently wanted to see Cyril before he died.

When Rescorla returned from the trip to England, he told Hill he had something he wanted to tell him, suggesting they meet off the base, at a nearby bar. Once they ordered their drinks, Hill asked, "How's your father doing?"

Rescorla paused for a moment, then looked at Hill. "He wasn't really my father."

"Oh, I guess I screwed that up," Hill said. "I thought you went to see your father."

"No, I screwed it up. He was actually my grandfather."

Hill let that sink in for a moment. "Then who the hell was your father?" he asked.

"I don't know," Rescorla replied.

Rescorla explained that the reason "Ste," the man he thought was his father, had wanted to see him before he died was to tell him that he was not his father. And the woman he thought was his mother was actually his grandmother. "Sis" was Rick's mother. She had become pregnant in 1938, and her parents had decided to raise the baby as their own to spare their daughter and the family the scandal of an illegitimate child. A few people in Hayle, of course, had known the truth. But no one ever said a word about it.

Hill was astounded. "Is your name really Rescorla?" he asked.

"Yes," Rescorla said. It was on his birth certificate. Written on the line for his father's name was "Unknown." His father had never seen him, Rescorla said. He'd been sent to France after the German invasion of Poland and was killed by German soldiers just before the evacuation of Dunkirk in 1940. That was all he knew.

Hill asked him if he'd asked his real mother about the circumstances of his birth.

"No," Rescorla replied. "It was too hard. I'd treated her like shit all these years, like an older sister. I didn't want to embarrass her."

Rescorla said the identity of his father didn't make much difference to him. He was an adult now, and he'd always thought he had a father, even if, as he had complained to Hill in Africa, he had felt the relationship was somewhat distant. But Hill wondered. He knew that Rescorla set great store in his Celtic heritage. Now he didn't know where his father had come from.

★

AS THEY HAD PLANNED IN AFRICA, both Hill and Rescorla applied for Officer Candidate School at the earliest opportunity, and both were accepted. But Rescorla, as a British subject, required a more extensive security clearance than Hill, so Hill arrived at Fort Benning, Georgia, in July 1964. Rescorla followed in November, the same month Lyndon Johnson was elected president in a landslide victory over Barry Goldwater.

Fort Benning, known to generations of officers as the "Benning School for Boys," occupies the site of a former Civil War plantation; its redbrick, white-columned nineteenth-century barracks form several quadrangles around a large parade ground. Besides housing the officer candidates, Fort Benning is the headquarters for the U.S. Army Infantry, the site of the paratroopers jump school, and Ranger training. It houses the secretive School of the Americas and is a laboratory for the development of infantry tactics.

The lives of the officer candidates were regimented around the clock. They were required to run between classes, spit-shine their quarters' tile floors, endure intense physical conditioning, then eat in rigid silence, staring straight ahead, lifting their forks in lockstep. So much as a glance during mealtimes earned another round of push-ups. They were scrutinized to see how well they held up under the intense and at times baffling pressure.

At age twenty-nine, Hill was older than most of his classmates. One of the youngest was a slender, intense eighteen-year-old from Pennsylvania named Larry Hess. In Hess, Hill saw many of the qualities he tried to cultivate in himself, except that he thought Hess was even more motivated. Hill predicted that if anyone in their class ever rose to the rank of general, it would be Hess. Besides being a dedicated soldier, Hess was affable, easygoing, and a talented musician who entertained Hill and other members of the class during their rare free evenings with his jazz guitar renditions of "Scotch and Soda" and "Am I Blue."

For some reason, the same qualities that endeared Hess to Hill seemed to rankle their tactical officer, who went out of his way to make life as miserable as possible for Hess. Hess excelled at the academic work, but in other areas—such as his assignment to spit-shine the tactical officer's office floor—he got demerits. He survived several reviews, but by the eighteenth week, enough demerits had accumulated that he was dropped from the class. He came to Hill near tears. Hill took Hess by the shoulders and gazed intently into his eyes. "You are not going to give up, and you are not going to accept defeat," he said. Then he took the poem from his wallet that Rescorla had given him and read it to him: "And so hold on when there is nothing in you / Except the Will which says to them: 'Hold on!' "

Hill told Hess he had gotten the poem from the best soldier he'd ever met: Rick Rescorla. Rescorla was in the class just behind them, the one Hess would now be joining. "He'll take care of you," Hill assured him.

As a member of the class ahead of Rescorla's, Hill was assigned the task of hazing the new candidates, administering demerits and inflicting punishments. But for Rescorla, Hill tried to return the favors Rescorla had bestowed on him in Africa. After one of the rigid dinners, Hill summoned Rescorla for what his colleagues assumed was more physical conditioning and make-work. Instead, Hill drove Rescorla to a picnic site, where he unloaded steaks and beers and built a campfire. He knew from his own experience that Rescorla was still famished after the requisite meals at Fort Benning. It wasn't the African bush, but it was a peaceful spot away from the intense regimentation, and they were able to resume their rambling talks.

Once, Hill jokingly replied to a provocative remark Rescorla made, saying, "You bastard, Rescorla." Then he stopped, and looked chagrined. But Rescorla just laughed. "That was an unfortunate choice of words, wasn't it?" he said in an impeccable British accent. When the outings were over, Hill drove them back to the vicinity of Fort Benning, and then, in case anyone was watching, Rescorla double-timed his way back to the barracks.

Hill graduated first in his class and won the class leadership award, the highest honor bestowed on an officer candidate. He was the first in his class to be commissioned a second lieutenant, which meant he had additional seniority. He also had his choice of assignments, and he chose the 101st Airborne Division, stationed at Fort Campbell, Kentucky. He wanted to resume his career as a paratrooper and ranger.

Rescorla didn't graduate first, but he came close, reaching the top 10 percent. Hess made it this time, too, and benefited from Rescorla's tutelage. Just before they graduated, in April 1965, President Johnson made one of the most fateful decisions of his political career. In response to an alleged North Vietnamese attack on U.S. Navy ships in the Gulf of Tonkin and a subsequent attack by North Vietnamese army troops on the South Vietnamese market town of Pleiku, he announced a major buildup of the U.S. military presence in Vietnam in a televised address. "I have asked the commanding general, General Westmoreland, what more he needs to meet this mounting aggression. He has told me. And we will meet his needs. We cannot be defeated by force of arms. We will stand in Vietnam."

The decision was immediately felt at Fort Benning. Rescorla, Hess, and many others among the newly commissioned second lieutenants were assigned to the legendary Second Battalion of the Seventh Cavalry Regiment, First Cavalry division, which had distinguished itself under its black-and-gold battle insignia in Korea and the Pacific during World War II. In the Korean War, it suffered so many casualties without blunting its fighting capacity that it earned the nickname "the Ghost Battalion." It traces its roots to the nineteenth-century American frontier and General George Custer, who had contributed the division's theme song and motto, "Garry Owen." Now it was being reconstituted as an air assault division, using helicopters instead of horses. On July 28, President Johnson announced that he was sending the division to Vietnam.

★

SAM FANTINO and the other members of Bravo Company, Second Battalion, Seventh Cavalry regiment, Third Brigade of the First Cavalry Division, didn't know what to expect from their new platoon leader when they assembled for training at Fort Benning. Rick Rescorla was unusual. He had a soft British accent, and though he was a "ninety-day wonder" fresh from Officer Candidate School, they knew he had combat experience in the British military. They liked that, given that none of them did and they were headed for combat in Vietnam. "Gentlemen," he said at their first meeting, "our mission is simple: It is to be the best."

They soon learned what that meant. When other platoons marched five miles under the midday sun, they marched ten. When other platoons ran five miles, they ran ten—and carried heavy packs on their backs. When others did fifty push-ups, they did one hundred. They had to take apart and reassemble their weapons blindfolded. They all had to learn map reading, coordinates, and radio signals, so that if the radio operator was killed or wounded, anyone could take his place. When they thought they were finished for the day, Rescorla had them belt out the battalion song:

> Once the Seventh rode with Custer,
> Against Sioux braves they did muster,
> Crazy Horse and Sitting Bull
> Have got their bellies full
> Of lead and steel from men of Garry Owen!

The men complained fiercely out of Rescorla's earshot. He never raised his voice, but there was something in his silent gaze that demanded absolute obedience. But gradually the grumbling subsided. For one thing, unlike some officers, Rescorla always did whatever he asked of his men—and often more. When they finished running and dropped to the ground, sweating and exhausted, he kept going. He did more push-ups. And as the weeks went by, the fierce training paid off. The men dropped their excess weight and grew strong and lean. In intrabattalion competitions, they won every one. The men realized that they had become the best, just as Rescorla had promised.

Rescorla assured them that he was training them this way for a reason. "Combat is terrible," he warned. "But if you believe in yourselves, and believe in me, we will come through anything." Their morale soared. Another second lieutenant, Patrick "Jim" Kelly, noticed that Rescorla's men ran everywhere.

"Why are you always running?" he finally asked one of them.

"Sir, we're getting ready for combat."

At the end of their training, Rescorla could look upon his platoon with evident pride. "Gentlemen," he said, "you are one hard corps." From then on, Rescorla was called "Hard Corps" by all of his men. And when it came time for the company to choose a radio call signal, Bravo Company chose "Hard Corps."

Rescorla reported to Hill at Fort Campbell that he was excited, thrilled to be leading men into combat against the Communists in Southeast Asia. It was what he and Hill had dreamed about years earlier. He quizzed Hill intensely on the nature of jungle warfare, which Hill had studied at the army's jungle warfare center in Panama and at Ranger school. Hill told Rescorla to read as much as he could—*People's War, People's Army* by Vo Nguyen Giap, who defeated the French at Dien Bien Phu; Mao Tse-tung on guerrilla warfare; and a book by Bernard Fall on the French experience in Vietnam, *Street Without Joy.*

"Know your enemy as well as you know yourself," Hill urged him. He was terribly envious that Rescorla was going into combat without him.

6

IN THE VALLEY OF DEATH

Rescorla in the battle of X-ray, November 15, 1965.
(Peter Arnett/AP/Wide World Photos)

O N AUGUST 14 at 3:30 A.M., the buses rolled into Fort Benning to begin the Second Battalion's journey to Vietnam. The men rode to Charleston, South Carolina, where they boarded the U.S. Navy Ship *Maurice Rose,* a troop transport ship of World War II vintage staffed by a crew from the Merchant Marines. As an officer, Rescorla was assigned to a two-man cabin just below deck. It was a bare-bones accommodation, furnished with two bunks, a desk, and a chair, but it had a porthole, and compared to quarters for the enlisted men, it was a *Queen Elizabeth II* stateroom. The enlisted men and noncommissioned officers were crowded into the lower decks, where they slept in canvas hammocks strung from the bulkheads four deep. There was no privacy. Since Rescorla and his roommate, David Patricelli, occupied only two of their bunk beds' four mattresses, Rescorla invited members of his platoon to take turns sleeping on the extra mattress to spare them the often sleepless nights in the hammocks. In the hierarchical American army it was unorthodox, but once Partricelli saw how much Rescorla's men appreciated the gesture, he began doing the same for members of his platoon.

Word of Rescorla's consideration toward his men spread throughout the ship. Rescorla was already an object of curiosity because of his British accent and reports that he was one of the few men on board with any combat experience. Dennis Deal, another second lieutenant and platoon leader, was more typical of the young officer corps headed toward Vietnam. Deal was a graduate of Duquesne University in Pittsburgh. He'd gone straight from college to Officer Candidate School, and then into Ranger training, hoping to become a paratrooper like Hill. But as soon as he finished his Ranger program, he was abruptly assigned to the First Battalion of the First Air Cavalry. He had spent only a few weeks at Fort Benning, participating in only one combat exercise, before receiving orders to report for duty in Vietnam. He was a little apprehensive about what awaited him in Vietnam.

Deal didn't get much information out of Rescorla other than that he had fought in Africa and Cyprus and had joined the British army at seventeen and a half. "They don't care how old you are as long as you can shoot," Rescorla had said by way of explanation. It was more his calm demeanor and aura of confidence that Deal and the others found reassuring. And sometimes he would get a look of such fierce determination that it was almost frightening. Deal was glad that Rescorla was fighting on their side.

Rescorla was friendly enough, but he maintained a certain British reserve, even with his roommate. Most platoons passed the ample spare time playing cards and sitting around talking. Not Rescorla. He spent all of his free time studying Vietnamese, listening to Vietnamese lan-

guage tapes, and reading the books about the military history of Indochina suggested by Hill. Rescorla could see the parallels between the
French colonial experience in Vietnam and the British experience in
Africa. By the time they landed, Rescorla was the only second lieutenant who spoke passable Vietnamese as well as French.

Many of the men had only the vaguest geographic sense of where
Vietnam was or how long the journey by sea would last. The ship
passed through the Panama Canal, traveled up the West Coast to Long
Beach, California, where it loaded weapons and provisions, then
headed southwest for the long Pacific crossing. The pace was so
leisurely that the ship was dubbed the *Ramblin' Rose*. Days were long
and tedious, interrupted by drills and exercise, though the cramped
space on the ship limited the options. Rescorla's platoon was the only
one that kept up a vigorous program of physical conditioning. Rescorla's platoon members shaved their heads into Mohawk cuts, and in
various athletic competitions, they continued to distinguish themselves
with an unbroken record of wins.

But the crossing soon turned eventful. About halfway between
Long Beach and the Philippines, a fire broke out in the hold and swept
through six decks. At one point it threatened the ship's cargo of fifteen
tons of live ammunition and grenades. Rescorla ordered his men to
don life jackets and they lined up at the lifeboats, awaiting the order to
abandon ship. Though none of their exercises at Fort Benning had prepared them for survival on the open sea, Rescorla reviewed the safety
measures in a calm, modulated voice and assured his men they would
be rescued quickly. Finally, the fire was brought under control.

Late summer is typhoon season in the South Pacific, and only a day
after the fire was brought under control, the USS *Maurice Rose* hit
a tropical depression of intense humidity and temperatures in the
nineties. Soon the ship was caught in its first major storm, with massive
ocean swells and high winds that grew so intense, the ship's officers
nearly gave the order to man the lifeboats. Seasickness on board was
rampant. Nearly all the men below deck were retching violently. The

ship's heads couldn't accommodate so many sick men at once, and the stench grew nearly unbearable. Rescorla was one of the few who showed no signs of illness. He spent the storm below deck with his men, trying to reassure them and ease their misery. After twenty-four hours, the storm faded and the cleanup began.

The ocean journey took a full month, and the portents weren't favorable. By the time they reached the coast of Vietnam, at Qui Nhon, everyone was desperate to get off the ship. They clambered into landing craft that looked like the ones Rescorla had seen in Hayle before the D-Day invasion. The American troops had no idea whether hostile forces might be awaiting them when they landed, so when the fronts of the craft dropped down, they charged the beach and ran for cover. But much to their surprise, swimmers and sunbathers enjoying a day at the beach greeted them. A young boy ran up to Rescorla's platoon. "GI, you want a Coke?"

Rescorla and his men were ferried by Chinook helicopters to the new base camp for American military operations in the Central Highlands at An Khe, forty miles inland from the beach where they had landed. The sight that greeted them was dismaying: acres of scrub vegetation baking under the intense tropical sun of the Vietnamese dry season. There was virtually nothing there; the American military was building the camp from the ground up. Their first assignment was to build an airfield capable of sustaining airborne military assaults on a large scale. Brigadier General John M. Wright, the assistant division commander in charge of the base, had decided that bulldozers couldn't be used because they scraped off all the vegetation and too much of the topsoil. This created landing sites that were easily whipped into dust bowls by helicopter and aircraft traffic during the dry season or turned into quagmires when it rained. The only alternative was to clear the proposed airstrip by hand, using axes and machetes. Rescorla and his men worked alongside thousands of Vietnamese laborers, and the immense task was finished in a matter of weeks. They nicknamed the airfield the "golf course," since General

Wright had decreed that the results of their labor had to be "as smooth as a golf course."

Despite their warm reception at the beach, An Khe was hardly friendly terrain for the Americans. North Vietnamese regular troops were operating in the area, the Viet Cong were even more prevalent, and they had plenty of sympathizers: the Central Highlands was an area notoriously friendly to the North Vietnamese. Sniper fire occasionally rang out near the camp, and once the airfield was built, the men cleared a wide, twelve-mile long fortified defense perimeter, which provided some peace of mind when the men were in the camp.

Bravo Company had its tents together near the perimeter. Next to Rescorla were his staff sergeant, Pete Thompson, his radio operator, Sam Fantino, and his medic, Tom Burlile. Living conditions were spartan: two-man pup tents, C-rations, and rainwater showers. They longed for hot food. One of the enlisted men in the platoon, Elias Alvarez-Buzo, from Puerto Rico, taught them how to catch, skin, and barbecue an iguana. An Khe was a far cry from the elegant officers quarters Rescorla had enjoyed in Africa, but he took steps to enhance the quality of life. He organized the other lieutenants, and in their spare time they built an officers club. By the standards of An Khe, it was luxurious: it had a poured-concrete floor, a tin roof, and louvered wooden slats for walls. More important, it had a refrigerator, which was generously stocked with cold beer.

The officers club quickly became the center of social life at An Khe, at least for officers and visiting dignitaries. Hess played guitar, and Rescorla started learning the instrument. There was singing just about every night, and Rescorla drew on his extensive repertoire of bawdy British fighting songs. He also sought out more serious conversation. He and Bill Shucart, a medic who had graduated from Washington University's medical school in St. Louis, spent hours discussing literature. Shucart persuaded Rescorla to read Faulkner, and Rescorla introduced Shucart to Kipling. Shucart was impressed with Rescorla's insights and intelligence and told him he should attend college.

Still, Rescorla spent plenty of evenings getting to know his men. He learned about their families, their lives in the States, their hopes for the future. Sometimes politics and military strategy cropped up. Rescorla didn't encourage it, but neither did he seem to object when his men asked questions about their mission in Vietnam. Tom Burlile, the medic, told Rescorla that he'd grown up in rural Ohio and had been working on a farm before joining the army. He missed his widowed mother and sister Delores, to whom he was very close and who depended on him. He loved animals and wanted to return to a life of farming. Though he'd grown physically tougher and shed some excess weight under Rescorla's intense training regimen, Burlile had a gentle nature that seemed ill suited for combat. He confided to Rescorla that he had trouble understanding why he'd been sent to Vietnam. "These people have never done anything to hurt me," he said.

In the sometimes chaotic conditions of An Khe, it didn't take long for Rescorla's platoon to stand out. Morale in most units of the hastily reconstituted First Cavalry was shaky. Captain Myron Diduryk, the commanding officer of Bravo Company, would periodically walk the line of the camp perimeter, checking the progress of his platoons. When he passed the section assigned to Rescorla, the men snapped to attention and saluted. They repeated their orders, shouting them down the line. No one could match them for polish and discipline. Use of the nickname Rescorla had bestowed on his unit at Fort Benning, "Hard Corps," spread throughout the base camp, and his platoon was proud of its reputation. Other officers began referring affectionately to Rescorla himself as "Hard Corps."

But this reputation meant that Rescorla's platoon was disproportionately assigned to the most dangerous missions. Just a week after their arrival, he was told to lead his men on a mission to Hong Kong Mountain, a forbidding redoubt not far from An Khe where enemy activity had been detected. None of his men had experienced any combat. Heavily armed, they cut their way through the brush and struggled through the rough terrain, moving in tandem with another platoon some distance ahead. The group heard gunfire, then a grenade explosion. Rescorla radioed for information, but he couldn't get a response. "I'm going up to see for myself," he told Sergeant Thompson, ordering his men to stay put. He disappeared into the bush. When he returned about a half hour later, he was gripping his arm, which was covered in blood. He reported that the lead platoon had indeed come under fire; Rescorla had been shot through the arm. He was the platoon's first casualty.

Burlile grabbed his medical kit and examined the wound. The bullet hadn't hit the bone, but the wound was fairly deep. He bandaged it to stem the bleeding. "You'd better get out of here," Burlile said.

"It's only a flesh wound," Rescorla insisted. But three hours later, the pain was too intense even for Rescorla. He made his way to the landing zone, and a helicopter flew him to a field hospital. His men knew that they might not see him again anytime soon. Soldiers with wounds no more serious had been sent back to the United States to recuperate. But Rescorla was back at An Khe when the platoon returned the next day. He had insisted that the injury not be reported to his superiors and dismissed it as a trifle.

Several weeks later, the platoon was on another mission in the Vinh Thanh valley, to the northeast of An Khe, an area riddled with Viet Cong and North Vietnamese sympathizers that had earned it the ironic nickname "Happy Valley." Bravo Company had taken up a position overlooking a village when gunfire burst out. Everyone dived for cover but Rescorla, who fixed his bayonet and walked straight toward the source of the fire. Then he had disappeared into the tall grass. Thompson was sure Rescorla would be hit and they would have to search for his missing body. But not long after, Rescorla returned to their position, slightly out of breath but unharmed. "Hey, Doc," he said to Burlile, "would you mind building a fire? I'd like a cup of tea." Burlile was wide-eyed with disbelief.

"He's not serious," Thompson reassured him.

Thompson couldn't help but notice that whenever a new mission was announced, Rescorla's platoon got the assignment as lead platoon. Finally he said something to Captain Diduryk, though he was only half-serious. "Do you have something against us? Every time you send us out, we're the lead platoon."

"I want to get the job done" was Diduryk's only reply.

★

THE EXCURSIONS TO Hong Kong Mountain and Happy Valley had given Rescorla and his platoon a taste of combat and served as valuable training exercises. But they knew this kind of minor skirmishing wasn't why they were in Vietnam. Word was circulating that reconnaissance platoons had made contact with what seemed to be significant troop concentrations west of Pleiku, near the Cambodian border, along the Ia Drang River. With its rugged mountainous terrain and dense jungle cover close to the Ho Chi Minh Trail, the region was ideal as a launching area for North Vietnamese offensives into central Vietnam and the south. Rescorla knew the area, especially its Chu Pong massif, as a center of Vietnamese resistance against the French and the site of a major French defeat.

On November 8, 1965, Rescorla and other officers were told to gather at headquarters. As two jeeps roared up in a cloud of dust, they snapped to attention. Major General Harry W. O. Kinnard, commanding general of the First Air Cavalry Division, stepped out, saluted, and told the men to stand at ease. He was the highest-ranking officer to address the battlion since Rescorla's arrival, which meant something was brewing.

Kinnard congratulated the men on setting up and securing the base camp, establishing lines of supplies, and flushing out Viet Cong on their missions into the countryside. "But the real mission of this division is to find the enemy, fix him in position, and destroy him," he said. "And I'm here today to let you know that we are beginning to do just that."

Kinnard indicated that their combat orders were being prepared and that they could expect to move into action sometime in the next three weeks. "I came down here to wish you good hunting and good luck in the next few weeks. I know you'll do your best when the time comes. And you can rest assured that we will support you from here as best we can. Thank you, gentlemen."

The officers snapped to attention. Kinnard and his staff returned to their jeeps, which roared off in another cloud of dust. Rescorla returned to brief his men. Something big was about to happen, and now their months of intensive training would pay off.

Three days later, the platoon boarded trucks bound for Pleiku, the largest city and headquarters for American military operations in the Central Highlands. They took the only paved road, Route 199, which led from An Khe into the mountains and through the Mang Yang Pass, which Rescorla knew as the site of one of the first major French defeats of the First Indochina War. The book Rescorla had read aboard ship, *Street Without Joy,* described how a seemingly impenetrable French armored column had been ambushed there and wiped out. It wasn't an encouraging precedent, and Rescorla's men were apprehensive, but they arrived on the outskirts of the dusty, sprawling city without incident. They established quarters at Camp Holloway, built on the site of a crumbling French fort just below a hill dominated by a stately white building with columns, the main house of a tea plantation abandoned years earlier by the French. Now it was the American headquarters, and the American flag flew over it.

On November 13, Lieutenant Colonel Hal Moore, commander of the First Battalion of the First Air Cavalry Division, briefed his officers on the impending operation. The more experienced First Battalion would launch the attack the next morning; Rescorla's unit, Bravo Company of the Second Battalion, would be held in reserve. The rugged terrain had offered a limited number of clearings suitable for large-scale helicopter landings, and Moore had chosen one about the size of a football field surrounded by scattered trees and brush. Air reconnaissance had detected a telephone line running nearby, evidence of an enemy troop presence. On the American military maps, the landing zone had been identified as "X," the letter known in the military's communications alphabet as "X-ray." Sixteen Huey helicopters carrying Moore and his men took off from Plei Me at 10:17 A.M. and flew southwest toward X-ray. Rescorla and his men returned to guard duty at Third Brigade headquarters.

Little more than two hours later, Captain Diduryk rushed up to Rescorla, telling him to ready his platoon for combat. After landing, Moore's battalion had come under heavy fire, and at least one platoon had been cut off and surrounded by NVA troops. Bravo Company was coming in to reinforce their position. Rescorla and his men hurriedly changed into jungle fatigues, donning their harnesses and weapons. As usual, Rescorla carried his M-16 rifle, M-79 grenade launcher, and .45 automatic pistol. He also kept a bowie knife strapped to his leg. Besides his dog tags, he wore the lion's tooth necklace. As they waited in the swirling red dust of the landing area for their transport helicopters to arrive, many of the men were tense. The noise of helicopters landing and taking off made conversation difficult. But during a lull Rescorla addressed his men, reminding them that all their training would now pay off. They were the best. Then Burlile, the unit's medic, stepped forward and began to speak. Rescorla was surprised. Of all his men, Burlile seemed the least enthusiastic about the war. But now, in the face of battle, his voice was steady and confident. He reminded the platoon of the four basic steps in first aid: clear the airway, stop the bleeding, protect the wound, and treat for shock. Then he reassured them that he would be there if they needed him: "If you are wounded, I may not be able to get to you right away, but I will do my best to get to you as fast as possible."

Thirteen Hueys arrived for the fifteen-minute flight to X-ray, and Rescorla and his men boarded. They arrived at the landing zone about 5:00 P.M., still daylight, but the smoke and dust made it difficult to see. As they descended, the helicopter crew warned that they were entering a "hot LZ" and should immediately run for cover. Rescorla and his men could see the khaki uniforms of NVA regulars perched in trees, aiming their rifles at them and firing. When they hit the ground, they ran to the right and made their way to Moore's command post. Diduryk saluted Moore. "Garry Owen, sir! Captain Diduryk and Bravo Company, Second Battalion, Seventh Cavalry, a hundred and twenty men strong, reporting for duty!"

Rescorla and his men were stunned by what they saw: a row of American bodies covered by ponchos, their boots sticking out beneath them. They were American fatalities waiting to be air-evacuated out. Scores of wounded men were being carried to the helicopters as gunfire continued. Moore ordered Bravo Company to assemble under a clump of trees about thirty yards away to act as reserves. Rescorla fixed his bayonet and led his men to the area, where a ditch had already been dug and more wounded men were waiting for evacuation. Burlile ministered to them as best he could. No one got much sleep; there was periodic fire throughout the night. Then, at dawn, it became eerily quiet. Just before 7:00 A.M., rocket and mortar explosions shattered the brief calm. Fire swept the landing zone. The North Vietnamese had mounted an intense attack to breach the perimeter, concentrating their forces on a Charlie Company platoon just two hundred yards from Rescorla's position. The entire platoon was killed or wounded, but enemy troops failed to take advantage of the weakness and push through the breach.

At about 8:00 A.M., Moore told Diduryk to move his men into position behind the devastated Charlie Company to restore the perimeter. Rescorla was crawling through the high grass of the landing zone, moving into position, when he saw two American planes that had been called in to strike the enemy positions just beyond the perimeter. But something had gone wrong; he and his men watched, horrified, as the planes dropped a pair of six-foot silver napalm canisters, which tumbled end over end through the air, heading straight for Moore's command post.

"Call that son of a bitch off!" someone screamed. "Call him off!"

It was too late. The canisters hit the clearing filled with American troops, and suddenly it was aflame. The heat was so intense that it singed the hair off the arms of Rescorla and his men. Screams rang out. Other men were on fire. Rescorla and his platoon scattered and ran, flames dropping around them. Once they were out of the burning grass, they dropped to their stomachs, gasping for breath. Enemy fire continued to ring over their heads. They could hear the cries of the wounded. "Medic, medic!" some yelled.

Burlile was at Rescorla's side. Nearby were Sergeant Thompson and Fantino, Rescorla's radio operator. They saw Burlile grab his medical kit, stand up, and head back toward the fire zone and the cries of the wounded. Thompson jumped up to go after him. The two disappeared into the tall grass. Twenty seconds later, Rescorla heard Thompson call out: "Come on, Doc. Let's go!" Then Thompson called Rescorla's name. He crawled forward, then stopped. He saw Burlile, lying face-down. Thompson was beside him.

"Tommy!" Rescorla called, but the medic didn't respond. When Rescorla reached his side he saw a bullet wound in his head. He turned Burlile over and gathered him in his arms. Burlile was still breathing. His eyes were open.

"Hold on, Doc," Fantino urged. But Rescorla knew it was too late for that. He didn't know if Burlile could hear him, but he held him closer, the blood from his wound covering his hands and arms.

"You're going to be all right," he said softly. "You're going to be all right."

Time seemed frozen, but less than a minute passed. Rescorla felt Burlile's breath falter and then stop. Another medic arrived and checked for a pulse. There was none. Still Rescorla held him. Then he stood and picked Burlile up, carrying his body to safety so it could be evacuated and returned to his family. A burst of enemy fire crackled nearby. Rescorla gently laid Burlile in the tall grass and covered his body with his poncho. Then he wiped Burlile's blood on his hands and arms. This was an African tribal ritual he had learned from his troops in

Rhodesia. Somehow it made him feel closer to the man he had just lost. Finally, he crawled to safer ground.

★

THERE WAS NO TIME to mourn Burlile's death. While enemy fire continued, Rescorla and his men advanced toward the perimeter positions they'd been ordered to reinforce. As dusk gathered, they reached a dried-up creekbed that formed a natural trench. They sprinted forward, then dived for safety. Rescorla landed hard on something relatively soft and then heard an American voice swear. He had jumped right on top of Dennis Deal, the First Battalion lieutenant from the USS *Maurice Rose*.

"Thank God it's you," Deal said, delighted that Rescorla and his unit would be protecting his right flank. Deal pointed out the positions Rescorla was supposed to occupy; then Rescorla and his men moved out of sight along the creekbed.

The next morning, when Rescorla surveyed the positions they were supposed to occupy and defend, the ones that had led to such heavy losses in Charlie Company, he was concerned. Their section of the perimeter consisted of a small clearing surrounded by forest and shrubs, which gave enemy troops plenty of cover. The clearing itself was deceptively open; there were large anthills, scrub brush, and trees, and some deep furrows in the terrain. Evidence of the previous night's raging battle was in plain view. The foxholes and defensive positions dug by Charlie Company had clearly been overrun. The American dead and wounded had been removed, but hundreds of Vietnamese corpses littered the battlefield, baking under the hot sun. Their bodies were bloated, and the putrid smell of decomposing flesh was so strong that some men vomited.

Rescorla told his sergeant, Thompson, that he was worried the positions dug by Charlie Company—positions they were meant to reoccupy—were too far into the clearing, too close to trees, for an effective defense. To Thompson's amazement, Rescorla strode across the clearing in plain view of any enemy snipers and into the trees, saying he wanted to get a view of the area from the Vietnamese perspective. For all Thompson and the rest of the platoon knew, those trees were infested with enemy troops.

But Rescorla returned unharmed. His men concluded there was some aura about him that acted as a kind of protective shield. Perhaps there was something to the lion's-tooth necklace that he wore as a good-luck charm. Still, Thompson thought at times that Rescorla's actions bordered on the reckless. The man was simply impervious to fear.

As Rescorla had suspected, the existing positions were too close to possible enemy lines. Although it meant duplicating an immense amount of labor, he ordered his men to rebuild the lines fifty yards farther back into the clearing. He ordered them to construct three- rather than two-man foxholes and insisted that they be deep enough to provide full cover. This enabled one man to operate his weapon continuously while another reloaded and the third repaired the inevitable jams that occurred during sustained gunfire. Then he had Thompson and his men rig booby traps and flares beyond the perimeter, along all the feasible avenues of approach.

As evening approached, Rescorla inspected his men's positions. He briefed Dennis Deal on his platoon's position, then walked over to the second platoon, which was defending the perimeter next to Bravo Company. "When the firing starts, are you guys going to stick around?" Rescorla asked one of the men, James Lamothe.

"Sir," Lamothe answered, "we'll still be here in the morning. Just make sure Hard Corps doesn't cut and run."

Rescorla was grinning. Another sergeant walked up. "I'm selling tickets on the next chopper to Pleiku," Rescorla told him.

"Shit, sir, I wouldn't miss this one," the sergeant replied.

This was the spirit Rescorla had hoped to see. He didn't want his men writing farewell letters to their next of kin on the eve of battle, as many soldiers in other platoons did.

Rescorla returned to his part of the line and gathered his men around him. There was no disguising the fact that however much they tried to hide it, they were tense and nervous. The North Vietnamese had failed to capitalize on their advantage the night before, but they knew they had inflicted heavy casualties at this point in the perimeter and were sure to return to what was likely to be its weakest link. Bravo Company would be waiting for them. Rescorla gave some last words of advice: "They will come at us fast and low. No neat targets. Keep your fire at the height of a crawling man. Make them pass through a wall of steel."

"What if they break through?" asked a private, his anxiety evident in his voice. Rescorla gave him a fixed gaze and made it clear that his platoon would fight to the end. "If they break through and overrun us, put grenades around your hole. Lay them on the parapet and get your head below ground. Lie on your back in the hole. Spray bullets into their faces. If we do our job, they won't get that far."

As darkness fell, the men returned to their foxholes and Rescorla, Fantino, and Thompson took up a command position behind an anthill, just twenty yards behind their men. The moon wasn't scheduled to rise for several hours, and they were soon in pitch darkness. Everyone had been ordered to remain on full alert and resist any temptation to sleep. Time slowly passed. Occasionally the men heard some strange, high-pitched whistling sounds from the forest. Then there was an ominous silence. It was almost too quiet. "Have the men fix their bayonets," Rescorla told Thompson, who issued the order. Then he repeated it. Tension mounted. "Have the men fix bayonets," Rescorla said again.

"Sir, you've given me that order three times," Thompson reminded him. That was the only sign that Rescorla, too, was nervous.

To ease the tension, Rescorla urged his men to talk back and forth between their foxholes. But when that faltered, Rescorla began to sing in his firm baritone "Wild Colonial Boy" and then "Going Up Camborne Hill." The men didn't know these old British and Cornish songs, but it didn't seem to matter. The steady cadence and melody in the heavy night air had a strangely calming effect. Between verses, Rescorla's men shouted in response, calling out, "Hard Corps!" and "Garry Owen!"

Around midnight there was some gunfire, and then some eerie green tracer fire arced over Rescorla's command post behind the anthill. Thinking an attack might be imminent, Rescorla moved forward and jumped into one of his men's foxholes. But an uneasy calm returned, and no attack materialized.

Several hours passed. Rescorla resumed his singing. Then, just after 4:00 A.M., the trip flares broke the quiet and some of the booby-trap grenades Rescorla's men had planted earlier exploded. Rescorla couldn't see the enemy, but minutes later he heard radio reports that the adjoining section of the line, where he'd been bantering hours earlier, was coming under waves of assault. Flares lit the landscape, and then Rescorla saw the enemy troops emerge into the clearing and head straight for their positions. He had to admire the discipline of the North Vietnamese. They moved forward, dropped to one knee, fired, then advanced again. Rescorla called in artillery and gave the order to fire. Since he'd moved their positions fifty yards back, the enemy had to cross the open terrain. They were easy targets, but as one was felled, others used the body as a shield and continued firing. Rescorla's men heard a bugle, and then the attack stopped. The North Vietnamese pulled back. It had all lasted little more than ten minutes.

Rescorla warned that they would be back, and twenty minutes later, they returned in greater force. Hundreds of enemy soldiers poured into the clearing. Bravo Company fired furiously as flares provided illumination overhead. The continuous machine-gun fire cut down waves of soldiers. None reached their line, though several were shot only five yards from it.

The last assault came at 6:30 A.M., as the sky was beginning to turn gray. Bugles sounded in the distance, and fresh waves of North Vietnamese troops and their Viet Cong allies poured from the slopes of the

Chu Pong massif. Rescorla's platoon again bore the brunt of the attack. Again the defensive line held as hundreds of enemy troops fell. After fifteen minutes, the attack began to subside. Rescorla saw enemy troops begin to retreat, dragging wounded comrades behind them. But one soldier persisted in the attack, marching forward into a fusillade of machine-gun fire. Rescorla had to admire the soldier's suicidal determination. The lone attacker fell only three paces from one of the American foxholes.

There was now no further sign of enemy activity, but Rescorla's men kept firing nervously into clumps of bodies. The battle was seemingly over. But then a young Vietnamese soldier leaped from behind a tree just forty yards away, plainly visible in the dawn light. He was limping but armed. He made no sign of surrender. Rescorla's men seemed dazed; no one fired. Rescorla reached for his pistol, aimed, and shot him.

★

SEVERAL HOURS LATER, with the battlefield quiet, Captain Diduryk ordered Rescorla and his men to move into the field of battle, bayonets fixed, looking for wounded survivors and any American dead. Peter Arnett, a reporter for the Associated Press, had arrived at X-ray that morning and was snapping photographs from a position near Diduryk's command post. He got a picture of Rescorla, helmeted and unshaven, with bayonet fixed on his M-16 rifle, as he moved out into the field with his men. The battlefield was a ghastly sight, with hundreds of enemy bodies lying where they had fallen. Many of the Vietnamese dead had whistles attached to strings around their necks, which accounted for the high-pitched sounds the Americans had heard during the night. The Vietnamese had used the whistles as a kind of code as they moved into position for the attack. Rescorla and his men moved through the bodies of the enemy dead in a zigzag pattern. Rescorla was moving cautiously in front, his bayonet drawn, with Fantino, his radio operator, about eight feet behind him. The tall grass and occasional anthill made the terrain difficult to search. About fifty yards from their foxholes, Rescorla approached a cluster of enemy bodies; the weapons indicated they had been a machine-gun crew. Suddenly he saw a motion and looked up at the crest of an anthill just a few yards away. Staring at him was a live North Vietnamese soldier looking down the barrel of his machine gun. The enemy soldier began firing, spraying bullets at Rescorla and Fantino.

Both men reacted instinctively, lunging for the ground. Rescorla leaped to the right, Fantino to the left, about twenty feet away. The rest of the platoon, farther back, dropped to their stomachs. Rescorla's mind was clear; he didn't feel panic. But he felt everything happen in excruciatingly slow motion. The firing continued. Incredibly, given their short distance from the enemy machine gunner, neither Rescorla nor Fantino was hit. When the enemy firing paused, Rescorla jumped up and fired. The enemy gunner ducked. Rescorla got off two rounds, but then his rifle jammed. He looked down and saw that his magazine was empty.

"Grenade!" he yelled back to Fantino.

Fantino loaded another magazine into his M–16 rifle and got close enough to Rescorla to toss him a grenade. As Fantino kept a steady round of fire aimed at the crest of the foxhole, forcing the enemy gunners to keep their heads down, Rescorla pulled the pin on the grenade and ran toward the machine-gun nest. When he was only a few feet away, he tossed it over the hill. Rescorla was so close he could see the heads of the enemy soldiers. The grenade exploded with deafening force. Rescorla's helmet and shirt were covered with the remains of the enemy gunners. Shrapnel from the grenade hit Fantino, injuring both arms.

Once it was clear the machine-gun position had been eliminated, Rescorla and his platoon raced back to their foxholes. Firing broke out along the line, indicating the presence of more enemy troops. Seven American soldiers were wounded besides Fantino. Rescorla told Fantino he should be evacuated, but Fantino refused. After seeing people blown apart, his own injuries seemed minor. But he stayed behind as Rescorla and one of his sergeants loaded up with grenades, then crawled back into the clearing beyond the perimeter, creeping up to anthills that might provide enemy refuge and tossing grenades behind them.

Then Rescorla spotted an American fighter-bomber bearing down on their position. Diduryk and Colonel Moore had called in air support. Rescorla raced back and ordered his men to lie facedown in their foxholes. A deafening explosion rocked the earth and sent dirt and debris flying. An American air bombardment leveled the area Rescorla and his men had just been searching.

The battle was over. Colonel Moore ordered one last sweep of the battlefield to make sure no American casualties were left behind. They found nothing. But the sight and stench of the human carnage on the battlefield made an indelible impression. By noon, the rest of the Seventh Cavalry's Second Battalion under the command of Lieutenant Colonel Robert McDade, the ones who had stayed behind when Rescorla's platoon had been thrown into action, arrived to relieve Rescorla's men and the exhausted First Battalion. Diduryk gave Rescorla and his troops the order to move out. They had occupied the landing zone for just three days and two nights, though it seemed like weeks. Rescorla settled into position as a helicopter lifted off for the trip back to Pleiku. But he couldn't stop looking back at all the bodies still visible on the ground below. Next to him, an enlisted man looked ashen and then vomited in Rescorla's lap. Rescorla told him not to worry; he knew how he felt.

Back in Pleiku, Rescorla showered, then headed to the officers club for a cold beer. Most of the officers gravitated there, gathering around Colonel Moore, the battle's commander. As Rescorla later recounted the scene, there was no jubilation. There was no singing that night. The men were mostly silent and grave. The only remarks were an occasional "shit" or "Garry Owen." There was a powerful sense of camaraderie from the shared danger they had managed to survive, but the realization was sinking in that so many of their comrades were dead. After little more than an hour, the exhausted officers drifted back to their tents and fell asleep.

In addition to Burlile, four of Rescorla's men died at X-ray, including Elias Alvarez-Buzo, who had taught them how to cook an iguana. Rescorla's platoon had the fewest casualties by far of any platoon in the Second Battalion, even though it had borne the brunt of the Vietnamese attack. A total of 79 American soldiers were killed at X-ray and 121 wounded.

Colonel Moore ultimately reported 634 Vietnamese dead, with an additional 1,215 estimated dead or wounded.

★

THE NEXT AFTERNOON, November 17, the battle-scarred men of Bravo Company were getting ready for the return trip to An Khe. Some were cleaning their weapons, others were writing letters home or enjoying some hot food. But mostly they were drinking beer. Rescorla was at the officers club when Diduryk came up to him, looking grave. "Get the company together," he ordered. The rest of the Second Battalion, the troops that had relieved them at X-ray, were "catching hell," he said. "We may have to go in." With the rest of the battalion in the field, and because of the heavy casualties at X-ray, Rescorla was the only platoon leader left in camp. "Help all the platoons get their shit together," Diduryk said, then hurried off to the enlisted club. "Saddle up," he ordered his men. "We're going off to rescue the battalion."

Thinking they were only hours away from being evacuated to An Khe, the men were stunned. But word quickly spread that the rest of their battalion—the companies led by Lieutenant Colonel McDade, the battalion commander, which had come to replace them at X-ray— was in dire straits, suffering heavy casualties. This was not because they had come under renewed attack at X-ray. The landing zone had been evacuated hours after McDade's troops arrived because a massive B-52 bombing strike had been ordered for the Chu Pong massif, and all American troops had to move beyond a two-mile perimeter of the designated attack area. McDade's troops were ordered to march to and then secure another landing zone, code-named Albany, closer to the Ia Drang River. Their five-mile route would take them past Landing Zone Columbus, where they would leave several units, then turn to the northwest.

Under a blazing sun and with the promise of a day of intense heat, the heavily armed troops had begun the march from X-ray at 9:00 A.M. To keep them awake after more than twenty-four hours of combat, they were given caffeine-laced tablets. With a reconnaissance platoon in the lead, the companies of the Second Battalion had fallen in behind them, forming a long column. At the rear was Alpha Company of the First Battalion, Fifth Cavalry, temporarily attached to the Seventh. One of their platoon leaders was Lieutenant Larry Hess, Hill's protégé and Rescorla's classmate. The reconnaissance platoon and Alpha Company reached the Albany clearing at about 1:00 P.M. It was about the size of a football field, covered with tall elephant grass, shimmering in the hot sunlight. McDade and his staff walked through the clearing and into a clump of trees. Several platoons split up and began to circle the clearing, intending to secure it. Suddenly a few shots rang out, then a torrent began. The attack spread all the way down the column. Enemy mortar fire began to hit the clearing with shuddering thuds.

McDade frantically radioed Colonel Tom Brown, the brigade commander, for help. Brown could hear rifle fire in the background. "Goddammit, what's going on out there?" Brown demanded.

But McDade didn't really know; he was now cut off from the other units in the column, pinned down by fire. "Got a couple of KIAs [killed in action] here and trying to get a handle on the situation," McDade replied. "Let me get back to you later."

Other radio reports of heavy casualties began to reach Camp Holloway. Though the situation was confused, a major attack was clearly under way. Brown ordered helicopters to drop Diduryk's units into the action and ordered units at LZ Columbus to march toward Albany.

Rescorla gathered his men. It was about 5:45 P.M. Despite their recent ordeal, they had dropped whatever they were doing, donned their uniforms and heavy gear, and stood at attention. Many of them hadn't had time to shave, but their weapons gleamed. Rescorla wondered how many other units could have been counted on to do the same. "I've never been so proud of any men in my life," he told Fantino and Thompson.

Rescorla radiated confidence, but he was blunt about their mission. "You know the battalion is in the shit," he told them. "We have been selected to jump into that shit and pull them out. If you fight like you did at X-ray, you'll come through it. Stay together. Come out of those choppers ready to get it on."

In the background, the first assault helicopters were approaching. "Head 'em up," Diduryk ordered.

Rescorla led the column as his men marched toward the landing area. Fantino was just behind him. "How are we looking back there?" Rescorla asked.

"No stragglers, sir," Fantino replied.

As they moved toward the helicopters, rear-area men from support units at Camp Holloway came out to watch them leave. They were wearing jeans, smoking, drinking beer. Some wore sunglasses or Hawaiian shirts, or were bare-chested. "What outfit are you?" one of them called out.

"The Hard Corps of Bravo Company, Second of the Seventh," Rescorla called back.

"Where are you headed?"

"To kick ass."

★

EIGHT HELICOPTERS LIFTED off for the forty-minute flight to the besieged landing zone. As they approached the clearing, dusk was falling. The sight from the helicopters was surreal. A cloud of smoke and the acrid smell of cordite and dead bodies hung over the area. Green tracers streamed through the darkness. There were orange flashes as mortars exploded. Rescorla looked out of one side of the helicopter; Fantino scanned the other. Rescorla saw plenty of bodies lying face up in the gravel of a dried streambed. They were dressed in the khaki shirts of North Vietnamese regulars. "Boy, they really got hit," he said to Fantino. "Look at all the Vietnamese over here."

But Fantino was looking at a grim sight on the other side of the helicopter. "There are all kinds of Americans down here, too," he said.

The enemy fire was too intense for a landing, so the helicopter pulled up and circled around for another pass. This time Rescorla could see what Fantino meant. In the ominous scar of a napalm attack, he saw plenty of American corpses and equipment. The helicopter began to descend slowly, but the pilot said he was worried; he wasn't sure he could touch down without getting hit. Rescorla crawled out onto the helicopter's skids to see how far off the ground they were. They were about twelve feet up, too far to risk jumping. Suddenly two bullets pierced the fuselage, and Rescorla pulled himself back in. He saw blood on the pilot's sleeve. The chopper lurched downward, then the wounded pilot began to pull up as more fire rang out.

"Jump out!" Rescorla yelled to his men.

Fantino watched in amazement as Rescorla leaped from the helicopter into the gathering darkness. He knew it was his duty to follow him, though he thought it was probably suicidal. He jumped, and the other men in the helicopter followed. As they hit the ground and rolled onto their stomachs in the high grass, they saw three soldiers in khaki shirts leap up in front of them and begin running for the tree line. Rescorla began firing, and the three fell face forward into the grass. In the other direction they could hear American voices yelling at them. Rescorla signaled to the others, and they sprinted toward them.

Rescorla and his men marched into the copse of trees that sheltered the remnants of Alpha Company. Rescorla had his M-79 grenade launcher on his shoulder, an M-16 in his hand, and bandoliers of extra ammunition strapped across his chest, and he looked determined. He could tell that the men of Alpha Company were exhausted and demoralized, gripped by what Rescorla described as a "dark malaise." Colonel McDade sat against a tree trunk in dazed silence. The badly wounded battalion sergeant major, James Scott, lay near him, his chest heavily bandaged. "We got hit bad, sir," he said. "Real bad."

But Rescorla's adrenaline was pumping. "Good, good, good," he said. "We'll wipe 'em up now! I hope they hit us tonight. We'll whip 'em good." And he gave the men a dazzling smile.

To Lieutenant Larry Gwin, Alpha Company's executive officer, it truly was as though the cavalry had come to the rescue. He rushed up and shook Rescorla's hand. "Thank you for coming, sir."

Rescorla's confidence and optimism were infectious. McDade's men went abruptly from feeling doomed to almost euphoric. They began yelling and shouting their determination. "Garry Owen!" cried Rescorla's men as the din rose.

Rescorla moved from man to man, speaking in a quiet voice, asking about their condition and what had happened to them. "You men have done a hell of a job," he assured them. Four of the eight helicopters that had left Pleiku with Rescorla were forced to turn back, but about eighty men, as well as Captain Diduryk, Fantino, and Sergeant Thompson, made it alive into Albany. Diduryk assumed command, and Rescorla and Thompson began organizing an effective defense perimeter, moving it out just beyond the trees. As they'd done at X-ray, they dug foxholes and braced themselves for further assaults.

While they waited, Rescorla spoke to Gwin and began to recognize the extent of the disaster at Albany. When McDade's troops marched out of X-ray that morning, an earlier helicopter reconnaissance run over the projected route had detected no enemy presence. Still, as McDade later conceded, he "really didn't know a goddamned thing, had no intelligence" when he left X-ray. But there were plenty of ominous signs. In moist spots along the route, forward troops had detected the telltale prints of tire-tread sandals worn by North Vietnamese troops. And despite the heavy casualties inflicted on the Vietnamese at X-ray, it was obvious that the Chu Pong massif had sheltered a significant enemy troop concentration. Unless they had been foolish enough to simply wait there for the inevitable American bombing runs, they must have dispersed somewhere in the immediate vicinity.

Then, as Lieutenant Gwin recounted the episode, the forward platoon had marched right into two North Vietnamese regulars resting beside an anthill. They had fresh uniforms, were well fed and armed, but they seemed to be shaking, from either fear or malaria. The column came to a halt as news of their capture moved down the line, and McDade came forward to interrogate the prisoners himself. He summoned the various company commanders to join him. None of the Americans spoke much Vietnamese, so the interrogation was confusing. The men indicated that they were deserters. This seemed implausible, given the state of their weapons and uniforms. But the Americans gave them water, food, and malaria tablets.

Gwin worried that so many of the company commanders were gathering in one place. Farther back in the column, discipline quickly eroded. Many of the men had gone the past sixty hours without sleep. Delta Company shed their weapons, lay down on the ground, or leaned against trees. They smoked and opened cans of C-rations. The men of Alpha Company, First Battalion, were resting. Then, with the rear units at ease, Gwin's Alpha Company began to move forward into the clearing at Albany, and the enemy firing began. After he ran into the trees, Gwin looked back to where they had emerged into the clearing. The area was now swarming with North Vietnamese troops. The first platoon, which had moved to the right around the clearing, had disappeared. The second platoon, which had been behind them, was now surrounded by North Vietnamese troops. Gwin pointed through the darkness to the southeast and told Rescorla, "What's left of the battalion is out there in three main groups, and then smaller teams." Gwin didn't know the fate of Charlie and Delta and First Battalion's Alpha

Companies. Occasional radio reports indicated platoons had been isolated or broken up, were surrounded, were engaged in hand-to-hand combat. The entire American column had been ambushed.

Rescorla was dismayed. He couldn't help but think of the French troops who had fallen into so many similar traps. Tactically, Americans had only themselves to blame for the disaster. Why had they marched overland to Albany without air support, when presumably they could have been ferried by helicopter? Why had there been no reconnaissance units, farther forward and on both flanks of the column? How could the men have been allowed to betray their presence, smoking and eating rations? And why hadn't they reacted immediately to the capture of two North Vietnamese regulars? No one had any answers, and in any event, they were irrelevant to Rescorla's mission, which was to rescue the remains of his battalion.

As Rescorla had predicted, the enemy attack continued sporadically throughout the night, but the perimeter defenses held. At one point, just after midnight, someone panicked and fired his weapon from a position well inside the perimeter, which infuriated Rescorla because it endangered his other men on the outer perimeter. He didn't want any casualties from friendly fire. He walked back to the group of soldiers there and said, "If I hear one more round out of you, we will turn our weapons around and open up. No one fires from inside the perimeter. If you want to fire, get out to the perimeter line."

Rescorla spent a good part of the night in a foxhole with Bill Shucart, his friend the medic. Shucart had been in the column marching toward Albany when the attack began, and he'd been cut off from the column. He had been wandering alone when he'd encountered two enemy soldiers and shot them with his M-16 rifle. Then he was rescued by a sergeant from the Fifth Cavalry. As a medic, he'd never expected to have to use his rifle; as a doctor, he was trained to save lives, not take them. He was badly shaken. Rescorla tried to reassure him. "This isn't cerebral," he argued. "This is more primitive than that. If someone is trying to kill you, there's no question that you kill him. This is basic to your survival."

Rescorla seemed haunted by the thought of more Americans like Shucart who'd been cut off, stranded in the darkness, alone and possibly wounded. At one point he discussed sending out night patrols to look for them, but Captain Diduryk worried that it was too dangerous and that sending men out would deplete the perimeter defenses. "Wait until dawn," he ordered. But late into the night, a badly wounded James Mullarkey, one of the men from the missing First Platoon, made it back into the perimeter. He reported that North Vietnamese troops were prowling in the darkness, executing wounded Americans. He knew that firsthand: an enemy soldier had come up to him, inserted a pistol in his mouth, and pulled the trigger. The blast had knocked Mullarkey out, but the bullet exited the back of his throat. He regained consciousness and crawled into the perimeter.

The report seemed to galvanize Rescorla. At about 4:00 A.M., he quietly approached Sergeant Thompson. They had made radio contact with some wounded men from Charlie Company and had been able to pinpoint their location. "They're wounded, they're dying out there," he said. "Let's go." Thompson didn't really want to leave the safety of the perimeter, but he and one other volunteer, handpicked by Rescorla, slipped out after Rescorla into the darkness. Rescorla never gave them a direct order, but they wouldn't have dreamed of letting him down. The three men crawled through the high grass, moving from anthill to anthill and in and out of brush and trees. It took them more than an hour to cover the five hundred yards to the vicinity of the stranded men. Frequently they lay motionless as enemy troops passed nearby.

When they neared their goal, Rescorla radioed the men to fire a single shot to identify their location. When they reached them, they discovered that all the men had been wounded. Of the 110 men in Charlie Company, they were among the 9 who had survived. One of them, Jack P. Smith, later described the scene: "The place looked like the devil's butcher shop. There were people hanging out of trees. The ground was slippery with blood. Men who were my closest friends were all around me, dead." Rescorla comforted them and assured them that help was on the way. He radioed for artillery support and a relief column, which arrived soon after to evacuate the wounded. Then he and his two men worked their way back to the Alpha Company perimeter. They never disclosed their expedition, and no one had noticed their absence.

As November 18 dawned, the men were told to remain in their foxholes, then open fire on command. The goal was to flush out any remaining enemy around the Albany clearing before venturing out of the perimeter. The command came, and the M-16 rifles and M-60 machine guns opened up. Rescorla was dismayed by the order; he knew there must be more Americans like those of Charlie Company lying wounded outside the perimeter. The firing was indiscriminate; how many of their own soldiers might get hit? Sure enough, frantic radio calls came in: "What the fuck is happening?" "Are you shooting at us?"

The firing did send some khaki-clad enemy soldiers running, but there was only sporadic return fire, and it was obvious the main Vietnamese force had pulled back. So the troops inside the perimeter moved out into the clearing, searching for American dead and wounded. They didn't have to go far. Hundreds of bodies, some beginning to swell from the morning sun and heat, littered the clearing. In the copse of trees where the First Platoon had been surrounded, bodies lay where they had fallen in what had obviously been hand-to-hand combat, based on the machetes, knives, and bayonets at the scene. A few men were found still alive. Gwin was astounded when one of his men from the Second Platoon, John Eade, was carried in on a stretcher, alive and smoking a cigarette. Eade had been hit in the legs with mortar fire and, unable to walk, had propped himself against a tree. Eade had watched as napalm canisters fell nearby, setting the area ablaze. Later, an enemy soldier had found him there, put a pistol to his head, fired, then left him for dead. The bullet had gone through one of his eyes and come out the back of his head. He had never lost consciousness.

Rescorla and several of his men worked his way back along what had been the column of the Second Battalion. American dead lay everywhere. Many were still sitting where they had paused to relax when the column had stopped. Rescorla noticed one dead soldier still holding a pack of cigarettes in his hand. Others had plainly been executed. They were slumped over, their hands still tied behind their backs, a bullet hole in the backs of their heads.

As Rescorla came around an anthill, he noticed a group of khaki-clad Vietnamese bodies. Suddenly something moved, and Rescorla fired twice into the clump of bodies. He cautiously advanced toward their position. There were three bodies. Two of the men were dead. The third, Rescorla later recalled, "was very young with a soft, round-featured face, lying belly up. He was dying, eyes flickering, shirt soaked with blood. They had all been wounded and had drawn close together. A team of some kind."

The young Vietnamese soldier must have been a bugler, since a dented but shiny brass bugle lay on his torso. Rescorla picked it up carefully and examined it. There was a bullet hole through the bell, but it was otherwise intact. Engraved on the instrument were the name and address of its maker: Couesnon & Cie, Fournisseurs de L'Armée. 94, rue d'Ancoième. Paris. Then the date: 1900. Beneath the French legend, the bugle had been further engraved with two Chinese characters, which, roughly translated, meant "long and powerful service." The bugle triggered Rescorla's strong sense of history. He wondered how the bugle had found its way to this remote valley in the Central Highlands, what battles it had heralded, what defeats it had endured. Had victorious Vietnamese soldiers seized it from the colonial French army as a trophy? If so, it was time for the bugle to change hands again. Rescorla put the bugle in his pack and moved on.

★

THAT NIGHT AT ABOUT 3:00 A.M., back inside the perimeter, Rescorla and his men again came under enemy attack. Rescorla had discovered that one of his men could actually play the captured bugle. He had him blew "charge," and his men began yelling and firing. It apparently demoralized the Vietnamese, because the attack ceased abruptly, and the enemy troops disappeared. The experience lent the bugle an aura of invincibility.

Rescorla and his platoon spent the next two days at Albany collecting American bodies, wrapping them in ponchos, and carrying them to the clearing to be picked up by helicopters. The stench of bodies in the afternoon heat of over one hundred degrees was becoming almost unbearable. Even the morale of Rescorla's Hard Corps turned somber as the stack of American bodies grew. Late that afternoon, Rescorla ran into a sergeant who had survived the assault on the rear unit of the Fifth Cavalry regiment and asked him about Larry Hess, the soldier he'd promised Dan Hill he'd look after. He knew the answer from the look on the sergeant's face: Hess was dead. He'd fallen early in the enemy assault. The young lieutenant, weapon blazing, had run straight into enemy fire after two of his men were killed next to him. A first bullet had broken his left shoulder. Hess had pressed on. A second tore through his lower right side. Still he kept firing. A third hit him in the forehead, and he fell.

Of the 400 men who set out on the march from X-ray, 155 had been killed, 142 wounded.

As Rescorla and his men waited to board the helicopters that would fly them out, the first members of the press were disembarking. "What's the official name of this place?" one asked.

"The Little Big Horn," someone answered, invoking the Seventh Cavalry's historic doomed battle under General Custer.

A captain quickly jumped in. "Don't say that," he sternly ordered. "There's been no defeat here."

★

BACK AT CAMP HOLLOWAY, Rescorla and his men washed and were offered fresh uniforms. But Rescorla wanted to keep the same fatigues, with the name tag and patches that had seen him through the intense combat. Though they were filthy, spattered with blood, and reeking, he donned his battle uniform again.

Despite their ordeal, Rescorla and his men were ready, even eager, to pursue the retreating enemy soldiers. They knew from intelligence reports and air reconnaissance that the units they had engaged at X-ray and Albany had headed due west, crossing the Cambodian border. But Colonel Moore's request for authorization to pursue the North Vietnamese was denied. President Johnson had decreed that there could be no military activity across the Cambodian border, even though it was increasingly obvious that North Vietnamese troops were using Cambodian territory as a sanctuary and staging ground. Rescorla was told to return with his men to An Khe.

Rescorla and his fellow officers were dumbfounded. As General Kinnard later told Colonel Moore, "I was always taught as an officer that in a pursuit situation you continue to pursue until you either kill the enemy or he surrenders. Not to follow them into Cambodia violated every principle of warfare. But the decision was made back there, at the White House."

After a night's rest, the surviving men of the Second Battalion, Seventh Cavalry, lined up for the ride back to An Khe. There were so few of them left that the entire battalion needed only four trucks. Rescorla did not want to let their departure go unnoticed, so he ordered his bugler to play taps on the captured French bugle. "Present arms!" he commanded, and his men snapped to attention as the mournful tune drifted through the camp.

They traveled back the way they had come just two weeks earlier, through the Mang Yang pass. As they reached their base camp at An Khe, darkness was falling. Still, the survivors of the First Battalion at X-ray lined the route and cheered them as they passed. Jim Kelly had just returned after spending the battle in the hospital, where he'd been treated for a serious case of malaria and blackwater fever. "Where are all the men?" he asked another spectator.

"That's all that's left," the soldier answered.

When the trucks reached brigade headquarters, the division band broke into the strains of "Garry Owen." Then Rescorla's bugler jumped on top of the truck and blew the tune in response. Momentarily euphoric just to be alive, the men broke into cheers and shouted, "Garry Owen!"

As Rescorla stepped down from the truck, Captain Diduryk came to shake his hand. "Rescorla," he said, "I know Hard Corps was your platoon nickname, but now I want to use it for the whole company. I'd also like to use that bugle as Bravo's bugle for the rest of our tour."

Rescorla saluted in assent. "Garry Owen, sir."

A light rain had begun to fall. Rescorla walked alone uphill toward the mess tent. He and his men had been greeted as heroes. But he could think only of the "bright young faces" of the dead he'd witnessed. Burlile, Hess—they would never grow old with the rest of them. His face grew streaked with tears, though he didn't want anyone to know he had wept. Later, he blamed the rain for the moisture on his face. "Hell yes," he insisted, "it was the rain."

★

THAT THURSDAY WAS THANKSGIVING. Rain continued throughout the day, and it was cold, muddy, and wet. In keeping with U.S. military tradition, Rescorla and his men were served a hot meal of turkey and dressing, along with a cup of real coffee. After weeks of C-rations, it seemed an almost unimaginable treat. He and Fantino had been to the mess tent, filled up their mess kits, and taken their mugs, and they were hurrying back to their tents to enjoy the feast. A long line of men was still waiting to be served. Suddenly they were all called to attention and ordered to move to an open area just down the hill. As they stood in the rain holding their plates of food, General William Westmoreland and an entourage of officers walked into view, and Westmoreland jumped onto a tree stump to address the troops.

"I salute you men of the Seventh Cavalry," Westmoreland said, and smartly lifted his hand to his brow. Then he praised their great victory in the Ia Drang valley and spoke of the greatness of the American cause.

As the general spoke, Rescorla looked down at his and Fantino's Thanksgiving dinners growing cold and wet in the rain. Then he turned to Fantino. "This is asinine," he said.

★

BACK IN THE UNITED STATES, the first of the telegrams went out notifying relatives that their husbands, sons, and brothers had died in Vietnam. They all began with the same language: "The Secretary of the Army regrets . . ." They gave no details, not even the locations of the deaths, which were considered military secrets. Delores Burlile, Tom's sister, was working her usual shift at a factory in Ohio when she was told she had a telephone call. When she answered, a stranger delivered the news: "I regret to inform you that your brother is dead." At first she didn't believe it. She and her mother had never even considered the possibility that he might die. As the news sank in, she became hysterical, then collapsed. She was taken by wheelchair to the emergency room.

7

CHARGE OF THE LIGHT BRIGADE

First Air Cavalry soldiers landing in the Central Highlands of Vietnam.
(Bettmann/Corbis)

A LETTER DAN HILL had sent to Larry Hess was returned to Hill the same week at Fort Campbell. Stamped on the unopened letter was "Search," meaning that the addressee couldn't be found. Hill knew that meant only one thing: Hess was dead.

After Rescorla, there was no man Hill had felt closer to than Hess. He had given Larry the copy of "If" that Rescorla had given to him. Now he was haunted by the notion that the heroism celebrated by Kipling and extolled by Hill had led Hess to his death. Hill knew Hess had just turned twenty. He thought of Hess's jazz guitar music that no one would hear again, and he wept. Late that night, Hill got a bottle of

112

Jack Daniel's bourbon, and he started drinking. He kept going until he had downed the entire bottle. He donned his camouflage fatigues, rifle, and pistol, painted his face with camouflage grease, and began rampaging through the house.

Hill awakened his wife, Pat, who found him fully armed with bloodshot eyes, looking crazed. She'd never seen him in such a state. "Leave me alone!" he yelled. He looked as if he were about to use his gun on himself. Frightened, she was about to call the military police. But then Hill passed out.

The next morning, he had a ferocious hangover and his memory was blank. "What happened?" he asked his wife.

"You nearly killed yourself," she said.

Soon after, Hill saw press reports about a major battle in the Ia Drang valley and saw that Rescorla's battalion was involved. On ABC News, General Westmoreland said, "I'd characterize this entire campaign as being the most successful of this conflict thus far. I feel that success is really unprecedented." But Hill was troubled by reports that there might have been more than three hundred American casualties.

Hill wrote Rescorla immediately, asking what had happened and if he knew anything about Larry Hess. From An Khe, Rescorla reported that the battles of X-ray and Albany were "the goddamnedest thing I've ever been part of in my life." Nothing he experienced in Cyprus or Africa had prepared him for warfare on this scale, with so many casualties. "Now I know why the guys in World War One and Two came back shell-shocked," he wrote. "I've never seen such carnage in my life." And he told Hill what he knew about Hess: that he'd been killed at Albany, charging valiantly into enemy fire, wounded three times before he fell.

Unlike his hangover, Hill couldn't so easily shake off his grief. He began badgering the assignment officer at the Pentagon, asking for immediate assignment to Vietnam. He wanted to avenge Hess's death.

★

HILL LANDED IN Saigon on January 19, 1966. From the air the land-scape was beautiful: verdant, lush, with rice paddies and irrigation ditches forming a patchwork quilt stretching to the distant mountains. After landing, Hill reported to Camp Alpha, the American base outside the city hastily built to accommodate the huge infusion of troops. Hill found it fly infested, filthy, the latrines overflowing. He left almost im-mediately to explore Saigon.

It wasn't the gracious former colonial capital he had expected, though he could see that it had once been beautiful, with grand boule-vards and palm-lined streets. But now it was noisy, dirty, and crowded, overflowing with refugees camping in the streets, fleeing the fighting in the countryside and drawn by the American dollar. After fighting off scores of pimps and ragged children begging for candy and cigarettes, Hill checked into the Saigon Hotel and had a shower. Still wet, he wiped the soap from his eyes and saw that a young woman had come into his room. She was naked. Hill said there must be some mistake and insisted that she dress and leave. He resumed his shower "in a rather disturbed state of mind," as he later wrote in his diary.

Four days later, Hill reported to the American base at Tuy Hoa, lo-cated about an hour's helicopter ride south of An Khe. It was even closer to the coast than An Khe, and Hill briefly enjoyed swimming in the South China Sea off of the beautiful white sand beaches adjacent to the base. But he was quickly thrown into action. Like Rescorla's pla-toon at An Khe, Hill's unit was so well disciplined and effective that it drew the heaviest assignments and was often the first to land in a hos-tile area. By now, "search and destroy" was standard operating proce-dure, and day after day, Hill and his men were sent by helicopter into unfamiliar landscapes, told to pursue and kill the enemy, then return for a short rest before being sent out again.

Hill kept a diary of those early months in Vietnam. Inside the front cover he wrote: "This book is dedicated to 2nd Lieutenant Larry Hess, who had all those soldierly traits and qualities, that great generals strive to achieve, and who demonstrated every one of them, right up to the day he valiantly gave his life for his country, leading his troops at An Khe, Republic of Vietnam."

In many entries Hill recorded the peculiar mix of excitement and dread that characterized their missions: "How men can thrill at the knowledge that soon they may be in pitched battle, struggling to stay alive or to kill their opponents, I don't know. But it was there. It came and went, now jubilation, now fear, now thrill, now anxiety. Maybe here is the very cause of war: the human lust for adventure, the slight touch of insanity within the normally sound mind that challenges one to risk death in a mortal contest with another man or nation."

It didn't take long for Hill to realize that Vietnam was a new kind of warfare, where the tactics he had learned in postwar Europe and the code of honor that went with them seemed irrelevant. The enemy was indistinguishable from the population they were meant to save; civilians one day were Viet Cong the next; areas supposedly "pacified" reverted to enemy control the instant the Americans and their rifles, grenades, and mortars left. On one mission, Hill's platoon was ordered to assault a village in which eighteen North Vietnamese regulars were reported to have taken refuge. Hill ordered his machine gunners to open up on the village, then he and his troops warily advanced to the first buildings, expecting the enemy soldiers to open fire on them at any moment.

Instead, "out of the houses came a bunch of women and children of all ages," Hill wrote. "There were a few old men, one so sick he couldn't move and had to be carried by two of the younger women. I held my breath and my heart stopped. I was sorry now I had the troops go in firing and feared that I had been responsible for many, many women and children being killed or injured. When we finished searching the village we found only a cow had been hit. I was weak with relief." On another mission he wasn't so lucky. As he and his men searched a village, a figure dressed in the black pajamalike garments of the Viet Cong had run into his path, carrying what looked like a rifle. Hill had shot instinctively. When he reached the body, it turned out to be a woman carrying a broom.

"Why do women and children have to get involved?" Hill wrote in his diary. "Soldiers have asked themselves this for centuries. This is the reason soldiers hate war more than anyone else. They see the torn and twisted bodies, smell the death, and rip themselves apart inside for the rounds they fire that kill the innocent, and the ones they don't fire that are the cause of some enemy soldier living to kill a friend."

On one mission, Hill's platoon was ordered into a valley to pursue a Viet Cong battalion that had reportedly taken refuge there. After jumping from the helicopters, they found themselves in "boggy muck" three to four feet deep, "covered in green slime" and infested with leeches. They immediately came under heavy enemy fire from higher positions and called for artillery support. Two volleys struck the enemy positions. Then, "my stomach knotted with the grip of stark naked fear," Hill wrote. An artillery barrage fell short, onto their positions. The explosion threw Hill into the air. When he landed intact, he dug himself into the muck as more rounds landed and shrapnel flew overhead.

"Get that artillery off my ass!" Hill yelled into his radio.

Then American planes arrived, dropping napalm and white phosphorus on the enemy positions, and the hillside erupted in flame. Hill's men began to cheer.

When the smoke cleared, they advanced into the devastated area, which contained a labyrinth of tunnels and caves that had been occupied by enemy troops. But now they were gone. Despite the intense bombardment, Hill was astounded that the caves were intact and there were no enemy bodies. The enemy "may well have suffered not a single casualty, which I now began to suspect," Hill wrote. He radioed for permission to pursue the fleeing troops but was told instead to withdraw. "We have another mission," a senior officer said. They marched back to the landing zone, and the helicopters returned to take them back to camp.

Filthy, hot, covered in sweat, and exhausted, Hill and his men returned to find a television film crew had arrived. The officer motioned Hill aside, out of earshot of the film crew and his men. "What's the big mission?" Hill asked.

"Now look," the officer replied. "You're not going to like this. You're going to take that hill again. They sent out this TV crew to get some film of an attack. I want you to take that hill the same way you did before."

Hill was speechless. He couldn't be serious.

"You understand?" the officer asked.

"No, no. I don't understand," Hill replied. "I took it once. We got away clean. Right now, Charlie is crawling back out of those holes and he's going to zap somebody on this go-around."

"That's enough, Hill," he said sharply.

Hill took a large swig out of the canteen of Jack Daniel's bourbon he always carried. Then he walked over and offered some to his men. "You gents better have a drink," he said.

The canteen was passed around, and no one said anything. Finally one spoke up. "Well, sir, how do the sons of bitches want us to take it for the camera?" he asked.

"How did you know?" Hill asked, incredulous.

"Sir, I've been in the old army, the new army, the modern army, and now this shit. I've seen the same assholes a million times. We knew when we saw you arguing with him. Just tell us how you want us to do it."

A sergeant chimed in, "The second time is always easier."

Hill was touched by his men's effort to make him feel better and their willingness to follow him back into such a dangerous situation. "How do you do it?" he later wrote in his diary. "How do you tell a man that he did a fine job so far, that nobody was killed and we lucked out. But now you want them to do it again and maybe this time get killed. What did I want them to risk their lives for? Our country? Our flag? The platoon? Their buddies? The freedom of Vietnam? No. Just a few feet of film."

"Okay," he told his men, "once more, just like before." The men laughed nervously.

"Ain't this a bitch," Hill said.

As Hill had feared, their descent into the valley was met with heavy enemy fire, duly recorded by the television crew. They fought their way up the same hillside, but before they again reached the abandoned caves and tunnels, they were ordered to form a perimeter they could defend overnight. There were numerous casualties among the American soldiers. A sergeant was shot in the chest and back and was paralyzed. When the medic came to the sergeant's aid, he was shot in the arm. Another man was killed by bomb fragments.

"You just got to be hard, Dan," another lieutenant told him when they gathered for the night. "You got to be hard."

★

GIVEN THAT HE faced enemy fire almost constantly, Hill was surprised that he himself managed to escape injury. In part this was because he had become such a keen observer of the enemy, trying, as he had advised Rescorla, to know the enemy as well as himself. He had learned to recognize the scent of canned mackerel, the standard ration for NVA regulars, as well as the tiny hot peppers they ate with them. If he detected a whiff of clove, he knew someone had been smoking the clove-scented cigarettes favored by the Vietnamese. In the morning, the air would drift from high to low ground, carrying with it any telltale scents. And yet, perhaps inevitably, Hill was hit.

Not long after returning from the expedition filmed by the TV crew, Hill's platoon was assigned to patrol a series of hamlets outside of Tuy An, a town about twenty miles inland from the coast. Though the area had supposedly been pacified and cleared of North Vietnamese troops, it remained infested with Viet Cong, and virtually every turn in the road marked the site of a potential sniper. Hill and his men were carefully moving single file along a road through one of the villages when a shot rang out and Hill felt something hot near his buttocks. The soldier behind him whirled around and fired, killing an armed Vietnamese man who had been hidden in a hole covered with sod.

Hill's medic came rushing over. "What did he hit?" he asked.

Hill had no idea. All he felt was a burning sensation. He felt along his rear end, then removed the fanny pack he'd been carrying. He reached down his trousers. There it was: the bullet had entered the pack, passed through a can of beans, and lodged in Hill's underwear. In all likelihood, the fanny pack had saved his life. "I'll be damned," Hill said. The medic removed the bullet but warned Hill that he'd be suffering from a fierce blister by the next morning.

★

AT AN KHE, Rescorla had been promoted to head a reconnaissance platoon, which was considered a high honor. Only the best platoon leaders were considered for recon. Word of Rescorla's performance at Albany had spread widely; some were calling Rescorla the best platoon leader they'd ever seen. The recon platoons were typically dropped into isolated areas to search for evidence of North Vietnamese troop concentrations and Viet Cong military activity. Then, if they made contact, they called in air support and troops for more of the search-and-destroy missions that had become the mainstay of the American war effort. Casualties in the units were high, since they operated in enemy territory so far from support units. Rescorla handpicked a group of his men to join him in the new platoon, including a new medic, Joe Holloway, and a sergeant named John Driver.

Driver was Irish, an immigrant like Rescorla, and he could hold his own with Rescorla at drinking, spinning yarns, and philosophizing over beers. He also obviously worshiped Rescorla. Others joked that in Driver, Rescorla had found a replacement for the British batmen who had served him in Africa. Rescorla developed a deep affection for Driver and later recommended him for Officer Candidate School. Of the men he invited to join him, only Sergeant Thompson turned Rescorla down, because he didn't want to leave Bravo Company bereft of experienced leadership.

★

BEFORE HE LEFT, Rescorla gave Thompson half of the platoon flag that Rescorla had designed and had made after the Ia Drang battles. It had a green field to symbolize the jungle of Vietnam, with British commando wings for Rescorla's British army experience and a cavalry saber across the wings. At the end of the saber was a Communist star with drops of blood on it. On the flag was inscribed, "Hard Corps, Ia Drang Valley." Rescorla kept the other half.

Rescorla thrived away from the regimentation of the base camp, where he was free to develop his own tactics. But not all of his men liked it. Fantino, his radio operator, hated the long forays into the jungle, the ambushes, the nights spent fending off insects, the constant threat of attack. But Rescorla brushed aside his complaints. "This is a part of war," he said. "You have to fight the enemy on the enemy's terms. We're not fighting the Second World War. It's not like there's a line, and the enemy's on the other side. We're in the middle of the enemy."

Rescorla's platoon headed north to Bon Song, a rugged area that bordered the South China Sea with some beautiful beaches and straddled Route 1, Vietnam's major strategic highway, which paralleled the coast. It was supposedly free of North Vietnamese Army regulars but filled with Viet Cong.

Rescorla excelled at reconnaissance, a skill he'd honed in both Cyprus and Northern Rhodesia. Reconnaissance allowed for far more autonomy. He trained his men to move undetected, to live off the land, to be alert to danger—in other words, to blend into the terrain like the enemy. On one mission, his recon unit was attached to Larry Gwin's company. Gwin's unit had paused on a march into a treacherous area known as the Crow's Foot, when Rescorla and his recon unit overtook them. Even though Gwin and Rescorla had become friends after Rescorla had come to Gwin's rescue at Albany, Rescorla passed him by with no sign of recognition. Gwin later recorded his impressions:

"Then I saw Rescorla, and all I can say is that I was glad he was on our side. Jesus, he looked mean. He saw me, too, and we were friends, but his mind was like a steel trap, tense and ready to spring, and he walked right by me as if I weren't there. He was walking slowly, watching where he put his feet. His people followed him like ghosts, gliding by me silently with their camouflaged faces, soft hats, eyes scanning the trees, weapons at the ready. Had it been dark, I doubt that I would have heard them. It was eerie."

Word of Rescorla's prowess soon spread. When Dennis Deal, the fellow second lieutenant Rescorla had landed on top of in the dry creekbed at X-ray, was also promoted to head a recon platoon, his commander sent him into the field to join Rescorla and learn his techniques. So in January 1966, Deal met Rescorla in Bon Song and joined him on a recon patrol. Though standard procedure called for patrols of fifteen to twenty men. Rescorla preferred smaller teams of five men and had pioneered long-range patrols, where the group would live off the land and stay away from camp for days or even weeks. He explained that he was simply imitating the tactics that seemed to work so well for the North Vietnamese.

On their first mission, Rescorla led Deal and their men, about ten altogether, through some dense vegetation toward a clearing of fields, banana trees, and a small village where there was rumored to have been some enemy activity. It was a warm, sunny day and they had gotten an early start. As they moved through the clearing and reached the beginning of the village, they cautiously approached a thatch-roofed structure, a typical hootch that dotted the Vietnamese countryside. The hootches could be deceptive; sometimes they turned out to have only two or three walls and were open at the rear.

This proved to be the case. Rescorla and Deal were in the front of their small column, and as they rounded the corner, they saw that the building had only three walls. In the same instant, they realized the building was filled with North Vietnamese Army regulars, all dressed in khaki uniforms. There were about thirty or forty of them, all sitting on benches facing away from Rescorla and Deal, looking at what seemed to be an instructor and the front of a classroom. Their weapons and other equipment were stacked neatly just outside the structure. In the next instant, the instructor saw them and looked shocked, and then everyone turned and stared.

Everyone seemed frozen. Rescorla broke the silence.

"Oh, pardon me," he said in an impeccable British accent. Then he turned and ran. "Follow me," he said to Deal.

Rescorla led his men through a zigzag course across the landscape, dodging bushes and banana trees. Fortunately the terrain was flat. He set a punishing pace.

Behind them, the North Vietnamese grabbed their weapons and poured out of the hootch. The first shots rang out.

A couple of the Americans stopped to return fire. "This isn't about time, mates," Rescorla wryly observed. "It's about distance." In other words, Deal realized, "Get the hell out of there." No one bothered to fire again.

Once they reached the cover of the tree line, the firing began to taper off. They continued running, and eventually all they heard was the sound of their own movement. They had eluded the enemy, at least for the time being. But it took them four hours before they found a suitable landing area for a helicopter to fly them to safety.

Deal was amazed by Rescorla's calm under pressure. When he and Rescorla had encountered the enemy, it was as if Rescorla had been interrupting a tea party.

He and Rescorla continued to patrol the area for the next several weeks. They hoped to find the location of the North Vietnamese encampment, so they could call in the air cavalry. But they never found any traces of the North Vietnamese regiment they'd encountered. They could have been anywhere, melting back into the local population, or nowhere, having moved rapidly to another supposedly pacified area. For as Rescorla had already realized, everyone in Vietnam was hostile to them. The enemy was just about everyone.

★

IN APRIL 1966, Dan Hill was eligible for his first week of R&R. He could have gone to Hong Kong, Bangkok, or Honolulu, like his fellow officers. Instead, he told his battalion commander that he had a friend at An Khe and wanted to head up there to visit him. His commander looked at him oddly for a moment, then shrugged. "Fine," he said. Though they'd kept up a steady stream of correspondence and each had the other's radio frequency in case they needed to reach each other in an emergency, Dan hadn't seen Rescorla since their last night together at Fort Benning. He put together some gear and hitched a ride on a helicopter going to An Khe. He watched intently as the lush vegetation of the southern highlands gave way to more rugged terrain and the Central Highlands came into view in the distance. Then the sprawling base camp materialized, and they landed in its dusty landing zone.

Hill asked for directions to Rescorla's recon unit and surprised him lying on a cot in his tent. Rescorla leaped up, gave him his big grin, and grabbed his hand. Hill was impressed by the sight of his friend. Rescorla had always been fit, but now he had no body fat, and when Hill grabbed his arm it felt like sinews of steel. Rescorla said he wanted to take Hill to a historic battlefield, as they had done so often while stationed in New Jersey, and told him to jump into a jeep equipped with a machine gun on the rear deck. Rescorla drove rapidly along Route 19 to the Mang Yang Pass. It was surrounded by mountainous jungle, shrouded by a triple canopy of vegetation. Here, Rescorla explained, was the spot where the French army lost an entire mobile army group. He took Hill to a six-foot-high obelisk with a simple inscription in both French and Vietnamese: "Here on June 24, 1954, soldiers of France and Vietnam died for their countries."

The next morning Hill and Rescorla boarded helicopters for an airborne search-and-destroy mission, which by now had become standard operating procedure. Rescorla would take his entire platoon, usually forty-four men, and they'd be dropped into a hostile area, hoping to lure the enemy into battle. There was little pretense that this would actually secure or "pacify" the region. Instead, it had become a war of attrition, with a strategy to kill so many North Vietnamese troops, Viet Cong, and their sympathizers that the enemy would be forced to surrender. This week, Rescorla asked Hill to serve as his point man, someone who patrolled just ahead of the platoon leader to warn of danger.

After landing, the men fanned out silently through the underbrush. If they had to talk, they whispered, taking care to speak only after exhaling, which made the whisper quieter and more distinct. They looked for signs of the enemy: wilted vegetation serving as camouflage, traces of food, signs of human defecation. Hill was especially effective. After a day of screening for the enemy, they ate before sundown, then moved to another location as soon as darkness fell. They set up an "ambush" for the night, prepared in case of an attack. They divided into groups of three; two slept facedown under a mosquito net while the third stayed alert for signs of the enemy. Once the ambush was established, no one could talk or move. The tension never let up.

The next day they were patrolling through the underbrush when Hill motioned for Rescorla to stop.

"What is it?" Rescorla whispered.

"I don't know." Hill had frozen. He scanned the landscape: the tall grass, the brush, the trees just beyond the clearing. He couldn't see anything. It was almost too quiet. "There's something out there."

"Do you have a feeling?" Rescorla asked.

"Yeah," Hill replied. "Someone is watching us. Someone is waiting."

Rescorla motioned for Hill and another man to stay where they were. Then he moved to their left, disappearing in the tall grass. Hill set up their machine guns in a defensive position. Suddenly they heard gunfire. Rescorla was firing, and it was being returned. His voice came on Hill's radio. "You got me spotted?"

"Yeah."

"Fire out ahead of me." Hill and the other soldier shifted their weapons and unleashed a barrage of machine-gun fire.

"Okay, move up to me." When they reached Rescorla, it was quiet. He pointed to the bodies of two men in NVA uniforms. A third, Rescorla said, had escaped.

The other soldier looked intently at Hill. "How'd you know?" he asked.

Rescorla grinned. "That's Hill," he said. "He's better than an English pointer."

Of Hill's week of R&R, he sent five days patrolling with Rescorla, eating C-rations, and setting up ambushes. When they returned to An Khe, they had two days to unwind. Hill accompanied Rescorla to the officers club. They ate steaks and chicken and drank beer. Rescorla played the guitar and sang. They shared Rescorla's tent, barely big enough for their two cots.

They hadn't been able to talk much while in the field, but even so, Hill sensed that his old friend was more reticent than he had been when they had been together in Africa. Since then they had no secrets from each other; they held nothing back. They had thought so much alike they could practically read each other's minds. But now something about Rescorla seemed different.

After one night of drinking and singing at the officers club, they were lying awake on their cots. Rescorla was quiet. His thoughts seemed far away. Then he turned to Hill. "What do you think of this situation?" Hill knew he was talking about Vietnam. As a professional soldier, Rescorla would never question the politics, strategy, or morality of the war in front of his men, nor would Hill. But Hill sensed that Rescorla needed to confide in him, to get something off his chest that he'd been holding back.

"It's not much of a war, is it," Hill said. "But it's the only one we got."

"Do you think we're right?" Rescorla asked.

"I don't give a damn," Hill said. He reminded Rescorla of their discussions of the U.S. Constitution. No one had more reverence for the Constitution than Rescorla, in Hill's estimation. As officers, Hill reminded him, their duty was to carry out the orders of their commander in chief, the president, elected by the people. Otherwise the United States would be no better off than a banana republic. Democracy—wasn't that what they were fighting for?

"How would you feel if you were Vietnamese?" Rescorla asked.

Hill pondered the question. He had little but contempt for the American puppets in the South Vietnamese government and officer corps. "I'd be a general or captain in the North Vietnamese Army," Hill conceded.

"I'd want my own country," Rescorla agreed. They launched into a discussion of Ho Chi Minh, how he'd sought the help of the Americans against the French but been rebuffed. He'd had no choice but to turn to the Communists. Now, they were involved in what Rescorla called an "internecine war," with "no solution and no end." There were no lines, no territory to hold, no captive people to liberate. "It's killing for the sake of killing," he lamented.

Nor was killing going to win the war. Rescorla had begun referring to the "rosy red hue," a phrase from Milton's *Paradise Lost,* through which the American commanders were viewing the war effort, but even accepting the inflated estimates of enemy casualties, it wasn't enough. Rescorla had calculated the North Vietnamese birthrate at nearly four hundred thousand a year, which meant that the enemy population was producing half as many male children every year—more than enough to replace those killed in the war.

Rescorla said he wondered at times if the real point of the war wasn't to generate profits for the military-industrial complex and drive up stock prices. He even entertained speculation that John F. Kennedy had been assassinated because he was going to stop the war. "I think this may just be to make money," he said. "I think they're running up stocks with these boys' lives."

Hill was used to Rescorla's use of rhetorical questions to make a point, but he'd never sensed such sadness and despair in Rescorla. Yet Hill knew what he meant. On more than one occasion, Hill had drafted his own letter of resignation from the army, only to tear it up. He was too much the professional soldier to walk out and leave his men behind.

Hours had passed, but still Rescorla wanted to talk. "How do you feel about the men you lost?" he asked. "Does it bother you?"

Hill thought for a moment of Larry Hess. But he put the thought aside. "No," he replied. "I don't let it bother me."

Since Hess's death, Hill had made it a point to learn as little as possible about the men he commanded. He couldn't even remember most of their names or faces. If they were killed, he wanted them to seem like strangers. Hill didn't dwell on the people he had killed, either. When his men asked, as they sometimes did, how many men he'd killed in his life, Hill said he didn't know. He'd stopped counting at two hundred. Hill realized that to people outside the military, this might seem hard-hearted. But for him, it was simply a matter of emotional survival.

"Could you have saved anybody?" Rescorla asked.

Hill shrugged. Maybe, but that would be Monday morning quarterbacking. He wanted as few casualties as possible, but he knew he'd lose some of his men. This was war.

Yet he knew Rescorla was different. Rescorla began to recite a series of names: "Tommy Burlile, Charlie McManus, Elias Alvarez, Eddie Brown, Richard Young . . ."

Rescorla could name them all, the men who'd died under his command. He knew their names, their faces, their hometowns, their family members. He knew what wounds they had suffered and how, where and when they had died. He told Hill he had held them in his arms, their young faces stricken with pain and anxiety and fear of death. "You're going to be all right," he had told them all, no matter how dire their condition. He would keep saying it until they died, and even after: "You're going to be all right." And then he had wiped his hands in their blood. Feeling their blood, he said, helped give him a sense of closure.

★

RESCORLA CONFIDED NONE of his growing reservations about the war effort to anyone but Hill. He stayed on at An Khe, rallying his men for the continuing search-and-destroy missions and teaching them the skills necessary to survive. He spent his free time at the officers club, where nearly every night he and the other officers gathered for beer, conversation, and singing, either a cappella or accompanied by one of the men who played guitar. But he never lost his competitive zeal. One night he asked for two full beer cans, then issued a challenge to his fellow officers: "Let's see if the strength you profess matches the bullshit I'm sure you're full of." Then he demonstrated his challenge. Rescorla backed up until the heels of his boots were firmly planted against the wall. He took the beer cans, one held vertically in each hand, and bent forward until they reached the floor. Then, using the cans to support his hands, he began walking his hands forward, supporting his weight on one as the other advanced. Soon he had reached a push-up position. Then he reached out one arm and deposited a can as far from the wall as possible. He brought this free hand back to the other and, supporting his weight on the remaining beer can, moved back toward the wall until he was again able to stand. The goal was to place a can as far from the wall as possible, then return to an upright position without ever touching the floor with the hands. Rescorla had a twinkle in his eye and looked smug.

Several muscular officers jumped at the challenge, eager to take Rescorla down a peg. The exercise didn't look that hard, but in fact it called for tremendous arm, back, and abdominal strength, as well as balance and coordination. Some managed to place the can farther than Rescorla's, then couldn't get back up. Others collapsed trying to place the can while fully extended. Finally Jim Kelly took up the challenge. Kelly not only had muscles of "coiled steel," as Larry Gwin later described them, but he was six feet four, which gave him a natural advantage over Rescorla, who was six one. Kelly took his cans, stretched to his full length, and managed to place his can ten inches past Rescorla's. There were tense moments as he struggled to return to the starting position, but when he finally succeeded, flushed from the exertion, the place erupted with cheers.

Then Rescorla returned to the wall, two cans of Budweiser in his hands. He dropped into position and quickly maneuvered into the push-up position. Then, incredibly, he kept going lower and lower, his chest nearly scraping the floor. Then he thrust his hand forward and left the can a good six inches past Kelly's. He was now stretched at nearly full length, his body supported by only one can, and he trembled slightly from the strain on his nervous system. He seemed about to collapse when he suddenly jerked backward and in a few powerful moves was on his feet.

The men went wild, cheering, yelling, clapping Rescorla on the back. For all the excitement, they could have been at the World Series or a world heavyweight championship. For a moment Rescorla made them forget they were in Vietnam.

"Beer walking," as Rescorla's game came to be known, became a regular event at the officers club, a rite of passage for new officers at An Khe. Despite his defeat at Rescorla's hands, Jim Kelly became the reigning champion. Having launched the competition, Rescorla himself gracefully retired, and his record was never surpassed.

★

ON JUNE 18, Hill was at Tuy Hoa when he got an urgent call that three platoons from the 327th Airborne Infantry were pinned down and suffering heavy casualties just outside the village of Trung Luong, in a wide valley near the Special Forces camp at Dong Tre. A substantial force of North Vietnamese troops was rumored to be in the area. After initial patrols yielded scant enemy contact, the Americans were ordered to sweep through the valley. Now it looked as though the Dong Tre incident had been a lure to draw the Americans into the heavily fortified area around Trung Luong. The three platoons under the command of Captain Charles T. Furgeson had suffered so many casualties that they desperately needed fresh leadership. Hill and two other lieutenants grabbed their weapons and jumped into the nearest helicopter.

The situation was far worse than had been reported. Furgeson had been ordered to advance on and take the village of Trung Luong, but it was heavily defended. North Vietnamese troops were concealed in thatched huts, barns, even haystacks. As Hill arrived, a medical evacuation helicopter was about to leave. It was loaded with casualties. Hill spotted a medic he knew. "Dan, you've got to get out there. They need leadership," he said.

Hill and the two other lieutenants raced through enemy fire to reach the American position on the outskirts of the village. "Jesus Christ, I'm glad to see you guys," Furgeson said when they arrived. He grabbed Hill's arm. "What do I do?"

Hill had already concluded that their position was indefensible, which meant they had to move somewhere, even at the risk of getting shot. "We got to do something," he said. "Go forward or backward and I don't give a damn which, but do something." As they flew into the village, Hill had spotted a nearby hill with a small pagoda on top. It looked like a position they could defend—if they could get there.

Captain Furgeson sent each of the platoons in a different direction, then told them to regroup at the pagoda. Hill led one of the platoons, which acted as a rear guard, covering the company as it split into two groups. Using rice paddy dikes for cover, the two groups made their way to the pagoda, and Hill's platoon followed. They dug in hastily, and Hill radioed for air support. Nothing was available, he was told. They braced themselves for what they knew would be a long night. Exhausted and frightened, they were running out of ammunition and could easily be overrun by the enemy force.

As the night wore on, enemy troops attacked in waves. Finally, in desperation, Hill used the radio frequency to reach Rescorla at An Khe. "It's Hill," he said breathlessly. "I'm down to about fifty men, and we've got the rest of the night to go. I think we're going to be overrun. I don't expect to make it."

"Oh, shit," Rescorla said.

"When you get home, take care of Pat and the kids," Hill said. "Tell them I love them."

"What are your coordinates?" Rescorla demanded, wasting no time.

"We're west of Tuy An, about thirty miles," Hill reported.

"I'll be there," Rescorla said.

Without authorization, Rescorla summoned his platoon members and commandeered four helicopters. He radioed his commander, Colonel Moore, that he was flying to Trung Luong, where American forces desperately needed assistance. Then he called Hill to say he was in the air.

Hill waited through the rest of the night as the battle raged. Tracers lit the sky, green for the North Vietnamese, red for the Americans. Rescorla reported that the air bombardment was too intense to risk a landing, and he had to touch down at Dong Tre. He told Hill to hang on; as soon as it was clear, Rescorla would land. More reinforcements were coming. The North Vietnamese continued to assault Hill's position, but each time they suffered heavy casualties and were stopped. During lulls, Hill's men ran out and seized weapons and ammunition from the dead bodies. Hill quickly taught his men how to use the unfamiliar weapons. Then, while the sun rose, the sky darkened as Rescorla and the entire Third Brigade of the First Air Cavalry Division commanded by Colonel Moore descended in scores of helicopters. It was the most incredible sight Hill had ever seen. His men began to cheer. Rescorla and the cavalry had come to the rescue.

The choppers set down, and hundreds of fresh American troops began counterattacking toward the village. Hill and his men rushed from their positions to join them. A few hours later, under a blazing sun and in intense heat, Hill was trying to cross a stream to direct an attack on a haystack that concealed an enemy machine gun. He had just ordered his men to fire a couple of antitank weapons and called for a flamethrower when he suddenly felt a little dizzy. He began to feel weak and wandered aimlessly in circles, an easy target for enemy fire. He felt a hand on his arm. Someone said, "We've got to get him out of here." He lost consciousness.

The next thing Hill knew, he was three thousand feet in the air in a medical evacuation helicopter, an intravenous tube in his arm, wounded men lying around him. When they reached Tuy Hoa, he was wheeled out on a stretcher. "I can walk," Hill insisted, and tried to stand up. Then he felt weak and wiped the sweat off his brow. When he looked at his hand, it was covered in blood. What the hell, Hill thought. Then he reached farther up along his scalp. A piece of shrapnel was protruding from his skull.

In the medical tent, a surgeon walked up. "What's wrong with you?" he asked. Hill pointed to his head, still bleeding profusely.

"Let me take a look," the doctor said.

"Are my brains oozing out up there?" Hill asked.

"Sit still," the doctor ordered. He grabbed a pair of pliers. Without any anesthetic, he put one hand on Hill's head, gripped the shrapnel with the pliers, then yanked it out. He spread open the wound with his hands to see how deep the shrapnel had penetrated. Hill yelped in pain.

"You're okay," the doctor said. "It didn't penetrate the skull." He washed and dressed the wound. "Drink a lot of water," he said as he moved to his next patient.

Hill got up and walked to the tactical operations center. "I want to go back out." He was on the next helicopter back to the battlefield.

When American troops finally entered Trung Luong that evening, the North Vietnamese had vanished. They found that the village sat atop an extensive network of tunnels, used by the enemy both to reach their positions and to disappear without detection. Of the 172 men in Hill's company, 50 survived. Total American casualties were about 300 dead and wounded.

★

SEVERAL DAYS LATER, Lieutenant General John A. Heintges, an aide to Westmoreland, arrived at Tuy Hoa for a debriefing on the battle of Trung Luong. Hill was told to act as the general's guide, and he accompanied him by helicopter, first to a provincial capital for lunch with a South Vietnamese colonel and then to the battlefield. When they arrived in sweltering midday heat, cleanup operations were in full force. Bulldozers were pushing Vietnamese corpses into large ditches, where they were soaked in diesel fuel and gasoline and then burned. The stench was awful. There were an estimated 850 Vietnamese dead. Hill pointed out the hill and what remained of the pagoda where he and his men had spent the night.

Then the helicopter touched down at the Special Forces camp at Dong Tre.

As Hill followed the general from the helicopter toward the command post, he heard an unmistakable voice ring out:

> *Here comes Hill!*
> *Half a league, half a league,*
> *Half a league, Hill!*

Hill's face lit up with a smile. It was Rescorla, quoting from "The Charge of the Light Brigade." He clapped Hill on the back.

"Am I glad to see you," Hill said. "You saved my ass."

"I heard you got hit," Rescorla said.

"In the head," Hill replied, pointing to his wound.

"Shit," Rescorla said. "Don't they know you can't hurt Dan Hill by hitting him in the head?"

8

HOME FRONT

Susan and her children.
(Courtesy of Susan Rescorla)

WHEN SUSAN AND ROBERT returned from their summer-long honeymoon in Europe, they moved into an attractive home in West Orange, New Jersey. Robert worked in his father's insurance business and also started his own brokerage firm; Susan returned to her public relations job at the advertising agency. They had plenty of money and time and made two trips to the Caribbean during the next year. In 1965, Susan was thrilled to discover that she was pregnant, and in 1966 her daughter Cristina was born. The name reminded Susan of Europe, especially Italy, which she had loved so much and where Robert's family had originated. Without giving it much thought, Susan quit her job to stay home with her new baby. She assumed she'd never work again.

Three years later, she and Robert had a second daughter, whom they named Alexandra. Both children were baptized Roman Catholics in deference to Robert's family, though Susan didn't convert. They moved into a much larger house in the more fashionable New Jersey suburb of Convent Station. The colonial-style house had four bedrooms and was on a large, beautifully landscaped corner lot. Every Wednesday, when many other doctors played golf, Susan's father took her, the children, and her mother to the Jersey shore for lunch. Susan loved being a mother, and she loved Robert for giving her the life she had dreamed of.

Preoccupied with her family and maintaining a large home, Susan felt remote and detached from the world events dominating the news. She and Robert read the papers, and Robert maintained an interest in politics and current affairs, but he didn't discuss his interests much at home. Susan was largely oblivious to developments in Vietnam. Since Robert was married with two children, he was exempt from the draft. None of his college friends fought in the war, and they didn't know anyone from their affluent suburb who had gone to Vietnam. Susan was vaguely aware of student protests against the war. She instinctively supported American soldiers and couldn't understand why anyone would want to burn the American flag. But she gave those issues little thought. Similarly, though riots in 1968 after the assassination of Martin Luther King devastated Newark, the outlying, nearly all-white suburbs were unaffected. Susan read the news reports but felt that the riots and demonstrations were far away, remote from her daily life.

In any event, she had more immediate problems. Her father's emphysema, diagnosed before her wedding, continued to worsen. Still he kept smoking. By 1967, he could no longer drive and was eventually confined to a wheelchair. Susan often picked him up and drove him to East Orange General Hospital, where he made his rounds in the wheelchair. Finally he had to retire from his practice. He was confined to their home, then to his bedroom. He had to breathe using oxygen tanks. Susan brought her daughters and stayed with him so Marian could get to her doll society meetings in New York. Cristina would play checkers with her grandfather propped up in bed. Susan and the children also stayed for extended periods while her mother traveled to Hawaii, Europe, and Morocco with a friend. Her father could no longer travel but had insisted that her mother not curtail the activities she loved.

Susan's father had his sixtieth birthday, in November 1970, in the hospital. Then he fell into a deep coma. Susan and her mother were at the hospital every day, hoping he would recover. "Please don't leave," Susan cried, holding her father's hand. Finally a doctor told her to stop.

"You have to let him go," he said.

Susan reluctantly pulled away and watched as her father struggled for breath. Then he died.

Susan's mother fell apart emotionally, and Susan made all the funeral arrangements. She greeted everyone at the funeral. Melvin Greer was buried in the family plot in Caldwell, New Jersey.

When her father's obituary appeared in his alumni magazine, Rufus Williams, a college classmate, wrote Susan's mother to offer his condolences. He and Susan's mother had dated during their college years, but then Susan's mother had met Melvin, and that was the end of it. Then Williams sent her mother a Christmas card. Soon they were talking on the phone about his upcoming open-heart surgery, and their phone conversations continued after he got out of the hospital. One day, her mother told Susan they were engaged.

They were married at an Episcopal church in Montclair, and Susan hosted a small reception afterward at the Manor restaurant in West Orange. Besides the bride and groom, the only guests were Robert, their children, and an old friend of her mother's.

Susan had mixed feelings about her mother's second marriage. She knew no one would replace her father in her mother's affections. But she felt Marian and her new husband had a good deal in common; he was a retired Pan American World Airways executive. He was affluent, a millionaire. He loved to travel as much as her mother did. Her mother was still vibrant and attractive, and she didn't want to face the rest of her life alone.

On the other hand, Susan's mother would be moving to State College, Pennsylvania, where Williams lived. The big, white-columned house where Susan had grown up, which had housed three generations of Greers, was sold. Having lost her father just two years earlier, Susan now felt she was losing her mother as well. After she moved, Susan saw her mother only three times a year, for visits just before Christmas, for her birthday in March, and during the summer. Her stepfather seemed to resent her mother spending time away from him and showed little interest in Susan's young children. They were rarely invited to Pennsylvania.

But Susan was busy with the children, trying to give them the advantages she had grown up with: lessons in dance, music, swimming; good educations; and travel. In 1972, when Cristina was seven and Alexandra four, she persuaded Robert to take time off from work. He was increasingly spending so much time at the office, frequently staying out at night for business dinners, that she felt she and the children were seeing much too little of him. He still pursued his hobby of photography, but she worried that his preoccupation with his financial business was crowding out the creative part of his nature. She felt they both needed a break. Susan made all the arrangements, and they spent part of the summer in Portugal, at the elegant Penina beach resort on the Algarve coast. It was Susan's first return to the country she had loved so much since she had broken off her relationship with the count. It was a beautiful vacation, and she gave the past little thought. She was too busy with her young daughters and handsome American husband.

In the ensuing years, the family took more trips: to Jamaica, Puerto Rico, Saint Martin, Bermuda. In 1974 Susan gave birth to another daughter, Bianca, and the house was again filled with the joy and preoccupations of a new baby. Robert seemed thrilled by the latest addition to the family. He gave Susan a stylish new Cougar automobile for Christmas.

Then, when Bianca was just two months old, Robert mentioned one day that he "hoped" a deal he was working on would come through. Susan paid little attention; it was odd that Robert even mentioned a deal. He never talked about business at home, she knew virtually nothing about what he did at the office, and she also knew nothing about the family finances. All she knew was that money was never an issue. When she needed to pay for something, she wrote a check. She had no idea what the checking account balance was. Robert handled all their financial affairs.

But Robert brought the subject of the deal up again a week or so later. "I hope this deal goes through so we don't lose the house," he said.

"What?" Susan was stunned. She thought she must have misheard, but he repeated that the bank was on the brink of foreclosing on their mortgage. She stared at him in disbelief. Somehow she held herself together; she didn't want to break down in front of Robert. She went to the phone, called her mother, and began crying hysterically. Her mother was equally stunned. She and her late husband had long ago lost their reservations about Robert and loved him as part of their family. There was little Marian could say.

Robert never explained what the all-important deal was, and it never materialized. Several weeks later, Susan stood by in horrified embarrassment as her car was repossessed. She hid most of their furniture at her mother-in-law's house, or that would have been taken, too. Then Robert told her they had to move. The house was going to be sold at a sheriff's auction. Robert was forced into personal bankruptcy.

Susan realized that her comfortable, affluent world was crashing around her. They hastily packed their few remaining belongings and moved to a rented house, a move made possible only through financial assistance from her mother. The bankruptcy filing and sheriff's auction were public proceedings; Susan knew their plight was the subject of local gossip and speculation. Still, she tried to hold her head high, saying nothing to add fuel to the rumors. She kept her children at their lessons and in school. Her mother paid for the children's clothing. Susan paid the rent on their new house out of a small inheritance from her grandparents. She wondered when the downward spiral would end. She figured things couldn't get much worse.

Nearly three years after losing their home, Robert told her that he was leaving her. He offered no explanation, other than to say he needed to "find" himself. It was the late seventies, when many men did seem to be going through midlife crises, but still Susan was baffled.

That same day, he took some of his things and left the house. He never returned. Susan was alone with three children, one of them a three-year-old.

Despite the shocks and setbacks of the past few months, Susan was floored. To her, marriage was forever, as it was in Robert's Catholic faith. It had never crossed her mind that it could come to this. It was true that Robert was rarely home, and there were times during the seventeen years of their marriage when she didn't feel loved by him, but she always felt she could make up for it by loving him more. In her world, it was the wife's duty to make a marriage work. Now she had failed. Instead of blaming him and venting her anger, she felt responsible. Her self-confidence was destroyed. She felt miserable, unattractive, and undesirable.

Susan and Robert were divorced in 1981. Susan shouldn't have been surprised, but she was, to learn that "finding himself" was a euphemism for something much more pedestrian: Robert had been having an affair with another woman. Susan was granted custody of the three children, but Robert took them every other weekend and had visitation rights. However she felt about him, Susan wanted her children to love their father and spend time with him. He was ordered to make child support payments, but soon they began arriving late, and then became sporadic. Susan thought she might panic but forced herself to get a grip on herself.

One morning Susan delivered her two older children to school, then took Bianca with her to the Town and Country travel agency in

Florham Park, New Jersey. She knew the owner; the agency had arranged their many trips to luxury resorts. She didn't know where she found the strength, but she felt like an animal mother whose only thought was to protect her endangered children.

"I want to learn the business," she told the owner, swallowing the shattered remnants of her pride. "You don't have to pay me."

9

NOT TO REASON WHY

Student protests at Kent State, May 4, 1970.
(Reuters NewMedia Inc. / Corbis)

RESCORLA'S TOUR OF DUTY in Vietnam ended in July 1966. He had thirty days' leave, which he spent with Hill's wife and children in New Jersey. He took Patricia to a performance of *Hello, Dolly!* on Broadway and then to dinner at Sardi's. Hill left Vietnam in January 1967. Both he and Rescorla returned to duty at Fort Benning as decorated combat veterans: Rescorla received the Silver Star for his heroism in the Ia Drang valley. He was awarded the Purple Heart for his injuries sustained near An Khe, two Bronze Stars, and the Vietnamese Cross of Gallantry with Gold Star. Hill received the Silver Star for heroism at Trung Luong, five Bronze Stars, the Purple Heart, the Army Command medal, and the Vietnamese Cross of Gallantry with

Palm Leaf. Both were senior tactical officers in the Officer Candidate School. Hill taught guerrilla tactics and unconventional warfare. In July 1967, both men were promoted to captain. As a married officer with two children, Hill could use his housing allowance to live off the base. He bought a duplex near the base. He and his family lived upstairs, and Rescorla moved into the ground-floor apartment.

One afternoon, a man knocked on the door and identified himself as James Hess, Larry Hess's father. He'd retired from the air force and was on his way to Florida with his wife when he decided to stop in to see Hill. Hill felt a pang of anxiety at the sight of Hess's father, who had forwarded to Hill a letter addressed to him that had been discovered, unmailed, among Hess's things after he died. In the letter, Hess had thanked Hill for his help and for giving him the poem "If," which he said was a constant inspiration. "I'm proud to be an officer commanding men," he had concluded. The letter renewed Hill's feelings of guilt over Hess's death. He told his father that he felt responsible and regretted giving him the poem.

"Don't be foolish," James Hess said. "He was a soldier. He said you were the best friend he ever had. I wanted to meet a man my son thought so highly of."

Foreigners were allowed to apply for American citizenship after two years of service in the U.S. military, and during the summer of 1967, Rescorla applied, taking citizenship classes in preparation. There was a brief awkward moment when he had to produce his birth certificate and fill out a form identifying his parents, but the clerk said it was fine for him to list his grandfather as his father. In July, Hill accompanied him to the federal courthouse in Columbus, Georgia, where he took the oath of citizenship and received his papers. "You can't call me a foreign SOB anymore," he told Hill proudly.

In their free time, Rescorla and Hill spent hours discussing a novel Rescorla was trying to write. He called it *Pegasus,* after the mythological horse that flew, and it was about a mobile air cavalry unit much like his own Hard Corps. But writing proved much more difficult than

Rescorla had anticipated. He struggled with the effort and consulted other writers, corresponding with John Masters, a retired British military officer who lived in New York City and wrote novels about the British colonial forces. Rescorla had read all his books: *Bugles and a Tiger, The Road Past Mandalay, Night Runners of Bengal,* and *The Deceivers.* Rescorla was especially impressed that *B'wana Junction,* set in Africa, had been made into a Hollywood movie. Masters told him he needed to study creative writing and, like Bill Shucart, urged him to get a college degree.

In January 1968, during Tet, the lunar New Year, North Vietnam launched a massive offensive against the cities of South Vietnam, successfully penetrating Danang and Pleiku, as well as the imperial capital of Hue, even Saigon and the United States embassy itself. Even though the United States claimed victory in rolling back the offensive and General Westmoreland called it a "sign of weakness," a "desperate diversion," it had a devastating effect on American public opinion and support for the war effort. It undermined Lyndon Johnson's presidency. In March, Johnson shocked the nation by announcing he would not run for reelection, but he committed even more U.S. troops to the war.

These events unfolded as Rescorla and Hill faced a decision about whether to remain on active duty for what would almost surely be another tour in Vietnam. Rescorla talked more and more about becoming a writer and less about pursuing a military career. He pointed out that Hill already had ten years of active service and would be able to retire from the army in just ten more years of service, at age thirty-six. But he, Rick, would be over forty. He didn't like the idea of working his way up the army bureaucracy for another fifteen years. Although Rescorla never said it in so many words, Hill felt he had never gotten over the loss of his men. He talked about them all the time. "I don't mind war," he told Hill. "If this was World War Two, I'd be out there. But all these boys are dying, and there's going to be no end to it."

Rescorla applied to and was accepted by the University of Oklahoma, one of the schools recommended by John Masters. One evening before he left, he came running upstairs to see Hill and proudly slammed two knife sheaths on his kitchen table. "They finally came," he said.

Hill looked at the handsome leather sheaths, then withdrew one of the knives. "Oh, man," he said.

It was a handmade Randall bowie knife, the most finely crafted knife available, for which there was a three-year waiting list. Each knife had set Rescorla back $300, an exorbitant sum. The steel blades were engraved with their names. In return, Hill gave Rescorla a 9 mm Browning automatic pistol adorned with their division patches and initials.

★

HILL RETURNED TO Vietnam in April 1968. As a captain, he now commanded a company of four platoons. One night they were assigned to assault a village that was a known Viet Cong stronghold, surprise the enemy soldiers, and take some prisoners for interrogation. As they crept through the darkness to the outskirts of the hamlet, they could see a single kerosene lamp burning inside a thatched hut. Outside, they could see a sentry, armed with a rifle. Standard operating procedure dictated that the sentry be killed to preserve the element of secrecy. "Wait here," Hill whispered to his men.

He crept silently into position behind the man, then sprang, covering the sentry's mouth and pinching his nostrils with his free hand as he stabbed him with the bowie knife Rescorla had given him. As the knife sank in, Hill had the horrifying thought that he was making a terrible mistake. For all the men he had killed, Hill had never stabbed anyone. He'd seen it in the movies, of course. It looked heroic, the ultimate in combat. He'd been trained at Ranger school to use knives, and he had taught his men. But even as he struck the blow, Hill desperately wished he hadn't done it. He couldn't believe how strong the man was, nearly writhing out of his grip even though he was small of stature and had a knife blade in his kidney. But there was no stopping now. Hill withdrew the knife and cut the sentry's throat. Blood spurted in all directions. The sentry went limp, and when Hill felt for a pulse, there was none. Hill was stunned and sickened by the experience. He quickly wiped off the knife on the dead soldier's uniform and put it back in its sheath. Still shaken, he signaled for his men to move forward and attack.

But the moment his men reached the lighted cottage, someone inside awakened and sounded an alarm. The element of surprise was lost. The Viet Cong soldiers inside reached for their weapons. His men opened fire and everyone in the cottage was killed. They took no prisoners. Hill was haunted by the thought that the sentry's death had accomplished nothing.

Days later, they returned to camp and Hill took the knife out of its sheath. He was shocked to see so much blood on the blade. He had obviously done a poor job of wiping it off on the man's shirt in the dark of the night. Now the steel blade was stained and slightly corroded where the blood had soaked in. He washed it repeatedly, oiled it, and even scoured the blade with steel wool. Nothing would remove the dark stain.

Sometimes when he was off duty, Hill left the army camp and drove his jeep into the village of Kon Tum. There was a small general store there, run by an attractive young Vietnamese woman named Mai. Her mother was usually there as well, and her young son. By now Hill had learned enough Vietnamese to get by, and they knew some English. Hill developed an attachment to the boy, who reminded him of Danny, and he found himself stopping in the store even when he didn't need to buy anything, bringing treats to the child and food left over from his rations for the boy's mother and grandmother. Eventually the young woman invited Hill to their home for dinner, and he accepted.

That evening, Hill drove alone into the village and parked outside their modest cottage. He entered, removed his pistol and knife, and hung his gun belt and rifle on a hook inside the door. Delicious aromas of spices and cooking filled the room. The young woman was cooking prawns and frog's legs, which Hill had mentioned were two of his favorite dishes. He wondered where she'd gotten them, since they were luxuries few Vietnamese could afford. Hill was touched that the family had made such an effort on his behalf.

Hill removed his boots and settled in at the low table that dominated the room. Suddenly two men walked in. Both were wearing the khaki shirts of the North Vietnamese Army. Hill realized he was unarmed and thought a trap had been sprung. How foolish he had been to trust these people. Oh, shit, he thought. This is it.

But instead of pulling out their weapons, they joined him at the table. The young woman introduced the younger of the two men as her husband and the father of their child. The other was clearly her father, and an officer. To Hill's surprise and relief, they were gracious, even courtly. The officer spoke excellent English. They broke out a bottle of Johnnie Walker Scotch, a costly status symbol among the Vietnamese, and offered toasts. The Vietnamese officer knew all about Hill's unit, its maneuvers, tactics, and skirmishes. Hill was impressed that he had such good intelligence.

"Tell me," he finally said, "why did you come all this way to my country to fight my people?"

"I'm a professional soldier," Hill answered. "They say 'go,' I go. The politics of the war, that's not my job."

"Do you know the politics of the war?" the man asked.

"Sure," Hill replied.

"How would you feel if you were me?"

"I'd have your job. I'd be fighting on your side."

The man pondered this. "What do you think will be the outcome?"

Like Rescorla, Hill had long ago abandoned the notion that America would "win." Hill told him he thought it would drag on and probably end in stalemate. He said he foresaw a divided country, something like Korea.

"The Vietnamese people will never allow that," he insisted. "Do you know how many Viet Cong are in South Vietnam?"

"Sometimes I think they're all Viet Cong," Hill said.

"The South Vietnamese Army will collapse once you leave,"the officer said, which he predicted would be soon. "Nixon is a great man." He was confident that if Nixon was elected, he would begin withdrawing American troops.

"You may be right," Hill said. "There's rioting in the streets in America."

Hours later, Hill rose to leave. The bottle of Scotch was empty. He realized he had to drive a long way back to camp alone through a jungle infested with enemy soldiers. He retrieved his weapons, then asked warily, "Am I going to make it back?"

His hosts seemed offended by the implication. "You will have guards watching you all the way back," the officer assured him. "You have never been safer in Vietnam then you are tonight." He bowed slightly, and Hill departed into the darkness.

The evening affected Hill profoundly, for now the enemy had a face. Whenever Hill heard an artillery barrage or an air bombardment, he hoped those men and their family would be spared.

★

NORMAN, OKLAHOMA, in the fall of 1968 was remote from civil rights and war protests, but boasted plenty of beer, drugs, sex, and rock and roll. Fred McBee, muscular and neatly dressed in a button-down shirt, was having coffee in the Hester Robertson cafeteria with other paraplegics, nearly all of them Vietnam War veterans. They made for an odd group, these young men in wheelchairs, using canes, missing an eye or a limb, recovering from bullet and shrapnel wounds. The few antiwar protesters gave them a wide berth, but so did everyone else: the fraternity boys and sorority girls, the campus athletes. They knew how some of them looked to them: disfigured, impaired, older than their years, conspicuous failures in the pursuit of wealth, beauty, and endless youth.

Jim Morris, a Special Forces soldier in Vietnam recovering from a bullet wound, came over with a new student, and the introductions went around.

"Rick Rescorla, First Air Cav."

"Ronnie Beets, Hundred and First Airborne."

"Fred McBee, RCA." Rescorla looked puzzled. "Rodeo Cowboys Association," McBee said, then laughed. Everyone assumed McBee had ruined his spinal cord in Vietnam, but he'd been thrown from a bucking bronco when he was sixteen, riding the junior rodeo circuit. Rescorla was fascinated that McBee was a real westerner, born in California, raised in the ranch country of West Texas. McBee also trained and competed in football and track with the university's wheelchair-bound athletes.

Rescorla had energy and charisma that immediately attracted McBee to him. Rescorla had chosen Oklahoma for its writing program, headed by Dwight Swain, who churned out mystery novels under the pen name Nick Carter. Swain boasted that he had deliberately called it a "professional" writing program, not creative writing. Both Morris and McBee were enrolled in the program, and McBee had already published a story, "Winchester for Killing." It had earned him both a check from *Great Westerns* magazine and an A from Swain, the sole criterion for an A being a sale for hard cash. Swain had nothing but contempt for self-absorbed artists who wrote prose that never sold and nobody could understand. What Swain liked was action, adventure, mystery, and romance. Some women students were already making $20,000 a year writing for *True Confessions* magazine.

McBee and Morris took Rescorla under their wing, and soon he, too, was churning out westerns, several of which he sold. He often consulted McBee for descriptive details, but he had a vivid imagination for the American West, as well as an excellent memory for all the B westerns he'd watched in Hayle. He recycled many of the plots into new settings with new characters. "Your B movies were our A movies," Rescorla told McBee. And he told him proudly that Cornwall was the

Texas of England. "A good hand and a trusty sword, a merry heart and true; King James's men will understand what Cornish men can do!" he sang heartily.

Rescorla also loved detective fiction, especially the novels of Raymond Chandler, which they studied under Swain's tutelage. Rescorla embraced Chandler's philosophy, which Chandler articulated in an essay, "The Simple Art of Murder":

> In everything that can be called art there is a quality of redemption. It may be pure tragedy, if it is high tragedy, and it may be pity and irony, and it may be the raucous laughter of the strong man. But down these mean streets a man must go who is not himself mean, who is neither tarnished nor afraid. He is the hero; he is everything. He must be a complete man and a common man and yet an unusual man. He must be, to use a rather weathered phrase, a man of honor—by instinct, by inevitability, without thought of it, and certainly without saying it. He must be the best man in his world and a good enough man for any world.

That, Rescorla told McBee, was how he wanted to lead his life.

Rescorla ended up spending three or four nights a week at McBee's apartment, talking and watching movies, teaching him to use and throw knives. Rescorla was willing to watch any movie that was on TV and had an amazing memory for obscure films and performances by long-forgotten actors. Then he'd leave for his night job, as a guard at a hospital for the insane, where, as he put it, he "wrestled homicidal maniacs into bed every night." At 5:30 A.M., he trained officers for the National Guard, bringing a new level of panache to the task. At their first session, he hired a bagpiper to pipe the new men in. Now nearly thirty, he conceded that it was getting harder to always stay out front, running faster, doing more push-ups and pull-ups. But he worked out religiously and managed to stay ahead of much younger men. During the day, he always attended Swain's classes, but he skipped most of the rest, spending the time with McBee and the Vietnam veterans drinking coffee in the cafeteria. People wondered when he slept.

On weekends, he and McBee would get into McBee's Jeep and roam the countryside, stopping for a beer or taking a picnic. In warm weather they swam at Lake Thunderbird. There was a rowboat near the swimming area, and once Rescorla jumped inside and maneuvered the boat expertly around the lake. He told McBee he'd learned to row from his grandfather, who took him fishing around the Hayle estuary.

One day Rescorla spotted an advertisement in the campus newspaper for someone with experience in martial arts. The Postal Academy was opening a branch at the university and needed an instructor in martial arts and riot control, subjects Rescorla knew well from his time in Cyprus and Africa. When he showed up for the interview, he was told they already had three candidates with black belts. "Do you have a black belt?" the interviewer asked.

"Let me make a suggestion," Rescorla countered. "Throw all of us into a bear pit and let's see who is the last man standing." He got the job.

Rescorla liked to tell McBee about a time in Cyprus when he felt he'd mastered all the wrestling holds and judo chops, and so, one day at the beach, he challenged an older soldier in his regiment, a man thirty years his senior. Rescorla had attacked him with a flying wedge kick to the chest, but the man just stood there, solid as an oak tree. Rescorla dropped to the sand. The man picked him up by the thumb and squeezed until Rescorla howled in pain and submitted. Afterward, the man said, "Ricky, my lad, I only know three holds. But I know them well." That became Rescorla and McBee's motto: "Learn three things well."

The war was naturally a constant topic of conversation, but the normally talkative Rescorla had little to say on the subject. One day they were throwing knives at Rescorla's apartment when McBee noticed a copy of *U.S. News & World Report*. Rescorla opened it and showed him the photo of himself that Peter Arnett had taken. Suddenly McBee could visualize his friend in combat: the fearlessness, determination, and intense concentration he had only glimpsed from time to time, brought to bear on a single mission. Rescorla said the photo had been taken in the Ia Drang valley. He added that he'd never been able to forget the smell of rotting human flesh or lifting up in a helicopter and looking down on acres of dead bodies. Otherwise, he said little about Vietnam.

Rescorla declined to participate in any of the antiwar rallies on campus. Nor did he join in any overt antiwar activism, though he wrote to Hill, describing the growing antiwar movement. All he said to others in the cafeteria was "If you're going to go to war, you need to win. Otherwise, don't go." To McBee he confided that he thought the American strategy was a losing one. "Political wars are a mistake," he said. "You either fight to win or you lose." Vietnam, he predicted, would be a "quagmire." In writing class, many of the veterans wrote about their war experiences, and some found it therapeutic. McBee encouraged Rescorla to write about his time in Vietnam, but he never did. Rescorla shelved his novel, *Pegasus*.

Hill wrote his wife and Rescorla every day when he wasn't out on patrol, and through his steady stream of letters, Hill kept Rescorla informed about progress in the war. Not long after his dinner with the Vietnamese, Hill shifted out of a direct combat role. He ran a training camp for newly arrived enlisted men, then trained South Vietnamese commanders to take over the war, part of the so-called Vietnamization of the campaign. The experience only confirmed the North Vietnamese officer's prediction that the South Vietnamese Army would collapse without the Americans. Hill grew increasingly disgusted by the corruption he encountered in the South Vietnamese Army and its unwillingness to fight. He reported to Rescorla that Vietnamization was a fiasco, little more than a way for corrupt commanders to siphon off even more American dollars for their own use.

Meanwhile, the American death toll continued to mount. Richard Nixon's election to the presidency in 1968 had not brought the rapid withdrawal the North Vietnamese had hoped for. Rescorla wrote Hill that both John Driver and Myron Diduryk, two of the soldiers he'd felt closest to, had been killed in action. Rescorla felt especially bad about Driver, whom he had encouraged to enroll at Officer Candidate School and pursue a military career. Hill again considered resigning from the army, but as his tour in Vietnam was coming to an end, he was told his chances for promotion were high, and he was chosen for the career officer training program at Fort Benning.

Hill returned to the familiar surroundings of Columbus, Georgia, in July 1969 and moved back in with Patricia and the children. He performed so well on the entrance examinations that he was required to take only one course, in nuclear weapons deployment. Toward the end of the semester, his assignment was to assume the role of a Soviet premier and supreme military commander whose goal was to launch World War III against the United States. How would you do it? Hill and his fellow officers were told to prepare and submit a written plan.

Nixon's 1970 State of the Union speech was a few weeks away, so Hill gave his plan the code name "State of the Union." He turned it in on a Friday.

The following Monday, he was on his way to class when he was stopped by a lieutenant colonel in intelligence. "I've got some people who would like to talk to you," he said. Hill protested that he would miss class. "Don't worry, we'll take care of it," the officer said. "Follow me."

Hill knew it was serious the moment he entered the room and saw Major General John Carley, the assistant commander of the infantry school. Six men in uniform and several others in dark suits flanked him. They were courteous, but they looked serious and got right to the point. "How did you come up with this?" the general asked. He had Hill's paper in hand.

"This is my area of expertise," Hill said. He explained that he had been trained in counterterrorism, unconventional warfare, demolition, and the use of explosives. His plan for starting a world war, he thought, was quite straightforward. He would recruit and train a suicide pilot, get a C-47 aircraft, and pack it with explosives. On the night of the State of the Union, the pilot would fly the plane straight into the Capitol building, through the rotunda, and into the House of Representatives, where the bombs on the plane would be set to explode. He'd take out the president, his cabinet, the members of the Supreme Court, the joint chiefs of staff, and most senators and representatives. At that moment, the Soviet Union would unleash its nuclear missiles.

The room was silent. Hill elaborated: "Everyone is watching TV, there's no air defense around the Capitol. By the time anyone realized an aircraft was near, it would be too late."

There was fidgeting in the room. Then the questions began, which Hill fielded for nearly an hour. Finally, the general said, "We'd prefer you forget you ever did this."

"Yes, sir," Hill said. "I was just trying to give an honest answer." He was dismissed.

Hill wrote Rescorla in Oklahoma, providing a detailed account of the exercise and the strange meeting. Rescorla immediately replied. "You evil-minded bastard!" he wrote. "When you have these thoughts, don't publicize them to anyone. The plan is tactically and technically proficient; it makes sense, but only to people like you and me. To the rest of the world, it looks like the workings of a deviant mind. This kind of thing terrifies people."

But Hill later learned that enhanced air defenses for the nation's capital were installed shortly after his meeting. Maybe some good had come from it, he thought.

When Hill finished the officer training course, he was offered the chance to earn a college degree at army expense. Years earlier, he'd bought a piece of land in St. Augustine, Florida, hoping to retire there someday. He had seventy-five days of accumulated leave, so he took Patricia, Gigi, and Danny there for an extended vacation. After a week or so of lounging on the beach and playing with his children, Hill used the time to build a house on his land. He moved his family to St. Augustine, and in 1970 he enrolled at Jacksonville University. Hill stood out among his classmates, since he was over thirty and wore his uniform to class every day at a time when other students were wearing bell-bottoms and peace medallions. In his spare time he built houses and condominiums.

Hill was just finishing his first semester when National Guard troopers killed four students at Kent State University and antiwar protests swept American campuses, including Oklahoma. Rescorla was deeply upset that fellow members of the National Guard had fired on American civilians, and he called Hill. Clearly, the National Guard members in Ohio hadn't been properly trained in riot control, let alone the Constitution, which guaranteed the very freedoms those students were exercising. "They're right about this," Rescorla said, referring to the student protesters.

"Yes, they are," Hill agreed. "They're morally right." But he reminded Rescorla that he was a captain in the army and Rescorla remained an officer in the National Guard. "Theirs not to make reply, / Theirs not to reason why, / Theirs but to do and die," he quoted from Tennyson. "We're professional soldiers. We have to stay subordinate to the elected government." Hill wondered how many of the protesters had registered to vote. "They can put in office anyone they want," he argued. "They can elect a new commander in chief."

"They're just dumb-assed, inexperienced kids," Rescorla said.

Rescorla earned a bachelor's degree and a master's in 1971. But he complained to Hill that he thought it was going to be tough earning a living as a writer of fiction. Unlike Swain, he couldn't see himself cranking out fifty pages a day for the rest of his life. Then he enrolled in law school. Not, he told Hill, because he wanted to practice law, but because he wanted to better understand the underpinnings of American democracy and the legal framework of police and detective work. Hill thought traitors should be summarily executed on national TV, but

Rescorla defended trial by jury. "We need the Constitution to protect us from people like you," he said, laughing.

During Rescorla's first year in law school, McBee met Jim Morris and his wife in the cafeteria, and they introduced him to Betsy Nathan, a friend of Morris's wife. She was blond, attractive, and well dressed. McBee's first thought was that Betsy was "too civilized" for their crowd. Nathan thought she was being set up by Morris's wife for a date with McBee, but that evening, Rescorla showed up at her door. Soon they were dating steadily. As graduation approached, Rescorla landed a job teaching criminal law at the University of South Carolina, which meant that he'd be leaving Norman at the end of the semester. Betsy was also graduating. That spring, Rescorla told Hill he was thinking of getting married. Hill was surprised, since Rescorla had never indicated any interest in marrying and settling down. "Why?" he asked.

"It's time," Rescorla said.

Rescorla and Betsy were married in 1972 in Dallas, her hometown. Her father was a successful oilman. They hosted a large sit-down dinner afterward in the hall adjacent to the synagogue where the ceremony was held. Hill drove to Texas from Florida to be Rescorla's best man. Both he and the groom were resplendent in dress blues with full decorations. As the reception drew to a close, Betsy looked ready to leave with her new husband, but Rescorla suggested they all go to a nightclub. He ordered several more rounds of drinks. Soon he and Hill were drunk. Rescorla got the band to play one of Hill's favorite songs, "Careless," and then he persuaded Hill to join the band onstage and sing it himself. Rescoria virtually ignored Betsy, who had stopped drinking hours earlier and was looking increasingly tired and forlorn. Finally, Hill suggested that Rescorla might want to leave with his bride.

"Why?" he asked. "She can leave whenever she wants."

"Goddammit, Rick. It's your wedding night," Hill replied.

Soon after, Rescorla and Betsy visited Hill and his wife in St. Augustine. "Where's your Randall?" Rescorla asked at one point, referring to the bowie knife he'd given him. Hill got the knife and pulled it from its sheath. Rescorla looked closely at the bloodstain. "What happened?" Rescorla asked.

Hill told him the story of the sentry. "Mine looks as new as the day I got it. I never got a chance to bloody it," Rescorla said, his voice tinged with regret.

"Be glad you didn't," Hill said. "I hope I never have to again."

Not once did Hill see Rescorla and his new wife kiss or hold hands. He thought they seemed more like an older brother and younger sister. He thought it odd, but Rescorla insisted he was happy, which was all that mattered to Hill.

★

THE RESCORLAS MOVED to Columbia, South Carolina, where Rick began teaching criminal law at the University of South Carolina. Their son, Trevor, was born in 1976. Hill earned a bachelor's degree in 1972 and was sent to Germany to command a tank company. After Nixon's reelection in 1972 on a premature promise that "peace is at hand" in Vietnam, the Pentagon began rapidly scaling back the size of the military. A cease-fire was reached in 1973, and the last American combat troops left Vietnam on March 29. Hill easily survived each successive "reduction in force"; officers were rated on a numerical scale, and Hill's combat record and awards for valor kept him near the top of the list.

Soon after Nixon's resignation during the Watergate crisis, the Pentagon concluded that the reductions in force had left in place too many older officers who were about to retire and collect pensions that would continue to tax the defense budget. So in 1975 the army conducted a series of armywide promotion reviews, in which a major criterion for promotion was a birthdate after 1940. Hill, born in 1938, was twice passed over for promotion to major, and due to the army's up-or-out retention policy, he was forced out in 1975, just five months short of being eligible to retire with a lifelong pension. Hill had been encouraged to think he had a shot someday at the rank of lieutenant colonel and, at the very least, a secure retirement pension. Now he was summarily discharged and offered a paltry severance package. Hill, steeped in a tradition of military honor, was stunned and deeply disillusioned. Fifteen generals wrote on Hill's behalf, to no avail. Rescorla, it turned out, had been right to get out of the military.

But he wasn't going to wallow in self-pity or let himself become bitter. He still had a family to support, so he returned to St. Augustine, where he started a construction business, built houses and condominiums, and tried to adjust to the strange world of civilian life. He spent more time with Patricia and his children: Gigi and Danny had grown into teenagers. He took them to London twice, to Europe to see castles and museums, and all over Florida. He introduced them to theater, movies, restaurants—all the things he'd missed growing up.

On television, Hill watched the humiliating collapse of South Vietnam. In April 1975 President Gerald Ford bluntly called the Vietnam War "finished." "Today, Americans can regain their sense of pride that existed before Vietnam." Then, just a week later, Saigon was evacuated as North Vietnamese rockets struck the city's airport. Mobs of South Vietnamese rampaged through the streets, desperate to get out. In one of the most telling scenes, cameras showed the American ambassador, clutching the American flag that had flown atop the embassy, boarding a helicopter to escape from the embassy roof. It was painful for Hill to watch. President Ford had failed to acknowledge the obvious: The United States had been defeated in Vietnam.

Soon after, Hill drove up to South Carolina to visit Rescorla, and they discussed the American withdrawal and rapid collapse of the South Vietnamese forces, despite the lack of a decisive battle, like Dien Bien Phu. "I can't understand it," Hill said. "We never lost a battle, yet we lost a war."

"Wars are not won by the side with the biggest battalions, or the most money, or the most sophisticated technology," Rescorla observed.

"They're won by those with the will to win. It was their homeland. They saw us as no different from the French. The North Vietnamese had the will. That's why they won."

They pondered the notion and mentioned several other examples: Napoleon in Russia, Hitler against the British, Castro in Cuba. Will won that war," Rescorla concluded of the American effort in Vietnam. "And it will win future wars."

After Trevor was born, Rescorla left South Carolina for Chicago, where he accepted a job in security for Continental Illinois National Bank and Trust Company. Though he coauthored a book on criminal justice and was finally a published author, academia was too staid and the pay was low. At Continental, then the nation's eighth largest bank, with $20 billion in assets, he became director of security, responsible for the safety of bank employees and physical assets in all the bank's local and international offices.

Though lacking the physical danger of the military, the job offered a fair amount of drama: there was an attempted robbery at a Continental branch office once a month, on average. Rescorla developed a system where tellers were instructed to withdraw all the currency in their drawer the moment they saw a weapon and received a demand. The cash drawers were wired so that the moment they were empty, an alarm sounded at police headquarters. Once the system was installed, there were no successful robberies during Rescorla's tenure. Negotiable securities were transported to the bank's vault from O'Hare International Airport each day by helicopter. Rescorla installed armed guards on the flights, and again, no successful robberies took place.

Rescorla had a staff of two hundred security officers. He also used informants and police officers, whom he paid in cash. He staged mock robberies and used decoys to test the readiness of branch guards. One of his more lucrative projects for the bank was a program to deliver up to $4 million in cash for use as ransom by companies whose executives had been kidnapped. In the early 1980s, there was a rash of such kidnappings in South America.

Rescorla was often the first executive to arrive and the last to leave at Continental's downtown Chicago headquarters. He and Betsy lived in the suburb of Park Ridge, and in 1978 their daughter, Kim, was born.

Hill, meanwhile, parlayed his knowledge of Arabic into remote but high-paying jobs in Saudi Arabia. He left his family in St. Augustine in 1979 to work for a subsidiary of Northrup Corporation building housing at the American air base at Dhahran and returned in 1980 to build oil pipelines for the Arabian Desert Company. He camped in the desert, the lone Westerner among 150 Yemeni Arabs and Bedouin workmen. He was soon fluent in Arabic and often found himself reading the copy of the Koran the iman had given him years before in Beirut, even after the project was finished and he returned to his contracting business in St. Augustine. In 1981, he got a job building a Waffle House restaurant, which came in so far under budget and deadline that the company hired him to build more of the outlets. The job took him on the road again for extended periods, but with Gigi and Danny now in college, he badly needed the money.

In 1982, Hill was in Atlanta building another Waffle House when his sister called to say that his father had been diagnosed with an inoperable brain tumor. After their early fights, he and Dan had become close. Dan, Sr., was proud of his son's military success, and in awe of his medals. Hill called Rescorla and told him he was going out to Las Vegas. "How are you fixed for money?" Rescorla asked.

Everything Hill made was going for his children's educations. "A little tight, but we'll manage," he said.

Hill's father died on Thanksgiving. Hill was at his sister's trailer home in Las Vegas when a Western Union telegram arrived. It was from Rescorla, wiring Hill $15,000.

Hill picked up the phone and called Rescorla. "That's a lot of money," he said.

"Unfortunately, these things cost a lot of money," Rescorla said. "That's all I've got at the moment, but if you need more, I'll find a way to get it."

★

FOR ALL HIS SKILLS with weapons and in the martial arts, Rescorla was congenitally hapless when it came to mechanical skills and simple repairs. In 1979, he asked Hill to come and enclose his covered patio. Dan drove up to Park Ridge with his tools in the back of a station wagon.

One day Rescorla invited Hill to join him at the Continental Bank headquarters located on LaSalle Street, in the heart of Chicago's financial district. When he arrived, Rescorla handed Hill a bulletproof vest and told him to put it on. He took Hill's 9 mm pistol, and they got in a taxi and drove west, to Chicago's notorious Cabrini Green housing project. Hill thought the tall buildings of the project looked impressive, but Rescorla told him to wait until he saw the interior. Bathrooms and kitchens had been ripped out, the fixtures and appliances sold to support drug habits. Copper pipes had been removed and sold as scrap. "Don't use the elevator," Rescorla warned as they entered one of the buildings. Whenever police arrived, residents threw flaming rags into the elevator shafts, followed by gasoline. They raced up sixteen flights of stairs, and then Rescorla kicked in a door. As it flew open, he aimed the pistol. "Freeze," he commanded.

There were four men and two women in the room, operating a machine that was making counterfeit Continental Bank credit cards. Rescorla seized the machine and the finished cards. A dozen uniformed policemen arrived and arrested them. Rescorla peeled several hundreds off a roll of bills and handed them out to the police.

"I don't get it," Hill said when the operation was over. "I thought you just called the police for something like this."

"That's not the way it operates here in Chicago," Rescorla said.

On another visit to the bank's headquarters, Hill asked Rescorla how things were going at the bank. "Things are a little shaky," Rescorla said.

"What's the problem?" Hill asked. Rescorla said something about an Oklahoma bank called Penn Square, but he didn't go into detail. He added that the problem was not "the guys with the guns. It's the guys in the thousand-dollar suits. That's where the banks' money goes."

Later, as they were leaving through a secured area in the basement, Hill noticed a stack of burlap bags being forklifted into armored cars. "What's that?" Hill asked.

"Sleeves of old money. There's one million in each," Rescorla said. "It's mostly worn-out twenties. We ship it to the Federal Reserve, which shreds it."

"How do you get it there?" Hill asked. Rescorla said it went by truck, fifty to sixty sleeves at a time.

"Jesus Christ," Hill said.

That evening, Rescorla took Hill to dinner at the Chicago stock-yards. They ate porterhouse steaks, drank beer, and ordered port wine with dessert, followed by brandy and Cuban cigars. The taste of the good life got Hill fantasizing about those sleeves of worn-out cash. "Think about this, Rick," he said, half-serious. "You could leave me the truck route and schedule. I'm a master at raids and ambushes. I know some noncommissioned officers, and we could knock this off. We'd take ten sleeves, bury them, and pull out a hundred thousand dollars a year apiece. We could safari, cruise, hunt, travel the world for the rest of our lives!" Hill could put his kids through college and never have to build another Waffle House.

Rescorla sipped his brandy and puffed on his cigar. He gazed at the ceiling as though he were pondering the possibility. "It would work," he finally conceded. But then he interrupted Hill's reverie. "Shit, Dan, These people are paying me to protect their money, not take it. I gave them my word. You wouldn't ask me to besmirch my honor and in-tegrity, would you now, Peachey my lad?"

Not long after Hill's visit, Rescorla met his deputy, Joe Barrett, a former Chicago police officer, for coffee at 7:30, as he did every morning. "The bank has big problems," he confided.

"What's the problem?" Barrett asked.

"We've got a loan officer in collusion with a bank down in Oklahoma," Rescorla said, referring to Penn Square, the same bank he'd mentioned to Hill. "I don't have it all yet, but I'll call you later."

The loan officer he mentioned, John Lytle, was in charge of its midcontinent oil and gas division. In the wake of the OPEC oil embargo, the value of oil and gas leases on the American continent had soared, and the Penn Square Bank, a modest storefront lending operation in an Oklahoma City strip mall, churned out loans to new oil and gas ventures, many promising exorbitant tax breaks. Penn Square's chief oil-and-gas lending officer was William Patterson, known to his Sigma Chi fraternity brothers at the University of Oklahoma as "Monkey Brains." Patterson persuaded Lytle to bring in Continental Bank as a participating bank on Penn Square's loans, at interest rates two full points above prime. Eventually Continental Bank had a Penn Square loan exposure of $1.075 billion.

Continental officers had asked Rescorla to investigate Lytle's connections to Penn Square after bank auditors discovered he had received hundreds of thousands of dollars in personal loans. He and Barrett examined Lytle's income and spending, his purchase of a ski house in Colorado, his ties to Patterson in Oklahoma. Rescorla's background was helpful; he knew people from his days at the University of Oklahoma, and his father-in-law had sold oil and gas rigs and knew the business. Rick thought Lytle had acted, at the least, unethically.

In 1982, Rescorla reported his findings, assuming that Lytle would be fired. Instead, to Rescorla's astonishment, although Lytle was ultimately fired, Continental chairman Roger Anderson initially reprimanded Lytle and kept him at the bank.

Penn Square collapsed later that year, leaving Continental with $1 billion in bad loans. Rick contacted a headhunter. He was frustrated by the events surrounding Lytle, and he felt he was no longer viewed as a team player. In 1984, Rescorla was hired by Dean Witter Securities to be its director of security. He sold their house, and the Rescorlas embarked for New York, where Dean Witter had its headquarters. Rick, Trevor, and Max, the family's Dutch keeshond, rode in one car, even though Rescorla detested Max. Whenever Rescorla got out of bed at night, Max would take his place, then growl at him when Rescorla tried to reclaim it. Betsy, Kim, and the cat rode in the other car. Rick said he couldn't stand to hear the cat howl while he was driving. They moved into a spacious two-story colonial-style house on Dale Drive in Morristown, New Jersey, about an hour's commute from his new office.

In September 1984, John Lytle was indicted by a federal grand jury on sixteen counts of conspiracy, misapplication of bank funds, and wire fraud. The Penn Square scandal rocked Continental to its foundations, triggering a bank run and eventually a sale of its assets to the federal government. It was later merged into Bank of America. John Lytle ultimately pleaded guilty to misapplication of bank funds in 1988 and was sentenced to three and a half years in prison.

★

HILL CONTINUED TO travel around the country building Waffle Houses. He lived in a small trailer, which he parked at the job site. He worked six days a week, and on Sunday did his laundry and wrote letters to his wife and Rescorla. It was a lonely existence, and he knew he was drinking and smoking too much. In his rare free time, he again found himself reading the Koran. One Sunday afternoon in Springfield, Missouri, where he was building a Waffle House on Interstate 40, he emptied a bottle of Jack Daniel's and fell asleep while reading the Koran. In his sleep he heard the chanting of the muezzin, as though he were back in Beirut. Oh, shit, he thought. He must have

died, and the afterlife was Muslim after all. Then he heard the chanting of the call to prayers again. He opened his eyes. He saw the inside
of his trailer and realized he was alive. He felt a wave of relief. He
got up and groggily stepped outside. There was a group of Islamic students kneeling in prayer outside his trailer. It was just after sundown,
and they had pulled off the interstate for evening prayer. Hill felt himself drawn to them. He knelt in their midst and began praying with
them.

That day, Hill stopped drinking and smoking. He grew a beard. He
began praying faithfully five times a day.

Back in St. Augustine, his wife, Patricia, welcomed the radical
change. Not that she would convert to Islam herself. She didn't accept
the subservience of women demanded by practicing Muslims. But she
was relieved that Dan stopped drinking and smoking.

In 1986, Hill read that the Muslim community in Jacksonville was
building the city's first mosque. That Friday, Hill drove the forty miles
to the city and arrived early at the site mentioned in the paper. So far,
the mosque was just a few walls of concrete blocks. A few people of
Middle Eastern nationalities arrived, and then one man approached
Hill. "What are you doing here?" he asked Hill, whose blond hair and
blue eyes were conspicuous.

"I'd like to pray with you," he said. The man looked a little skeptical and asked Hill where he was from.

"St. Augustine." The man still seemed curious, but he shook Hill's
hand and invited him to join the group.

Hill quickly became a fixture in the small group, traveling every
week to Friday evening services. After years of travel and working on
his own, outside the structured life of the military, Hill found that he
enjoyed this newfound community, so isolated from the north Florida
mainstream. He took the Muslim name of Abdullah Al Amin, which
means "Servant of God, the Faithful." He learned all the prayers in
Arabic. He volunteered to help build the mosque, later taking off eight

months and organizing a ten-man crew to work on it full-time. And he became a close friend with two brothers, the Mojadidis, medical doctors who had emigrated from Afghanistan to the United States and settled in Jacksonville. The brothers alternated, each spending half the year in Florida, the other half in Afghanistan, earning money to send back to Afghanistan and helping the Mujahadeen in the war against the occupying Soviet military. Their other brother, Sibgatullah Mojadidi, was a leader of the Mujahedeen forces.

Hill was naturally fascinated by the valiant struggle of the Afghan people to throw off their Russian oppressors. Much of Hill's military education and countless training exercises had focused on the prospect of a war against the Soviet Union, yet Hill himself had never fought a Russian. He plied the Mojadidis with practical suggestions for guerrilla warfare, his major area of expertise, and finally, bowing to his obvious zeal, they suggested he go to Afghanistan himself and fight as a volunteer with the Mujahedeen. He would take no pay. Finally they said they could arrange it.

Hill was breathless when he reported the news to Rescorla. "All my life, I've never gone head-to-head with the Russians," Hill said. "This would be the real thing."

Hill was a little disappointed that Rescorla didn't seem more enthusiastic. "Dan, you're not as young as you used to be," he said cautiously.

Hill was forty-eight years old. He was still running every day, working out at the gym. "Hell, I'm still in good shape," he said. He offered to prove it, and Rescorla invited him to his new home in New Jersey.

When he arrived, Rescorla picked him up at Newark Airport and drove him to the house in Morristown. "Uncle Dan!" Trevor and Kim exclaimed, excited by the surprise visit. They were fascinated by his beard and the news that he had converted to Islam; they didn't know any Muslims. "Why can't you drink?" Kim asked, noticing that he ordered nonalcoholic beer. "Why can't you eat pork?"

Hill confided to Rescorla that he sometimes found it embarrassing to be a Muslim. "I don't see why," Rescorla replied. "Hitler and Mussolini were Catholics." Rescorla said he was leaning toward Buddhism, and Hill gave him a copy of *Understanding Islam*.

Hill impressed Rescorla by running each morning from the house to the train station and back. One evening, Rescorla had Hill sit outside on the deck while he got out a BB rifle. Then he tossed an aspirin in the air and told Hill to hit it. He threw one up, and Hill fired and shattered it. Another, still higher. Hill blew it away. He'd always been a keen marksman, competing once in the thousand-yard national rifle championships. "Well, your reflexes are still good," Rescorla conceded.

Finally, Rescorla gave his friend his blessing. "I've got something for you," he said, then disappeared into the house. When he returned, he had something that he carried with great reverence. "Bend down," he told Hill. Then he placed a cord around his neck.

"That's the lion's tooth!" Hill exclaimed.

It was Rescorla's treasured talisman, the thing that had always protected him, even in the darkest moments in Vietnam. Hill stroked the tooth. He sensed the magic in it. "It will give you the heart of a lion," Rescorla reminded him. "The only thing that can kill you is a .577. And they don't make them anymore."

★

USING HIS MUSLIM NAME, Abdullah, Hill arrived in Afghanistan in January 1987, crossing on foot through the high, snow-packed passes of the Hindu Kush mountain range. The scenery was spectacular, with peaks reaching 24,300 feet in altitude, marked by deep ravines and steep crags. Hill felt exhilarated: he was in Nuristan at last, the remote, northern Afghan province where Dravot and Peachey had been crowned kings in Kipling's tale.

As they continued on foot through the rugged terrain, Hill scrutinized the people he met. A few were light haired, with fair skin and blue eyes. Perhaps they were indeed descendants of Alexander's forces. Hill wore the loose-fitting clothing and headgear of the Mujahedeen

166

over his thermal underwear and the lion's tooth necklace. Given Hill's physical appearance, some Afghanis assumed that he was Nuristani.

Hill had traveled first to Islamabad, Pakistan's capital, which was teeming with Army Special Forces and CIA operatives. It reminded him of the Congo, though on a much bigger scale, now that the United States was training Afghan forces in Pakistan and supplying them with shoulder-held Stinger antiaircraft missiles and other sophisticated weaponry. With American assistance and money, the Mujahedeen campaign against the Soviets was rapidly gaining steam, and reinforcements were pouring in from all parts of Afghanistan and throughout the Muslim world. Afghanistan was increasingly being referred to as the Soviet Union's Vietnam. This time, Hill wanted to be on the winning side, fighting a just war.

After traveling along mountain trails mostly at night, resting by day in caves and small villages supporting the Mujahedeen, Hill and his fellow travelers arrived at a field hospital in the mountains northwest of Kabul, where the Mojadidi brothers treated the wounded. Hill worked at first as a hospital assistant, but he angled for opportunities to get into the field. Eventually his coworkers asked a visiting Mujahedeen commander if he would take Abdullah with him. The commander sized him up. "Is he CIA?" he asked. If so, he didn't want him.

"No, he's a brother Muslim from Florida," he was told. "He helped build a mosque there."

"Does he know anything?"

"He was an army Ranger."

The commander's face lit up. "Ah," he said. "Any Mujahedeen is welcome to come with me."

The commander ran a group of about sixty soldiers, part of a larger company of about two hundred men. Rarely were they together. They would disband and break into groups of four or five, sleeping in caves. Then they would reform into platoon-size units, communicating with each other by radio. Their mission was to lure Soviet forces into ambushes. They would disseminate false intelligence about a Mujahedeen meeting, then hope to attract Soviet troops and helicopter gunships, which could be shot down with the Stinger missiles. They would attack, then retreat into the mountains. The Soviets rarely pursued them; they were wary of the treacherous terrain and the likelihood of further ambushes.

During the past year, the Mujahedeen had been operating with remarkable success. Hill was impressed with the toughness and dedication of the men, many of whom slept close together under a single blanket for warmth and had nothing but cloth-covered sandals for footwear. Hill had a warm sleeping bag and insulated boots in addition to his thermal underwear. Even then, he felt the bitter cold.

Hill rapidly absorbed their tactics and methods, shared his own expertise, and soon joined in their combat operations. Though the terrain and climate were different, he was an expert at ambushes, was comfortable with the weapons, and soon gained the respect of his fellow soldiers, especially a young Afghani named Said Nader Zori. Hill had been drawn to Nader almost as soon as he arrived at the camp. Nader had a dark shock of hair, an olive complexion, and a big smile. He was open, friendly, and curious about the American; at the same time, he was a fierce and dedicated fighter. Hill had learned some Farsi while still in Jacksonville, and many of the fighters spoke at least rudimentary English. One Friday evening, Hill delivered the weekly *khutba,* or sermon. He stressed that the Russians were trying to prevent them from worshiping as faithful Muslims, and thus it was right to fight them in a holy war. He quoted extensively from the Koran.

At one of the company gatherings, Ahmed Shah Massoud, the legendary Lion of Panjshir, who later commanded the Northern Alliance against the Taliban, paid them a visit. Hill was standing with some other fighters when Massoud noticed him. "Who's he?" he asked in Farsi.

"He's a brother from America," someone said, adding several phrases Hill couldn't understand.

Massoud came over and shook Hill's hand. "Thank you for coming," he said, smiling. "Allah will grant you many blessings. And if you die, you will go straight to paradise."

One night Hill's unit received a radio message that a Russian armored personnel carrier was moving under cover of darkness along the road to Kabul, just a few miles from their location. They hastily donned their gear and moved down the mountain into position for an ambush. They waited silently, then heard the rumble of approaching heavy vehicles. It was a small Russian convoy, more heavily guarded than they had expected. Then, at a signal from the commander, they unleashed a barrage of grenades. Hill began firing his Russian-made AK-47.

One of the personnel carriers burst into flames. The convoy halted as Russian soldiers leaped out, scrambled for cover, and began returning fire. Then they heard the sound of helicopters approaching. The Mujahedeen halted the attack and, after dividing into small groups, scrambled back into the mountains. Hill raced alongside Nader and three other men as they leaped over rocks and climbed the steep slopes in the darkness.

But this time the Russians followed their attackers. The helicopter swept alongside the mountain slope, training its searchlight. Hill took refuge behind a large boulder as Nader moved forward across a small plateau. Suddenly the roar of the helicopter was upon them, and Nader was caught in the glare of the searchlight. Bullets kicked up spurts of dust around his feet. Hill aimed and began firing at the Russian helicopter, but he was sure Nader would be killed. Then, suddenly, Nader vanished.

The helicopter circled, its searchlight sweeping the area, but by now other Mujahedeen were firing on it. The helicopter lifted up and disappeared in the night sky. Hill felt his heart racing and fingered the lion's tooth around his neck. There was silence.

Then shadowy figures began to emerge onto the plateau. Hill moved to where he had last seen his friend and fellow soldier. "Nader!" he called.

He heard a sound from somewhere far below their position. Hill moved cautiously forward and saw that the plateau ended in a steep drop-off. "Nader!" he yelled into the abyss. "Get your ass out of there."

"La la la," Nader answered. "No, no, no. My legs."

Hill scrambled down the side of the cliff. When he reached Nader, he saw that his legs were shattered. Nader, blinded by the intense searchlight, had run off the edge of the cliff and broken his legs on impact. He was gasping in pain.

Hill summoned six other fighters. They assembled an impromptu stretcher, using sticks and a poncho. They slowly made their way back to the cave, where Hill gave Nader a shot of morphine directly into his legs. Then he and the other men used a winch to stretch his broken legs so the fractures wouldn't start to knit improperly. But they couldn't stay there. Their company was moving, and Nader couldn't fight. He needed urgent medical attention, the pain was intense, and the supply of morphine was limited. Hill volunteered to get his friend out of the country. He was determined to take Nader back to America, where he could receive first-rate medical care.

When dawn came, they stayed in the cave, sleeping and resting. Hill, a guide, and one of Nader's brothers, all on foot, and Nader, strapped to the back of a mule, traveled by night. When the liquid morphine ran out, Hill gave him morphine tablets. And when those were gone, Hill bought pure opium along their route, held it over a flame, and had Nader inhale the smoke.

Eleven nights later, as dawn broke over the snow-covered Hindu Kush, Hill and his small party emerged from a high mountain pass and saw a Toyota Land Cruiser parked in the distance ahead of them. They had reached the Pakistani border, and the vehicle was waiting to take them to safety.

10

TOWERS IN THE SKY

The World Trade Center at night.
(Getty Images)

THE WORLD TRADE CENTER, its distinctive twin towers rising 110 stories and 1,350 feet, dominated the lower Manhattan
skyline even before it opened in 1973. It was the last work of monu-
mental architecture proposed by former New York governor Nelson
Rockefeller, conceived at a time when skyscraper height was a measure
of civic pride and commercial achievement. It was a building of su-
perlatives: thirteen million square feet of office space housing more
than one hundred thousand workers, 104 high-speed elevators, more
than thirty thousand windows. The World Trade Center claimed the
title long held by the Empire State Building as the world's tallest skyscraper until Chicago's Sears Tower eclipsed it.

Designed by architect Minoru Yamasaki, the World Trade Center did not attract much critical or architectural acclaim, but no other tall building so seized the popular imagination. It was still the tallest building in New York, the financial capital of the world, and it consisted of two matching towers, not just one. They seemed to spring right from the waters of the Hudson River, and their stainless-steel cladding shimmered in the shifting morning and evening light. Droves of tourists were drawn to the site and its top-floor observation deck.

In a commercial sense, the World Trade Center never achieved the status or commanded the rents of Manhattan's most prestigious addresses, like Rockefeller Center, the Seagram Building on Park Avenue, or Nine West 57th Street. In part, this reflected the overall decline of the Wall Street area, as well as the ebbing notion, at least in America, that taller and bigger were necessarily better. Still, the World Trade Center attracted its share of prestigious tenants: an array of financial companies, law firms, and public agencies, including the offices of its owner and operator, the Port Authority of New York and New Jersey. Dean Witter, the brokerage firm founded in San Francisco, chose the building for its New York headquarters in 1985. The firm occupied forty floors in 2 World Trade Center, the south tower. The firm installed an elaborate marble entrance and reception area in the tower lobby where guests were screened before being whisked to the forty-fourth-floor sky lobby. There was a spacious cafeteria on the forty-third floor with views of the Statue of Liberty, connected to the sky lobby by escalators.

Rescorla liked being in New York and working in the World Trade Center. He felt he'd arrived: he enjoyed the panoramic view from his office and was proud of the building's status. He sent his friend McBee a T-shirt that read, "New York. It ain't Kansas." Rescorla insisted that his entire security staff of nearly two hundred people dress every day in suits and ties, to command respect and enhance their self-esteem. Some of them were relatively low-paid contract workers from an outside security firm and showed up for work shabbily dressed in worn or ill-fitting suits. Rescorla paid for new ones out of his own pocket.

As a securities firm, Dean Witter didn't face the obvious risks of a commercial bank like Continental. It had fewer offices, less exposure to the public, and far less cash and negotiable securities on hand. But client confidentiality was critical and commercial espionage was a concern, along with the usual array of employee security issues. Rescorla installed guards on every floor of the building and continued to gather intelligence and pay informants. He limited public access to the offices and developed an evacuation plan and drills, which were nonetheless widely ignored. His measures sometimes irked the firm's best-performing brokers, who occupied luxurious quarters on the firm's top floors in the building and didn't want their wealthy clients inconvenienced.

Over the years, Rescorla became less concerned about routine theft and increasingly worried about employee safety, especially after Pan Am flight 103 was downed by a terrorist bomb over Scotland in 1988, a tragedy that brought the seemingly distant threat of Islamic fundamentalism frighteningly close to America itself. "You know," he said in a call to Hill, "with all this terrorist activity, I'm getting concerned. I don't think the U.S. will be sacrosanct forever. I'm not sure how much longer we're going to be safe." The World Trade Center "is awfully big and visible. We're a symbol, an obvious target."

"You're probably right," Hill said, "but what can you do about it?"

"Probably nothing in the way of deterrence," he said. "But I want to do all I can to protect my people. Come on up here and be my consultant," Rescorla suggested.

"Why me?" Hill asked.

"Because you're an evil-minded bastard," Rescorla said, laughing. "If anyone can figure out how to hurt this building, you can." Rescorla told Hill he wanted him to adopt the same diabolical approach Hill had used in the exercise to start World War III. "I want to know the worst," Rescorla said.

Rescorla picked up Dan Hill at Newark Airport, and they spent the night at Rescorla's house in Morristown. The next morning they rose early and took the train, changing to the PATH train at Hoboken. They emerged on escalators into the lower concourse of the World Trade Center, which even at seven was thronged with commuters. Hill was surprised to see a vast underground shopping mall. Then Rescorla took him to the 107th-floor restaurant, Windows on the World, where he treated him to a breakfast of steak and eggs. Rescorla was a regular at the popular restaurant, and Hill was dazzled by the striking decor, the efficient, white-jacketed staff, and the amazing views.

Rescorla explained the basic engineering of the towering buildings, although he was by no means an expert on the subject. But the World Trade Center had attracted considerable attention for its unusual structure. The earliest skyscrapers, including the Empire State Building and Rockefeller Center, had been built on the principle of load-bearing exterior walls, in which the enormous weight of the building was transmitted by beams between floors to the steel-reinforced exterior walls. The steel was often encased in concrete and the exterior clad in heavy materials, such as limestone or granite. The buildings were solid and fire resistant, but the heavy exterior framework limited windows and views. A new generation of structures, starting with such landmark buildings as the Seagram Building and Lever House, both in midtown Manhattan, had been built on the principle of glass curtain-wall construction, in which the weight of the building rested on an interior core and supporting interior pillars. The exterior walls were merely a skin for the internal structure of the building and didn't support the building's weight. The entire exterior could be glass. But structural columns punctuated interior spaces.

With the World Trade Center, the engineers had chosen an innovative alternative. The building had a load-bearing central core and load-bearing steel exterior columns. The weight of the floors was transmitted to the load-bearing supports by relatively thin steel trusses that ran under each floor. The load-bearing exterior walls, which gave the World Trade Center its distinctive stainless-steel sheen, limited the size of the windows to tall but narrow vertical openings. There were complaints about this, but not from the architect himself, who suffered from acrophobia, especially in glass curtain-wall buildings with nothing standing between him and free fall but a pane of glass. An advantage was that the wide floors of the Trade Center had no interior columns, which was ideal for housing Dean Witter's large open trading floor. "Let's start at the bottom and work our way up," Rescorla suggested.

They returned to the ground level, and Hill took out his clipboard and pencil. They circled the entire sixteen-acre compound on foot. Besides the towers themselves, there were five relatively low buildings flanking an open plaza at the center, dominated by a steel-and-bronze sculpture, *The Sphere*. The plaza, providing access to the mezzanine level of the towers, served as the roof of the underground concourse and entrance to the PATH trains. Two subway lines also converged in the complex.

Hill wondered about the logistics of supplying the huge complex. Where, he asked, were the loading and docking operations?

Rescorla took him to a large ramp leading to the basement levels. There were no doors visible. When he looked more closely, Hill saw that there were metal doors that rolled up into the ceiling. He and Rescorla walked down the ramp, past a large loading dock, and into a parking area. Hill saw no one. "Where are the guards?" he asked.

"There are no guards," Rescorla said. Hill scribbled in his notebook. He looked around. Every major column and supporting beam was visible and exposed. He made some more notes. He thought for a few minutes, then did some quick calculations.

"Hell, Rick. This is a soft touch," Hill said. "It's not even a challenge. Here's what it would take to drop this son of a bitch." Hill said he'd bring in a stolen truck, painted like a delivery truck. He'd fill it with a mixture of ammonium nitrate and diesel fuel, then drive down the ramp and park. With four or five men dressed in coveralls, he could plant additional charges near key supporting pillars within fifteen minutes. Then he and the men would walk out and disperse, and he'd remove his coveralls. He'd have a taxi take him to another location, where he'd have a van waiting. Inside the van, he'd want a woman, two kids, and, if possible, a dog. Then he'd use a cell phone or beeper to detonate the truck bomb and charges. "Nobody's going to stop a family and a dog on Interstate 95," he said.

"You are an evil-minded SOB," Rescorla said. "But it would work."

That night, Hill and Rescorla stayed up late, analyzing Hill's findings and incorporating them into a report for the Port Authority. Rescorla didn't type, so Hill incorporated his and Rescorla's comments into a rough typed draft. The thrust of it was simple: The Port Authority needed to drastically increase security at entrances to the underground levels of the complex. "Jesus," Rescorla said. "Sometimes I wish I was back in the military and I had the power to go in and command that these things be corrected. But I've got to persuade the Port Authority."

The next morning, they again came into Manhattan early, and Rescorla took Hill to breakfast at a restaurant close to the center. Hill had corned beef hash and eggs. "I don't know how the hell you stay so thin," Rescorla observed.

Hill had noticed Rescorla had put on a few pounds, which surprised him. He'd always been so careful about fitness. "Metabolism, I guess," Hill said, as he polished off the platter with another cup of coffee. Hill had some errands to do while Rescorla met with Port Authority officials. They agreed to meet again for lunch.

When Hill met him in the lobby of the trade center, Rescorla looked discouraged.

"So what happened?" Hill asked.

"They blew me off," Rescorla replied. "They said, 'You worry about your floors, and we'll worry about the rest, including the basements and parking,' " he said.

"They're that dumb?" Hill asked.

Rescorla made sure that copies of their report reached Port Authority officials, even the New York City police. But he received no official response.

Unknown to Hill and Rescorla, Port Authority officials had already faced similar warnings and recommendations from its own planning staff. The Port Authority's Office of Security Planning had submitted a 150-page report that posited a terrorist bombing scenario strikingly similar to the one Hill had dreamed up. The report specifically identified the underground parking levels as a point of serious vulnerability and called for enhanced security as well as the elimination of public parking under the complex. According to one participant in the study, top Port Authority officials concluded that "world terrorism has subsided," that there was no justification for the loss of parking revenues, and that "the public would not stand for the capitulation to fear of terrorists." No steps were taken to increase security or limit access to the sub-basement levels.

★

IN JULY 1990 Saddam Hussein invaded Kuwait, and America mobilized for an invasion. Hill was galvanized by the prospect of war, and he and a friend, John C. Reade, another retired army captain, called the army officers' desk at the Pentagon and volunteered to serve in any capacity. A young officer took the call and said he'd pull their records and call back.

"Captain Hill?" he asked. Hill turned on the speakerphone so Reade could listen. "On paper you have outstanding records, excellent reports. But good God! You're fifty-three and he's sixty-three years old."

"We're not that old," Reade insisted. "We're in good shape. We'll do anything. We don't care about rank."

"No, no, no, no," the man said. "How can I put this euphemistically? Watch it on CNN, you old farts."

Rescorla was moving in the opposite direction, further away from the military. When Rescorla moved to Dean Witter, he had contacted the New York National Guard, expecting to resume active duty in the reserves. Though he had been promoted to full colonel, he was told to appear for an interview at the National Guard Armory on Park Avenue in Manhattan. When he arrived, wearing his uniform and medals, he met a panel of three colonels. He could tell from their decorations that none of them had any combat experience. They began asking questions, and Rescorla didn't like the tone of the interview. They seemed cool, skeptical of some of his answers. Finally he said, "What, exactly, am I doing here?"

"We're evaluating you," one said.

"Gentlemen, I don't believe there's anyone in this room qualified to evaluate me," Rescorla said. Then he stood up and left. He resigned his commission.

When he reported the incident to Hill, he said it was time to sever his connection to the military and put the past behind him.

He had already stopped talking about Vietnam, deflecting questions even from his children. He had ignored periodic invitations to attend reunions of veterans of the Ia Drang valley battles. But about the time Hill came up to consult on security at the World Trade Center, Rescorla heard from Hal Moore, now a retired general, asking him if he would submit his recollections of the battles at X-ray and Albany for inclusion in a book Moore was writing along with Joe Galloway, a United Press International journalist who had been present in the Ia Drang valley. Moore had gotten Rescorla's number from someone at the last Ia Drang reunion, and he was asking many of the veterans to submit their recollections of those tumultuous events. Rescorla was reluctant, but he confided in Hill that he was bothered by the efforts of so many to rewrite history so they could be nominated for awards for bravery. So he wrestled with the distant, painful memories and submitted something to Moore and Galloway. Even then, he skirted the most painful moments, like the death of Tommy Burlile.

Moore and Galloway's book, *We Were Soldiers Once . . . and Young,* was published in October 1992 and quickly became a best-seller, eagerly purchased by Vietnam veterans who felt their efforts and heroism in a doomed cause had never been adequately recorded or acknowledged. Hill read it immediately and spoke to Rescorla, who said he had liked the book. "Was that really me?" he wondered. He felt it exaggerated his heroism but acknowledged that he couldn't be sure. His memory of such traumatic events was too hazy.

McBee told Rescorla he should write his own book, but Rescorla dismissed the idea. "*Platoon. Apocalypse Now. Hamburger Hill.* Acts one, two, and three. It's already been done."

Rescorla told his children he didn't want them to read the book. "When you have to wake up and kill thirty people before breakfast . . . that's something you wouldn't understand," he told Kim. "You wouldn't recognize your daddy. It was a different time. I'm a different man now."

Kim and Trevor got a copy of the book anyway and read it aloud to each other. But they found it confusing, and it didn't make much of an impression on them. "What's the difference between a battalion and a platoon?" Kim asked, but her mother said her father didn't want to discuss it. One day she took some of his medals to school for show-and-tell. "This is what my daddy got," she told the class.

The teacher seemed stunned. "Your father earned a Silver Star?" she asked incredulously.

Later, their father took them to visit the Vietnam War Memorial in Washington, D.C. Rescorla grew very somber and took several rubbings of names carved on the wall: Tom Burlile, John Driver, Myron Diduryk. But he didn't discuss the visit and was quiet during most of the drive home.

Even though he didn't discuss the book with his family, Rescorla did reach out to others who were mentioned in the book and had been his friends: Bill Shucart, Jim Kelly, Sam Fantino. He hadn't seen any of them since 1966, their last days together at An Khe.

Fantino, the radio operator who had thrown Rescorla the grenade at X-ray, returned to his home outside Chicago late one night, and his

wife said, "Honey, you got a call from a guy named Rick Rescorla."
Fantino had to think for a moment. He, too, had tried to put Vietnam
out of his memory. He now owned an insurance business. He hadn't at-
tended any reunions. Then his wife showed him a copy of *We Were
Soldiers Once,* which she'd just bought for him that day. There was
Rescorla's photo, the one taken by Peter Arnett, on the cover.

Fantino called Rescorla the next morning at his office in New
York. The book had unleashed a flood of memories. They talked for
hours. Finally Rescorla said, "I want to see you."

"I'll get on a plane," Fantino said.

"No, I'll come see you," Rescorla insisted. He said he wouldn't stay
at his house, so Fantino made a reservation at the airport Hyatt Hotel.
The next evening, Fantino picked him up and took him to dinner at
his favorite Italian restaurant. They talked for four hours, not just about
Vietnam, but about everything that had happened to them in the inter-
vening twenty-six years. Late that night, when it was time to leave, they
argued briefly over who would pick up the check. Finally Rescorla
gave in and let Fantino pay. "Come back to my hotel room," Rescorla
said. I've got something for you."

Fantino followed Rescorla up to his room, where Rescorla handed
him a copy of *We Were Soldiers Once.* In it he had written, "To Sam
Fantino: You're a man who saved my life, and a good soldier." Fantino
felt tears well up. He put his arms around Rescorla. Then he felt him
reach around and slip something into his pocket. Fantino hoped he
wasn't still trying to pay for dinner. But when he reached in, he felt
something small and hard. "This is something that you should have
gotten," Rescorla said. It was a Bronze Star.

That November, both Fantino and Rescorla attended the Ia Drang
reunion, and Rescorla agreed to be one of the speakers. When he
reached the event, he milled around in the crowd, looking for familiar
faces. At one point he noticed a heavily decorated veteran looking intently in his direction. Rescorla looked back. Suddenly he realized it
was Lieutenant Colonel, now General, Hal Moore. Rescorla had put

on a few pounds, and he thought Moore didn't recognize him. He walked up to him introduced himself, and shook his hand. "The title of the book should be *We Were Soldiers Once . . . and Thin*," Rescorla said.

The following summer, Rescorla received a letter from Delores Call, the now married sister of Tom Burlile. After hearing about the book on an ABC television show, she had bought a copy and read it, then had written to Joe Galloway. He had sent her Rescorla's address. She wrote, "I always felt it was unusually cruel that I was called at work and told by a complete stranger that my brother had been killed. Because of the shock, to me it was totally unreal . . . until he came home to us, and then I realized my best friend was really gone. And my only thought was that he had died alone."

On the July Fourth holiday, Rescorla wrote a reply:

"I realize that the pain caused by the loss of a loved one never goes away, and I therefore approach the details of Tom's death with some hesitation. But I know I would want to know exactly what happened, if I were in your place. You have a right to know, and I have a duty to tell you.

"I remember Tom as a man who performed his job well, even though he did not care for the Army or the war. He used to say he never lost anything in Vietnam, therefore he had no reason to be there. A serious man with a dry sense of humor, Tom was well liked by all members of the platoon. This was remarkable, since we were composed of a wide cross section of America: white, black, brown. Tom was never afraid to speak up for what he believed in. He often said the war was crazy. Yet if there was work to be done he would be among the first to do it."

Rescorla described how the platoon had first come under fire in Happy Valley and how Burlile had stepped forward to speak to the men before they lifted off for the Ia Drang valley. He described in painful detail how Burlile had run forward in the face of enemy fire to answer the cries of men burned by napalm. Then he had disappeared, and when Rescorla reached him, he was lying facedown in the tall grass. "I held him, and in less than a minute he passed on. Tom was unconscious from the moment he was wounded, and I can assure you that he felt no pain.

"I know you have asked yourself, as I have, why Tom, a fine man, was taken. Why not some person less worthy? I don't know the answer to that, even after thirty years.

"Tom was as valid an American hero as anyone in any war that this country has ever fought. I know he would be the last to think of himself as a brave man. Tom would say, 'I was just trying to help someone.' But that day in the Ia Drang valley his sense of duty was so strong that he gave his life trying to save his fellow soldiers. This is the way I remember 'Doc' on Veterans Day and the Fourth of July. Whenever I visit the Wall in Washington with my son, Trevor, we always go up and touch Tom's name. It is a way of putting America in perspective, and to remember what it meant to serve alongside a real patriot in a desolate mountain valley a long time ago."

11

THE TARGET

Ahmed Shah Massoud (with machine gun) and a Mujahedeen in the
Hindu Kush mountains of Afghanistan, 1990.
(Webistan/Corbis)

IN THEIR ALMOST daily conversations, Hill and Rescorla spoke
often about their teenagers and, as the years passed, their grown
children. Hill's children, both older than Rescorla's, had graduated from
college. Gigi graduated summa cum laude at Florida State, and Danny
graduated with honors from the University of Florida. He was working
in computers, and Hill was putting money away to help set him up in
his own consulting business. Rescorla didn't want his own children to
miss having had a father the way he had. He took them to Shakespeare
plays, encouraged them to read, and, in Trevor's case, introduced him to
a wide array of sports, from rappelling, kayaking, and marksmanship to

rugby and soccer. Rescorla's competitive zeal remained undiminished, and he became so agitated at soccer matches that he was removed as a coach from his son's team and told not to attend games. He tried to interest Trevor in Cornish wrestling and took him to Hayle to compete in a match. But, relatively unpracticed in the sport, Trevor was trounced. Rescorla told Hill he just didn't understand why Trevor showed so little interest in his father's passions.

Hill hadn't always had such an easy time with Danny, either. He had struggled to find the right balance between encouragement and tolerance on the one hand, and firmness and discipline on the other. He let his children have an occasional drink at home, a glass of wine or beer, so they wouldn't sneak out and drink somewhere else. Hill financed several trips to New York so Danny could attend Broadway shows and a Diana Ross concert. But Danny ran up what to Hill were enormous bills on his credit card, and Hill reprimanded him. One day a bill came addressed to "Daniel Hill," and only after he opened it did he discover it was another credit card bill for his son. He summoned Danny from Gainesville, where he was still in college. "Danny," he said, "you and I are going to go for a little walk." When they were alone, he pulled out the bill and said, "What the hell is this? You can't pay this. You're going to be in debt even before you get out of college. Let me tell you: Never carry a debt you can't pay off by the end of the month." Then Hill pulled out a wad of cash and gave Danny enough to pay the bill and $200 to spare. "Pay that damn thing off," he said.

"You're a saint," Danny told him. Rescorla told Hill he was a softhearted SOB.

A month later, another bill came. "If this happens again, I'm taking one of these guns and I'm going to shoot you," Hill told his son. He refused to pay, and Danny's spending sprees came to an end.

Hill was surprised at how strong their bond had become, given how much he'd been away and how he had never wanted to have children to begin with. Danny wasn't interested in guns, hunting, or the military, but he shared his father's sense of adventure and curiosity about life. He was handsome, with his father's blond hair, which he wore long, and blue eyes. He had numerous friends, including good-looking women at whom Hill occasionally cast an envious eye. Hill was proud that he'd been able to give Danny some of the advantages he'd never had and that Danny seemed to be using them to build a promising future.

In July 1992, Hill returned to Fort Benning for a ceremony commemorating the fiftieth anniversary of the founding of the army Rangers. He wanted to meet several World War II veterans, including the few survivors of the D-Day assault on Pointe du Hoc, where four enormous German cannon had been trained over the English Channel. Of the three hundred men in the Ranger battalion assigned to assault the position, six had survived the battle. To Hill, they were the embodiment of the Ranger creed. As they sat in their wheelchairs, a new generation of Rangers shouted in tribute: "Though I be the sole survivor, I will not cease until the mission is accomplished."

But Hill's visit was cut short by a call from home. Danny had been skydiving when he had developed a hernia. When he was examined, the doctor told him he had a serious heart murmur.

Hill wasn't unduly alarmed, but he left immediately. When he reached the hospital in Jacksonville, Danny was tested and told that he suffered from a rare congenital heart condition. He would need open-heart surgery to replace a heart valve and aorta.

The operation was set for August 25. It began at seven in the morning and lasted hours. Hill waited anxiously and was relieved when the doctors indicated it had gone smoothly and they were removing Danny from the heart and lung machine that had kept him alive during the operation. But then he developed an infection. On September 10 he underwent more surgery and the surgeons were about to close the incision when Danny's heart and lungs stopped functioning. He was reconnected to the machine. Hill waited at the hospital with mounting apprehension. Two hours later, he saw the chaplain approaching him. He looked grave. "I lost him, didn't I?" Hill said. The chaplain nodded. Hill started to sob.

When he could collect himself, he called Rescorla from the hospital. "Oh God, no," Rescorla said. "I'll be right down."

Hill had to break the news to Patricia and Gigi. They were shattered. Later, Patricia reminded him that he'd promised her that Danny would be there to take care of her after Hill was gone. "You lied," she said, weeping softly.

Danny was twenty-nine years and six months old when he died. Hill remembered the prophecy of the gypsy fortune-teller all those years ago: Daniel Hill wouldn't live to see his thirtieth birthday. Of course he thought she had meant him.

When Rescorla arrived that same night, Hill came rushing into the driveway to meet him. Rescorla put his arms around him and then started to cry. In all of their times together, it was the only time Hill had seen Rescorla weep. Then Hill started to cry, too. The two men stood in the driveway, hugging each other and sobbing, unable to speak.

Rescorla went with Hill to the funeral home the next day, where Hill picked out a coffin. Hill brought Danny's favorite suit and told the undertaker exactly how Danny's hair should be arranged. Danny had always been proud of his hair. Hill had nothing to wear himself, so Rescorla drove him to a shopping mall and bought him a new dark suit.

The next day, Hill said he wanted to return to the funeral home to see Danny, to check to make sure everything was perfect before the ceremony.

"Dan, he's perfect as he is," Rescorla said.

"I want Danny," Hill insisted and started to cry.

"That's not Danny," Rescorla said gently. "That's just the container that Danny came in. Danny is gone."

★

DANNY HAD HAD NO medical insurance, and Hill had no policy to cover him. The doctor and hospital bills were over $400,000. Hill used all his readily available assets and had to remortgage their house to make the payments. One night he removed one of his guns from his case and put the barrel in his mouth. He didn't feel life was worth living. But then he remembered that his life insurance wouldn't pay if he committed suicide. Patricia and Gigi still depended on him.

Danny's death wrought a profound change in Hill. He was no stranger to death, of course. He had killed many men, and many men he had counted as friends had been killed. Death hadn't affected him much, or so he had thought. But now he felt devastated. Each man he killed had been someone's son, as Danny had been his. And to what end? God, country, honor, to "free the oppressed," which was the motto of the Special Forces. Now Hill just didn't know. For the first time in his life, he fell into a deep depression. He stopped working, and the bills mounted. One afternoon he came home after gathering some crab traps he'd set in the bay near their house. "Dan, we're going to have to sell the house," Patricia told him. "We're out of money. You're not working. We're going to lose our home."

The next day, Hill rose early, loaded his tools into his truck, and went out looking for work.

The next summer, Hill hiked the Appalachian Trail, deep in thought. And he got out sculpting tools he'd acquired after visiting the 1963 World's Fair. He'd never used them, but now he thought again of Michelangelo's *Pietà,* the sculpture of the virgin cradling her dead son that had so moved him all those years ago. He set up a shop in a room next to the garage and began carving wood. His first effort was a large sculpture of a hunter with his dog, and even Hill was surprised at how good it was. When Rescorla visited and saw it, he exclaimed, "Hill, you're as good as Michelangelo. You just don't know it." Rick encouraged him to enter art competitions and advertise.

So Hill photographed the sculpture and ran an advertisement in *Sporting Classics* magazine, offering to reproduce the work for $1,750. Soon after, he received a call from the president of the Hartford Insurance Company, a hunting enthusiast, who said he'd like to order the sculpture.

"Do you want your face on the hunter?" Hill asked.

"No," the man replied, but he wanted the dog to be a springer spaniel. Hill completed the work, using Gertrude, his own springer spaniel, as a model. He packed it carefully and shipped it to Connecticut. Later, his patron called to say how pleased he was. He reported that an appraiser from New York City had placed a value of $6,000 on the work. The appraiser had added that if anyone had ever heard of Dan Hill, it would be worth $12,000. Hill immediately doubled his asking price to $3,500.

One weekend, Hill was at an art show in Fort Lauderdale when he heard a familiar voice from his childhood. He looked over at an elegant, well-dressed, elderly blond woman. My God, he thought. He went over. "Are you Juju?" he asked. The woman looked startled.

"Who are you?" she demanded.

"Why, I'm Danny Hill," he said.

Her face lit up. "Good God!" she exclaimed. "It's little Danny!" She smothered him in a big kiss.

Hill began making regular trips to see Juju, who now used her real name, Judith Jones, and was a widow in her mid-eighties. "You can't tell anyone" about my past, she said coyly. "I'm a respectable society matron down here." She had married one of her clients, a successful medical doctor, and moved to Fort Lauderdale and a comfortable retirement years earlier. But with Hill, there was no need to maintain any pretenses. She loved reminiscing about her colorful life in Chicago with him. On one of his visits she mentioned the nickel-plated revolver he'd shot behind the whorehouse. "I only had to shoot one man with it," she said, and laughed. He was a Chicago policeman, trying to shake her down. Even then, she didn't shoot to kill, just to scare him. "Here," she said, pulling it out of her purse. "I want you to have it."

A year later, Judith Jones died quietly in her sleep.

★

ON FEBRUARY 26, 1993, a Friday, Barbara Williams was having her lunch at the security console she manned just outside Rescorla's office on the forty-fourth floor of the World Trade Center. In her early fifties, Williams had been born in Jamaica, and Rescorla enjoyed the lilt in her voice, a reminder that she, too, was from a corner of the old British empire. Williams's job was to watch the security monitor, and the console was filled with television screens transmitting images from security cameras located in the lobby and throughout Dean Witter's floors. Suddenly there was a loud, ominous noise and she felt vibrations in the building. It sounded a little like a crack of thunder.

"What's that sound?" Rescorla called from his office.

"I don't know," she said.

Wesley Mercer hurried out from his office and stopped at the console. He'd just gotten back the night before from a vacation in Barbados. Rescorla had met Mercer in 1987, when Mercer had been working at Dean Witter as a contract security guard. He had close-cropped hair, a mustache, and glasses, and people often said he looked like Johnnie Cochran, O. J. Simpson's lawyer, though he hated the comparison. "You must be a military man," Rescorla told him, impressed by Mercer's handling of the men who worked under him. He was right: Mercer had earned a Purple Heart and Bronze Star in both Korea and Vietnam. Rescorla had invited him to Windows on the World and had offered him a job working for him. Rescorla had told Mercer that the building garages were "the soft spot."

Rescorla joined them, studying the images on the console screens. They could see the ground-level lobby filling with smoke. Then the phone rang, and Rescorla answered. When he hung up, he said, "The World Trade Center has been bombed." The intercom started buzzing. "We'd better get out there."

Mercer called his companion, Bill Randolph, an associate organist at the Cathedral of St. John the Divine. They'd been living together since 1976, though Mercer also had a wife, from whom he was long separated, and a child. "I'm all right," Mercer reported. "The building swayed." But then he said he'd have to call him back.

People were milling in confusion in the forty-fourth-floor lobby.

Some Dean Witter employees had come down from higher floors; others had stayed at their desks. No fire alarms had gone off, and even if they had, employees had been for the most part ignoring the fire drills. There were no directions or guidance over the intercom because the blast had knocked out the Port Authority's emergency communications and power center, located near the blast in the sub-basement of the complex. The elevators had been shut down. When Rescorla checked the emergency stairwells, they were filling with smoke and were dark. The emergency generator had failed, and the stair treads weren't marked.

Rescorla shouted to get the chattering throng's attention. They ignored him. Finally he stood up on a desk and yelled, "Do I have to drop my trousers to get your attention?" He had them wait until he received word that the smoke had cleared; then he distributed flashlights and had them walk down the dark stairs to safety. Rescorla manned one of the two interior stairways, Mercer the other. Then they climbed the stairs, stopping at each floor to make sure everyone was out. "Sweep the floor, secure the premises," Rescorla told his staff.

Later, policemen arrived on the floor to report that the building was safe and people could remain inside or leave. But by then Rescorla had gotten everyone out.

★

HILL RETURNED HOME from a job at about three in the afternoon and was looking forward to a weekend of wood carving. Patricia was out. The phone rang; he knew it was his usual afternoon call from Rescorla.

"Hill here. Good afternoon."

"Did you see it?" Rescorla asked breathlessly.

"Did I see what?"

"The sons of bitches bombed us," Rescorla said.

"Where?"

"Right under my ass, you idiot. Exactly where you said it would happen. In the basement."

"No shit," Hill said.

"Turn on your TV," Rescorla said.

Hill quickly turned on the set and was shocked by the pictures: smoke pouring from a gaping crater in the sub-basement parking area, the surrounding area choked with fire trucks, ambulances, and police cars.

"What were the casualties?" Hill asked after he absorbed the images.

"Not that bad," Rescorla said. "Maybe a dozen at most." He said he'd gotten all of his people out of the building.

Hill observed that the building was still standing. "Yeah, but I felt it," Rescorla said. "If you'd been in charge, we'd all be in one big heap in the basement. Pack your shit and get up here," he continued. "I'm going to hire you again as a consultant." Dean Witter would pick up all his expenses, even a new winter coat, which Hill would need in New York in February.

Rescorla knew how badly Hill needed extra money. Still, Hill felt his pulse quicken at the prospect of getting to the scene of the terrorist attack. For the first time since Danny's death, he felt his spirits begin to rise.

On Sunday, Rescorla met Hill at Newark Airport, and after a night at Rescorla's house in Morristown, where Hill visited Betsy and the kids, they checked into the Marriott Financial Center hotel, located just south of the World Trade Center. Hill's room was on such a high floor that it made him nervous to stand too close to the window. It had a minibar, and Rescorla told him he was welcome to order anything from room service. Hill was amazed that the room cost $400 a night. He'd never paid more than $60 for a room himself.

As soon as they checked in, he and Rescorla walked to the site. The ramp that had given Hill and Rescorla such easy access to the basement levels in 1990 was now cordoned off by police and FBI agents, who wouldn't let them through. But Hill didn't need to go any farther to know what had caused the blast. "Ammonium nitrate and diesel fuel," he said, just as he had predicted.

"How can you tell?" Rescorla asked.

"The smell," Hill said. "You can always tell."

Later, back in the room, Rescorla asked, "Who did this?"

"Muslims," Hill said. "I suspect Iranians or Palestinians." Rescorla agreed, though he thought it might be Iraqis, retaliating for the Gulf War. Rescorla suggested that Hill try to gather some intelligence. He was a Muslim, after all, and he spoke Arabic. Rescorla had drawn up a list of mosques in the New York area, many of them located across the Hudson in New Jersey. Each day Hill donned a scullcap and carried his prayer beads and a copy of the Koran. He used his Muslim name, Abdullah Al Amin. He took the PATH train to New Jersey and timed his arrivals for *zuhuh,* noontime prayer. A meal and conversation, giving Hill a chance to gain information, typically followed noon prayer. When fellow Muslims viewed him skeptically, he explained he was visiting from Jacksonville, where he had helped build the city's mosque. To explain his Nordic features, he sometimes added that he was Nuristani.

Each day he visited a different mosque, often returning for a second visit. Most of the people he met at the mosque in Patterson were Turkish. They were friendly and pro-American, and they welcomed Hill into their midst. They stressed repeatedly that they hoped the perpetrators didn't turn out to be Muslim terrorists. Hill felt he didn't need to spend any more time there. But at every other location, Hill was struck by the intense anti-American hostility he encountered. Though these were not his own views, he barely had to mention that he thought American policy toward Israel and the Middle East was misguided, or that Jews wielded too much political power, to unleash a torrent of anti-American, anti-Semitic rhetoric. Many applauded the bombing of the World Trade Center, lamenting that it hadn't done more damage.

"Those are the towers of Jews" he was told at several stops. Then his hosts quoted from the Koran: "Wherever you are, death will overtake you, though you are in lofty towers in the sky." Only at the Brooklyn mosque of Sheikh Omar Abdel Rahman did Hill glean nothing. No one invited him to stay for the meal following the noon prayer, and he felt stares of hostility during the service. There was no sign of the blind mullah himself.

"We've got a problem," Hill said to Rescorla, referring to the New Jersey and Brooklyn mosques. And it wasn't going to go away simply because the World Trade Center had been bombed once but remained standing. As the symbolic "tower of the Jews," it was likely to remain a target for the foreseeable future. Indeed, Rescorla began routinely referring to the Trade Center as "the target" and "ground zero."

Rescorla also enlisted Fred McBee, his friend from Oklahoma. He said he assumed the terrorists' goal had been to take down the towers. Since a truck bomb had failed, what would they try next? Rescorla mused that a small, portable nuclear weapon might do it. Another possibility, he said, which he'd drawn from Hill's plan to start World War III, was to fly a cargo plane into the building. McBee happened to have a Microsoft flight simulator on his computer at that moment. He'd been experimenting with it using a Cessna light plane, but with a click of the mouse he changed it to a Boeing 737. Then he pulled up the image of lower Manhattan and simulated a crash into the World Trade Center. "This would be a piece of cake," McBee said. Then he tried it on the Statue of Liberty and the Empire State Building, with the same results. Then he switched to Washington, D.C. But the White House and Capitol were blacked out. "It looks very viable," McBee concluded.

As they had done in 1990, Hill and Rescorla stayed up late at night working on a report that incorporated Hill's findings, Rescorla's analysis, and their warnings of future risks. It warned that because the World Trade Center was the tallest building in New York, located at the heart of Wall Street, and a symbol of American economic might, it was likely to remain a target of anti-American militants. Rescorla quoted the passage from the Koran referring to the "lofty towers in the sky." Although the bombing of the trade center and numerous other acts of Islamic terrorism had been relatively unsophisticated, Muslim terrorists were showing increasing tactical and technological awareness and were getting more adept. Numerous young Muslims were living in the United States studying engineering, chemistry, and medicine, which meant there was a potential enemy within. Hill's research had identified certain *dawah* groups, connected to some of the New Jersey mosques, whose goal was to travel around talking to young people, recruiting radical firebrands. Rescorla said that terrorists would not rest until they had succeeded in toppling the towers, which had plainly been the ultimate goal of the truck bombers.

Rescorla sketched a scenario of what the next attack might look like: an air attack on the twin towers, probably a cargo plane traveling from the Middle East or Europe to Kennedy or Newark airport, loaded with explosives, chemical or biological weapons, or even a small nuclear weapon. Besides New York, other cities might be targeted, such as Washington or Philadelphia. Perhaps terrorists would attack all three.

Rescorla's report concluded that Dean Witter should leave the World Trade Center and build new quarters in New Jersey, preferably a low-rise three- or four-building complex spread over a large area. He pointed out that many employees already commuted from New Jersey and would welcome the change. He warned that Manhattan's limited bridge and tunnel connections meant it could be easily cut off and transportation and communications disrupted. Moreover, the World Trade Center space was expensive compared to prices for real estate in the suburbs.

As they put the finishing touches on the draft of the report toward the end of the week, Hill noticed that Rescorla was again planning to spend the night in his hotel room. Rescorla had been dealing with security issues at Dean Witter all day, skipping meals, staying up late working on the report, then tossing and turning at night, interfering with Hill's sleep. Earlier, Hill had noticed him flirting overtly with a waitress, which didn't seem like him.

"Don't you want to go home to see Betsy and the kids?" Hill asked.

"I may never go back again," Rescorla replied angrily.

Hill was shocked. "What do you mean?"

"The marriage is over. We haven't slept together for years."

★

IN 1993, Susan's stepfather died suddenly, leaving her mother a widow once again. Marian took his death in stride, but at eighty-two, she didn't want to live alone in Pennsylvania, isolated from Susan and her grandchildren. So Susan suggested her mother come and live with her, even though she knew it would enrage her second husband.

Susan had remarried in 1981, still depressed by the failure of her first marriage. She had met a forensic psychologist, who had an uncanny instinct for saying the right things to someone whose self-esteem had been battered. He promised to love her, to ease her financial burdens, buy her a new house, and take care of her children. He may not have been as good-looking as Robert, but he was brilliant and stimulating, and said he loved her madly.

They did move into a spacious new house, which came as a relief after Susan's moves from one rental property to the next. But she soon realized that she had made a terrible mistake. He did not, as he had claimed, care about her children, and he was jealous of her time with them and irritated by their presence in the house. He verbally abused her and the children. Their relationship deteriorated into a series of arguments that Susan invariably lost.

Susan lived for thirteen years in a quiet state of desperation, trapped in the marriage for financial reasons and by the need to support her children. She had made a success of her travel business, arranging tours for corporate, church, and educational clients as well as individuals. But her commissions were modest. When Robert stopped making regular child-support payments and her second husband refused to contribute, she found a job as administrative assistant to the dean at Fairleigh Dickinson University in Madison, New Jersey. The salary was modest, but Bianca, her youngest daughter, was eligible to attend the university tuition-free. Everything she made went for the children; she relied on her husband for her own support, to the grudging degree he was willing to provide it. It was a humiliating position to be in, and over the years, her self-esteem sank even further.

Still, Susan's two older children had gotten through college. Cristina married, and Alexandra moved to Manhattan. Bianca was at Fairleigh Dickinson. Periodically Susan tried to breathe some life into her marriage. For Christmas one year she bought her husband a golden retriever puppy to complement her three Siamese cats. He named the dog Buddy. She knew how much he had wanted a dog, and she came to love Buddy, too. But not even a puppy could salvage the marriage. When Susan's mother moved in with them, it didn't take her long to assess the situation. "We are going to get out of here," Marian told Susan. "I'll buy you a town house." Susan knew exactly the place: Convent Mews in Morristown. She had been eyeing the development for years, hoping to escape her marriage. It had a vaguely Spanish-colonial flavor to the architecture, which reminded her of her happy days in Spain and Portugal.

Susan left with her mother, Bianca, and the three cats. Buddy stayed behind. Almost as soon as they moved in, Marian's health began to deteriorate. She was suffering from the early stages of Alzheimer's disease and was soon confined to a wheelchair. Susan hired caretakers by day, then did the cooking and cleaning when she returned from work. Marian was in the hospital several times. Susan loved her mother, and she wanted to maintain her quality of life. At the same time, she recognized she had no time for herself. In one of Marian's lucid moments, Susan held her mother's hand and asked, "Will anyone ever love me again?"

Her mother squeezed her hand and smiled. "I know they will," she promised.

In 1995, when Susan felt she couldn't take the daily routine much longer, her mother agreed she should take a vacation. Susan rented a small house in France at the base of the Pyrénées on the Mediterranean coast. She and her friend Terry Caprio traveled to Barcelona and drove along the Riviera. Terry had gotten a degree in nutrition, and she and her husband had opened a holistic clinic in Westport, Connecticut. Over the years she had introduced Susan to many new ideas about organic food and healthy living.

One day, Terry mentioned that she knew some Buddhists who lived in the mountain village of Sainte-Agnès, France. They stopped and discovered that Terry's friends were hosting a group of Tibetan monks. What am I doing here? Susan wondered. It was awfully exotic by her standards, but they spent the night, and she found all the chanting curiously soothing. While she considered herself a Christian, she conceded there was more than one way to feel the power of the universe.

Susan phoned her mother every day. With each call, her mother became more upset, crying and demanding that Susan return, complaining that the caretakers were abusing her. When Susan got home after the trip, her mother asked if she'd had a good time. "How could I?" Susan asked. "You were acting out."

Her mother looked apologetic. "I was jealous," she said. "I couldn't go, not in a wheelchair."

Susan had vowed she wouldn't do it, but she had to put her mother in a nursing home. Susan visited every day, making sure Marian's hair was done properly and that she was clean and well groomed. She knew how important her appearance was to her mother.

In July 1997, a nurse called, urging Susan to leave work and come immediately. When she arrived, her mother's frail body was ashen. Susan took her hand and told her mother that she loved her. She began reciting a prayer, then noticed that her mother had stopped breathing. In some ways it was a blessing.

A few months later, the neighbors reported that they hadn't seen Susan's second husband for several days. Susan's daughter Cristina called the police. When they arrived, they found his body. He had suffered a massive stroke and been dead for three days. Buddy was sitting by the body.

Susan went to a neighbor's home and collected the dog. With Bianca about to graduate from college, she figured Buddy might be the only companionship she could look forward to.

★

IN 1997, Dean Witter merged with the even more prestigious Wall Street securities firm of Morgan Stanley & Company to form Morgan Stanley Dean Witter, Inc., and the headquarters was moved to Morgan Stanley's offices in midtown Manhattan. Rescorla thought there was a good chance he'd be offered a buyout or retirement package as part of the merger, but instead he was promoted to executive vice president. Many of the merged firm's operations remained in the World Trade Center, where Dean Witter's lease didn't expire until 2006.

Rescorla's report was apparently one of a number of factors that led Dean Witter to sue the Port Authority both for damages related to the bombing and to be released from its lease. A confidential memo dated October 27, 1993, to, among others, Philip Purcell, Dean Witter's chairman, described the World Trade Center as "damaged goods" that "is and will remain a target building." It concluded that the Port Authority's "current actions do not significantly increase Dean Witter's level of security" and recommended an "aggressive posture" toward the Port Authority. But in the meantime, Rescorla's office stayed on the forty-fourth floor, and he remained responsible for the security of the firm's 3,700 employees in the World Trade Center. Twenty-seven hundred worked in Tower Two, and 1,000 worked in one of the low-rise buildings in the complex. Rescorla felt frustrated that he couldn't do more, but within the twenty-two floors that were under his jurisdiction, he introduced strict new security procedures.

Kathy Comerford had noticed the changes immediately when she and other employees returned to the World Trade Center offices about eight weeks after the bombing. Comerford, a cheerful, heavyset, dark-haired woman, had worked at the firm since she had graduated from college, starting as a paralegal and working her way up to a vice president and event planner. She loved the fact that she could take the Long Island Railroad from her home in Bethpage, get on the subway at Pennsylvania Station, exit into the World Trade Center, and take the elevator to her office on the seventieth floor, changing from sneakers into dressier shoes, all without stepping outside.

At Rescorla's orders, no visitors were allowed into the offices without an escort from Morgan Stanley. There was grumbling that even food deliveries had to be picked up in the lobby. New security ID cards were issued, which employees had to pass through turnstiles before gaining entry. All packages and mail had to be inspected on the ground floor. Fluorescent tape was installed in the interior stairwells. Rescorla expanded his security staff, with two guards patrolling each floor. And he doubled the number of employee fire marshalls. He asked Comerford to be one of the marshals for her floor.

Fire and evacuation drills were implemented immediately and held every other month. At the sound of an alarm, all employees were required to gather in a hallway that connected the two interior stairways, remain quiet, and await further instructions from one of Rescorla's staff. In the event they were ordered to evacuate, they were to choose a partner and descend the stairs in pairs, side by side, to the forty-fourth floor, where Rescorla would issue further instructions. At their first few drills, Rescorla reprimanded them for talking and for not moving quickly enough. He, Wesley Mercer, and other deputies began timing them with a stopwatch. The idle chatter stopped, and their performance improved rapidly. All employees were told specifically to obey orders from Rescorla and his staff rather than announcements from the Port Authority; Rescorla had lost all confidence in the authority after his and Hill's experience in 1990.

Participation in the drills was mandatory, though after the bombing, most people needed little persuasion. All, that is, except a few people on the opulent seventy-third floor, occupied by the some of the firm's top-performing brokers like Lindsay Herkness, a member of the elite "chairman's club." Fun loving and irreverent by nature, Herkness had been vacationing in Paris the day of the bombing and saw no reason to take the new drills any more seriously than he had before the attack. He liked to say that the World Trade Center was the safest building in America, and the fact that it had withstood the bombing proved it.

Given the commissions the top brokers generated for the firm, there was little Rescorla could do to enforce discipline on the seventy-third floor, and in any event, like just about everyone else, he liked Herkness. Maybe he saw the obvious similarities: Herkness had grown up in a military family; he was fiercely competitive, physically fit, had a good sense of humor, and chafed under outside authority. His Christmas cards were legendary: a photo of him ballooning over the Swiss Alps ("Dropping in on Swiss clients . . . with more hot air!"); being arrested outside Buckingham Palace ("I only recommended to Her Majesty that she fund an IRA account"); and, in 1993, a photo of his beloved basset hound with an enormous blue ribbon, with Herkness working out on a NordicTrack in the background ("Best in Show and Wanna Be").

At the same time, Herkness led the privileged life of a successful Wall Street broker, something beyond Rescorla's means and experience. A bachelor, Herkness lived on Manhattan's Upper East Side and belonged to the exclusive Union Club, the oldest men's club in the country, and the Piping Rock Club on Long Island. He loved the opera and expensive restaurants, and he sometimes made the rounds of three cocktail parties in a single night. He began his mornings with a shiatsu massage from his personal trainer and played squash at the Union Club nearly every evening, winning the club's annual mixed doubles tournament for five consecutive years. Though he was only a few years younger than Rescorla, he barely looked forty, if that.

Inevitably, as the years passed and there were no further terrorist incidents, the bombing receded from people's memories and the urgency of the drills began to fade. Still, Rescorla kept telling people to be alert and continued to warn of a potential threat. During the summer of 1998, Bob Edwards, a freelance film producer, interviewed and video-taped Rescorla in his office on the forty-fourth floor. "Hunting down terrorists—this will be the nature of war in the future," Rescorla predicted bluntly. "Not great battlefields, not great tanks rolling. Terrorist actions can bring conventional forces to their knees." He warned of the sometimes "cavalier" actions abroad of American companies and the U.S. government, and he warned they were creating a "residue of hatred" that "will come home to roost."

To some, Rescorla came to be viewed as a discomforting figure, a Cassandra, always warning about possible attacks on "the target." Comerford would see him during her lunch break, when she sometimes ate outside on the plaza between the two towers. He would be walking around, reconnoitering, scanning the crowd, taking up positions where he wouldn't be noticed. She thought it odd that he was often singing to himself.

★

IN 1995, Hill helped design and build a mosque in St. Augustine, which was closer to home than Jacksonville. There were only a dozen or so Muslims in St. Augustine, but enough to sustain a small mosque. Nader Zori, the Mujahedeen Hill helped rescue in Afghanistan, helped him build it. After he left Afghanistan with Hill, Nader Zori had gotten a green card and emigrated to the United States thanks to Hill's contacts in the Special Forces in Islamabad. His fractures had been repaired at hospitals in Islamabad and Jacksonville. After his release, he spurned welfare and got a job as a janitor at a Ryan's Restaurant. He rented a garage where he detailed cars to earn extra money. Hill helped him install a toilet, shower, and sink, and he lived in the garage. Nader managed to send $100 a month back to his family in Afghanistan.

One afternoon, after working on the mosque, Hill got his usual call from Rescorla. "I've got some bad news," Rescorla reported. "I've got prostate cancer."

"What are you going to do about it?" Hill asked, worried.

"It's pretty advanced," he said. "I'm going to have an operation." Hill offered, but Rescorla said there was no need for him to come up.

After the surgery, Rescorla called Hill from the hospital, sounding cheerful. "I've been through the center of the earth," he reported. "I've seen all the great canyons and the abyss. . . ."

"What the hell are you talking about?" Hill asked. Rescorla explained he'd had a proctoscopy and had watched as a camera had moved through his body. He thought the surgery was a success and the cancer eradicated. But later he reported that it had spread to his bone marrow.

"You've got to die of something," Rescorla said. "It looks like I'm going to beat you to the barn, Hill," he said, quoting Gary Cooper's famous comment to Ernest Hemingway just before Cooper died of cancer in 1961. But then he vowed, "I'm going to fight it."

And if he had only a short time to live—he estimated four to six years, maybe less—he intended to make the most of it. After the surgery, he'd moved into a separate room from Betsy, and the marriage had deteriorated. It wasn't that they quarreled or raised their voices with each other, it was that there wasn't any passion at all. He told Hill that if it hadn't been for the children, he would have gotten divorced years before.

Even then, it was Betsy who proposed it, though Rescorla was never sure she really meant it. One evening they had been discussing the loveless state of their marriage, when Betsy had said almost wearily, "We might as well get a divorce."

"Good idea," Rescorla replied. "You get a lawyer, and I'll get one."

Kim overheard parts of her parents' conversation and was shocked. The next morning, her mother broke the news to her and Trevor. She said that they had decided it was better for them "to pursue their own goals and interests." Kim thought she'd never seen her father look more upset.

Since he thought he wasn't going to live long, Rescorla granted nearly all of Betsy's demands, acquiescing to alimony and support payments. They were divorced in 1996 but remained on relatively friendly terms. Initially, Trevor stayed with his father at the house on Dale Drive and Kim moved with her mother to a condominium in the Convent Mews development in Morristown. Max, the ill-tempered family dog, also stayed with Rick and Trevor. But then Rescorla sold the house, and he and Trevor moved into an identical condominium down the street, so it would be easier for Kim and Trevor to go back and forth. Rescorla asked Hill to take the Dutch keeshond off his hands. "You've got all those guns," he said. "I'll pay you one thousand dollars to shoot the animal." Hill took Max but declined the money. "The only unconditional love you'll ever get is from a dog," Hill said.

Hill couldn't accept the fact that Rescorla might be mortal after all. They still had so much they wanted to do together. Then, after the August 1998 bombings of the American embassies in Nairobi and Dar es Salaam, Hill heard on CNN that the United States and Saudi Arabia were jointly offering a $15 million reward for the capture of the suspected mastermind of the attacks, Saudi millionaire Osama bin Laden. This might be an opportunity to finance a last great adventure together. Hill got excited and called Nader, who now ran a pizza business that Hill had invested in with him. Nader's brother-in-law was now living in exile in Islamabad. He had served briefly in Afghanistan's defense ministry after the Soviets abandoned the country in 1989 and still maintained numerous contacts in the country.

"Is your brother-in-law still going in and out of Afghanistan?" he asked

"All the time," Nader said.

"Does he have Taliban contacts?" Hill asked. Nader assured him he did. "Can you talk to him?" Hill asked.

Nader told him it wasn't safe; the phones were tapped. Mail was routinely opened. The only safe communication was by courier. But someone from the mosque was often scheduled to travel through Islamabad. "Then I've got an idea," Hill said.

Hill outlined a plan to enlist Nader's brother-in-law as the commander, organize an ambush, and attack and kill bin Laden. Hill and Nader would join the operation, Hill with his military expertise and Nader with his knowledge of the language and terrain. If they succeeded, they'd split the reward: $2 million for Hill, $2 million for Nader, $2 million for Nader's brother-in-law, and the rest for the additional men they'd need in Afghanistan. Nader wrote a letter in Farsi outlining the plan and gave it to the courier for delivery to his brother-in-law. Several weeks later, the courier delivered the response: The brother-in-law was interested. He had Taliban contacts; he knew the locations of three compounds bin Laden used in Kandahar, and he knew that bin Laden made regular trips between Kandahar and Kabul. He traveled in a small convoy of just three vehicles. But he wanted assurances of U.S. government support.

Hill made contact with the FBI office in Jacksonville, and an agent there, Leo Morris, seemed enthusiastic. He'd said he'd check with his superiors in Washington and get back to him. Hill called Rescorla to report on the latest developments. They discussed various permutations of the plan in detail. Hill offered to split his share of the reward with Rescorla, and they could both retire, travel, go on safari—just as they'd always dreamed of doing.

"I don't know," Rescorla said. He said he thought Hill might succeed in killing bin Laden, "but I don't know if you'll get out alive. I wouldn't want you to end up like Peachey."

"I'm sixty. I'm not risking that much," Hill replied. "If I don't get out, you would make sure Pat and Gigi got the reward money. Anyway," he continued, "it's better than being an old man. I'd go out in a blaze of glory." Hill paused thoughtfully. "But I'm going to make it out, Rick. I feel it. Plus I've got the lion's tooth and the .577."

12

SOUL MATES

Rick and Susan, 1998.
(Courtesy of Susan Rescorla)

ON A SUNDAY MORNING in July 1998, Susan Greer and
Buddy were again on their early morning walk on Dorado
Drive when a dark green Lincoln Mark VIII glided alongside them.
The passenger window lowered, and she heard a voice say, "Hello." She
knew immediately that it was the voice of the intriguing man she had
met the day before, the one running in his bare feet. Susan felt excited,
but a little nervous.

The man leaned over toward the window, and she got her first real
look at him. He was smiling. He had a broad, open, friendly face and
blue eyes with a distinct twinkle in them. "Why not come to breakfast?" he asked.

"I can't—I have the dog," she replied instinctively. He looked disappointed. Susan reminded herself that she had vowed just the day before to take more risks in life. So what if they hadn't been introduced and she barely knew him? She took a deep breath. "Why don't you come have coffee on my patio?"

He readily agreed, and she gave him the address of her town house, just around the corner. He said he'd have breakfast and then be right over. She finished walking Buddy. As she and the dog returned to the town house, she glanced around to see if any of the neighbors was out. She wasn't sure she wanted anyone seeing a strange man going into the house.

In less than an hour, he walked through the rear garden to her covered patio, exclaiming over the beautiful plants and a small fountain Susan had installed. Within the confines of a town-house complex, she had done her best to reproduce the ambiance of the Mediterranean hotels and villas she had so enjoyed when she was young. She had vines tethered to the roof and terra-cotta urns she had brought home from France. The patio floor was covered in Italian tiles.

Inside, the house was filled with antiques and paintings, many of them inherited from Susan's mother, others purchased by Susan on her many foreign trips. Susan stepped into the kitchen to make coffee, which she served on beautiful china she had found in Portugal.

She hadn't even put the coffee down before he started talking, eagerly telling her about his upbringing, his writing, his military career. The screenplay he had mentioned the previous morning, *M'Kubwa Junction,* was set in Northern Rhodesia and was based on his experiences in the British colonial police force. Few of the native Rhodesians had worn shoes, he explained, which was why he had had to feel what it was like to run barefoot. He mentioned the incident with the lion. He talked about growing up in Hayle, a tiny village on the coast of Cornwall. When he wanted to, he could really turn on a Cornish accent, softer and more lilting than the standard British accent, or even speak the Cornish dialect. He knew some other languages as well:

French, Vietnamese, even some Arabic, which delighted Susan. She herself was so interested in foreign cultures and travel, yet she found few Americans who shared her interests, let alone knew foreign languages.

He had also been running to keep his weight down, he said. Susan thought that he was simply a big man, and he carried himself well. But he seemed dismayed that after having been extremely fit nearly all of his life, he had recently gained so much weight. He was matter-of-fact about the cause: he had been diagnosed with prostate cancer, and it had spread to his bone marrow. The cancer treatments he'd been undergoing made him extremely thirsty and had caused his body to swell. He said he didn't know how much time he had left to live, but he intended to make the most of it. Since his divorce, he'd thought of registering with a dating service, and he'd gone on several dates.

He spoke almost constantly, moving from topic to topic in no coherent order, as though he had been starved for someone to listen. He had friends he had promised to meet that afternoon in New York City, but as he rose to leave, he said, "I know we are going to be friends forever."

Susan said, "You're a rogue."

After they parted, Susan cleared the cups and led Buddy back into the house, her head spinning. When she glanced at the kitchen clock, she was surprised to see that it was eleven-thirty. Four and a half hours had passed.

It was a lot to absorb. Yet there was so much that Susan didn't know, starting with his name. Had he introduced himself? Maybe he had mentioned his first name when he was in the car, but if so, Susan didn't remember it. Did he have a job? She wasn't sure. Perhaps he worked at home as a writer. Susan assumed he knew even less about her. He had talked so much that she doubted he heard much of what she had to say, not that she said all that much. She hoped it had registered that she, too, was divorced and wasn't seeing anyone. For she wanted to see him again.

The next day, Susan took Buddy for his regular walk, half expecting the man to be out jogging or to drive by in his car. But she didn't see him. Still, she thought of little else for the rest of the day. At work at the bank, she had an uncharacteristic Cheshire Cat smile on her face. When her friends asked about her weekend, she said, "I think I met my soul mate." Given that she'd gone five years without a date, they stared at her in disbelief.

Several more days passed. Susan walked every morning, hoping for a glimpse of him. She was sure he wouldn't just disappear. Then, on Thursday, she was driving home from work, and as she turned into Dorado Drive she saw a green Lincoln coming toward her from the opposite direction. He drew up alongside and lowered the window. "Where were you?" he shouted. He told her he took the 6:10 morning train to Manhattan and looked for her each day on the way to the station. She had been walking at 6:30, which meant she had just missed him. "I'd like to take you out," he said. "Wherever you'd like."

He scribbled his name and phone number on a piece of paper, handed it out the car window to her, and asked her to call. Then he drove on.

Susan looked at the paper. There, at last, was his name: Rick Rescorla.

At work the next day, Susan reported that she had called Rescorla and made a date for brunch that coming Sunday. "But you don't even know him!" one said worriedly. Others chimed in that she should be more cautious. Susan didn't care. She was throwing caution to the winds. This might be her last chance.

★

THE FOLLOWING SUNDAY Susan rose early, walked Buddy, then bathed and dressed carefully. This time she wanted to look her best. She chose black-and-beige chiffon pants and a silk sleeveless tank top. On her feet were thin-strapped gold sandals. She wore a necklace with two leopards in gold with green emerald eyes, holding a circle of diamonds. For good measure she added several bracelets and rings. At 10:00 A.M., when Rescorla had agreed to pick her up, she was waiting outside by the curb. "Why are you waiting outside?" he asked. "You don't ever have to wait outside. I'll always come in to get you."

"Oh, my God," he said, when she got in the car and he got a good look at her. Had she overdone it with the leopard necklace? It wasn't exactly understated. She worried momentarily, but then he said, "You look lovely."

They drove to Frenchtown, a picturesque community on the Delaware River. Rescorla again told Susan she looked beautiful, and Susan complimented him on his safari jacket, which he said reminded him of his time in Africa. He loved the fact that the previous Sunday she had called him a "rogue." The lion he had killed, he explained, had been a rogue lion. Even though he had had to shoot the animal, he had admired the lion's courage, its great leap into the face of death.

Susan also admired his cowboy boots. Rescorla told her that he kept a knife concealed in the boots. Later, he showed it to her, a sharp blade in a leather sheaf. If he was trying to impress her with his derring-do, Susan thought he was wasting his time. After all, he'd killed a lion. She already knew what kind of man he was.

When they arrived at the Inn at Frenchtown, a nineteenth-century inn with views of the river, they ordered drinks at the bar. Rescorla quickly struck up a conversation with another couple sitting there. Susan grew quiet. When they moved to their table in the dining room, Rescorla asked Susan if she was shy. Susan was not shy, but she felt his conversation with strangers was taking away from their date. Already she felt that every moment with him was precious, and she didn't want to share them.

During their brunch, they discovered their mutual interest in movies. Rescorla seemed delighted at Susan's interest in foreign films and told her about his trips to the Palace cinema in Hayle. He'd loved the westerns, the war movies, the Hollywood musicals. In fact, he confided in Susan something he rarely mentioned to anyone: At one point, he had longed to go on the stage himself. Though he'd never gotten any encouragement in Hayle, he thought he had a decent singing voice. And he'd long harbored a desire to take dancing lessons. He even wanted to learn Latin dancing, which, though she was rusty from years of inactivity, was still one of Susan's favorites. Would Susan like to take them with him? He seemed like a sixteen-year-old, boyishly excited at the prospect of a first date.

During this conversation, Susan had more of a chance to speak of herself. Somewhat to her surprise, she discovered that Rescorla had been listening to her the previous Sunday; he remembered everything she'd said. She pointed out that despite her sheltered background, so different from his, she had an adventurous streak, too. Among other things, she enjoyed a cigar now and then and had traveled to Africa, Central and South America, had ridden on a camel in the Sahara, and parasailed in Acapulco.

When they left the restaurant, Rescorla darted into a nearby bar and emerged with two cigars. He gave Susan one, lit it, and then lit his own. They strolled onto a pedestrian bridge that spanned the Delaware. Rescorla pointed to the boulders visible in the rushing water below.

They stood together quietly, leaning on the railing, savoring their cigars, gazing into the water. Then Rescorla said, "This is the beginning. I think this is more than a casual date."

The next day at work, Susan was practically giddy with excitement. "It's making us sick," one of her coworkers said. "You're smiling and happy all the time."

Rescorla's colleagues at Morgan Stanley noticed a change in him, too. He was smiling and singing to himself, and he couldn't wait to catch the train. As usual, he called Dan Hill that Monday afternoon at about 3:30 P.M. "I met an interesting woman," he told his friend. Hill wondered what he meant by "interesting."

"What kind of breast line does she have?" Hill asked.

"No, this is a nice lady," Rescorla insisted.

"You better be careful of nice ladies," Hill said, laughing.

Rescorla told Hill that he'd met her while he was running in his bare feet and that she'd been walking a golden retriever.

"What are you going to do about the dog?" Hill asked him. He knew Rescorla wasn't a "dog person," not after the incident with the Dutch keeshond.

"Shit, he'll go," Rescorla predicted confidently.

That evening, just after Susan got home from work, the phone rang. "Have you eaten?" Rescorla asked. "Let's go out." The next evening, he called again. "Have you eaten? I'll bring something over."

On the third evening, they finished dinner and were sitting together on the sofa. Susan had lit candles and turned on the tiny white lights that were threaded through the vines covering her patio. She felt his hand touch the back of her neck. A thrill went down her spine. Then, with his other hand, he gently but firmly pushed her back into the sofa. He leaned over and kissed her.

Susan had never experienced such a feeling. She felt a wave of emotion wash over her.

The next night, Susan heard the doorbell ring. When she opened the door, no one was there. She looked down, and there was a single white rose.

Susan called Rescorla. "I'm so thrilled," she said. "What are you doing?"

"Waiting for you," he replied.

★

RESCORLA AND SUSAN spent every night together, except when Rescorla had to travel on business. He confessed that his given name was not Rick but Cyril, which he hated. Nor was he a professional writer, though he hoped to become one as soon as he retired, which might be soon. He worked on Wall Street, as first vice president for security for Morgan Stanley Dean Witter.

The week after their brunch in Frenchtown, Susan and Rick enrolled at the Arthur Murray Studio in Chatham. Before class, Susan put music on the stereo, and they practiced some steps on the patio. Rescorla was awkward at first. He was so much taller than Susan that it was hard for her to get her hand comfortably around his neck. But what he lacked in experience he made up for in enthusiasm. At the lessons, they worked on the waltz, something relatively simple. They learned the importance of posture. To compensate for their difference in height, Susan wore higher heels. Soon they were whirling about the floor with poise and confidence. By the eighth lesson, they were tackling the rumba, the samba, and, finally, the tango. As soon as the lessons were over, they returned to Susan's town house and kept dancing.

Several weeks into their lessons, they had brunch at another inn in western New Jersey, and as they left Rescorla grabbed Susan and began dancing to the jazz standards playing on the stereo. He whirled Susan out of the restaurant, onto the porch, and down the steps into the parking lot. Similarly, at a local delicatessen he began dancing to the piped-in music. Susan was oblivious of the onlookers. But it began to happen so often that strangers would mention to her that they'd seen her dancing.

Rescorla loved the tango. Susan suggested they watch the popular Italian film *The Postman,* about the life of the poet Pablo Neruda. They especially liked the scene where Neruda and his wife begin dancing the tango, and they watched it over and over on video. Susan began reading Neruda's poetry and then other Latin American poets. When their class at Arthur Murray ended, they signed up for more lessons at a local public school.

On weekends, Susan introduced Rescorla to many of the cultural activities she loved, taking him to art galleries, museums, and antique shops. One of her daughters lived in the Chelsea neighborhood in Manhattan, and they'd often combine a visit to the neighborhood's many galleries, antique shops, and flea markets with a visit to her. Susan persuaded Rick to undergo a Chinese massage from a man who had his clients sit in a chair just outside one of the flea markets. They both enjoyed it so much that they returned every time they came into Manhattan. Nearly every week they patronized the independent cinema.

Rescorla was an excellent mimic and would often reenact snippets of the dialogue. With Susan, Rescorla shared his love of nature and history, and he took her to parks and many of the historic sites he'd visited with Hill, as well as used-book stores.

Sometimes they went shopping together, and Rick helped Susan choose new clothes. Rescorla had finally mentioned, very gently, that perhaps Susan had been a little overdressed for their first date. She not only accepted the criticism, she let him go through her closet, discarding many of her more flamboyant outfits. He discouraged her from wearing so much jewelry and bought more modest pieces for her. He said she didn't need all those accessories to bring out her natural beauty. Susan gave some of her antique jewelry to her daughters.

And sometimes they went to look at houses with a Realtor. They hadn't formally decided to live together, but it seemed a natural, even inevitable, evolution. They were spending all their free time and every night together. On one foray into Hunterdon Township, in western New Jersey, they saw a beautiful old stone house on a creek. It had a studio where Rick could imagine himself writing once he retired. They got so excited that they nearly made an offer, but then they discovered the house was in a floodplain. In any event, with their five children all in Morristown or nearby, it didn't make sense to move so far away.

In their many discussions, the word *cancer* was never mentioned, but Susan was acutely aware of Rescorla's condition. She was no doctor, of course, but she was firmly convinced that her love could help restore his health. He was undergoing periodic treatment at a clinic, which required painful injections of interferon directly into his stomach or his arm every month. He never complained about them, but Susan knew they were an ordeal. He would have to lie quietly for hours after receiving the injections. He also took a regimen of pills. They made him constantly thirsty, and the fruit juices and other fluids he drank were what had caused his body to swell.

Susan suffered from lower back pain but had benefited from visits to a holistic practitioner, Brad Snyder, in Lebanon, New Jersey. In mid-August, she persuaded Rick to accompany her. They spent an hour talking about their lives and explaining Rick's condition to Snyder, and he prescribed a regimen of rest, diet, meditation, and Chinese liquids. When they were finished, Rick returned to the car while Susan stayed behind. Snyder took Susan's hand and said, "Let's pray." They said a prayer. "I promise you the cancer will leave and he will never feel pain," he said. Under Susan's watchful eye, Rick adhered strictly to Snyder's program, while continuing to get the injections and take the medication.

For Labor Day weekend, Rescorla was planning to visit Sam Fantino and his wife in Chicago, and a few days before, he called and asked if he could bring a date. Fantino was surprised; Rescorla had mentioned dating some women, but he had never proposed bringing any of them to visit. "I've met someone, and I like her," he told Fantino. "If you don't mind, I'll bring her with me."

Fantino and his wife met Rescorla and Susan at the airport. On the ride to Wayne, Illinois, the horse-country suburb where the Fantinos lived, Rick and Susan sat in the backseat. Fantino could see them in the rearview mirror, kissing. "We're going to have to put you two in a separate wing," he joked, "so you don't keep us awake at night." Susan made sure Rick took his medicine. Fantino thought Rescorla was already looking much better than the previous time he'd seen him. He'd lost some weight and positively radiated happiness. Fantino was thrilled that he had met someone mature, who so obviously admired him. He noticed that Rick and Susan held hands constantly.

★

THE WEEKEND SUSAN was in Chicago, her old friend Anne Robinson happened to call. Susan's daughter Bianca answered the phone.

"She's in Chicago with Rick," Bianca said.

"Rick? Who's Rick?" Anne asked.

"Oh, I wasn't supposed to tell you," she said.

Anne was worried. She didn't want to see Susan hurt again. But when Susan called, she said, "I met him, and I love him. We love each other. It was instant."

"Are you really happy?" Anne asked.

"Yes," Susan said. "I have truly met my soul mate."

Hill, too, decided he had to take Susan seriously. Not only did Rescorla talk about her constantly, but Hill noticed that despite Rescorla's prediction, the golden retriever remained on the scene. Rick mentioned that he had taken to walking the dog himself. He began referring to Buddy by name. When Buddy developed a tumor on his back, Hill thought the dog could have been one of Rescorla's children, the way Rescorla worried over his prognosis.

Finally Hill said, "Christ, Rescorla. This looks serious. This isn't just some roll in the hay."

"I think I met the woman of my life," Rescorla replied.

"Get off my ass," Hill said. "You sound like some sophomore in high school."

In September, Hill decided he'd better check out the situation in person. He was driving up to the national side-by-side shotgun competition in Rhode Island, hosted by the Society of Edwardian Gunners, and en route, he and Patricia stopped off to see Rescorla. Susan fixed an elegant dinner and later smoked a cigar. Hill was impressed by Susan and how crazy she was about Rescorla. The relationship was indeed serious. He'd seen his old friend with many women over the years, but he'd never behaved like this, certainly not with his first wife. Hill also recognized that Susan came from a wealthy background and was from a higher social class than he and Rescorla were. In a way, he wasn't surprised. Rescorla had always gravitated toward the finer things in life, whether it was the finest bowie knife, good brandy, or beautiful women. Still, Hill could tell that Susan was madly in love with Rescorla and he with her. They couldn't keep their hands off each other. Having been married so long himself, Hill had trouble understanding this in a fifty-nine-year-old man, but there was no denying it.

After they left, Patricia said, "It's a shame he didn't meet her thirty years earlier."

Rescorla and Susan had kept up their house hunting, and one day in October a Realtor took them to a town-house development in Morristown called Windmill Pond. The Realtor took them up the walk, then opened the front door. The house was empty. Susan could see straight through to the rear, where huge windows and sliding glass doors opened onto a terrace and a view of a pond and waterfall. She turned to Rick, her face aglow. "This is it!" she said.

"You're right. We're buying it," he said. They returned to the Realtor's office that afternoon, made a bid, which was accepted, and left a deposit.

Susan oversaw a renovation of the town house. The floors were stripped and stained, everything was painted, the carpeting and appliances were replaced, draperies and slipcovers made. The attic was lined with shelves for Rescorla's collection of books: his works on Cornish history, literature, philosophy, and the American Indian, as well as his language books, tapes, and dictionaries. Rescorla had been studying Zen Buddhism and meditation, and he urged Susan to simplify her life. She got rid of most of the antiques and furniture she'd inherited from her mother, keeping only a few favorite pieces and paintings.

One afternoon, as she was going through her things, she came upon the metal box in which she had placed the photograph of Enrique, the Portuguese count. In the photograph, of course, he'd never aged and was as handsome as ever. Susan thought back to that romantic interlude so many years earlier. Over all these years, three children, and two marriages and divorces, she had never been able to part with the photograph and the youthful dreams that went with it. Now, finally, she put the box and its contents into the trash.

Rick and Susan moved into their new home on December 5, 1998.

Susan took the week off from work to unpack and organize. Rick told her to take her time. "Don't think you have to do everything at once," he said. "You don't have to kill yourself." But she couldn't wait to get settled. While unpacking, she came across a shadow box filled with Rick's military decorations—the Silver Star, the Bronze Star with oak-leaf cluster, several Bronze Stars, a Purple Heart, and the Vietnamese Cross of Gallantry. Susan mounted the shadow box on the wall of the den.

Susan also came across photographs of Rick in uniform at age twenty-five, with army buddies, with Vietnamese officials. He looked so young, thin, and wiry, with his thick hair cut in a military buzz. But he had the big smile she'd recognize anywhere. There was Dan Hill, too, just as thin, with his head shaved and his ears sticking out. She wondered about those years. Despite all their conversation, Rick had said almost nothing about Vietnam. Busy being a wife and raising three daughters, Susan had paid scant attention to the war while it was going on. Now she wished she had.

When Rescorla got home that evening, Susan showed him the shadow box in the den. He stared at it momentarily, then tersely told her to remove it. "I don't want any of this stuff out," he said. He threw away most of the photographs and put the rest in a closet.

In three days, Susan was finished. She lit the candles and prepared dinner. She put Barry White and Andrea Bocelli on the stereo. When Rick came home, he was amazed that she had finished so quickly and everything looked so lovely. He told her he finally felt he had a home, and he was proud of her.

Rick and Susan's life settled into a comfortable routine. Every weekday morning, Rescorla rose early and showered. He was always singing in the shower—a Cornish ballad or military song, or something from a movie they'd just seen. Susan had coffee and breakfast waiting for him, made sure he took his medications, and then he drove to the Morristown station and caught the 6:00 A.M. train. He was at his desk in the World Trade Center by 7:30 A.M. and invariably spoke to Susan at 8:15, after he had checked to make sure all of his security staff were at their posts. Sometimes he was so buoyant after their calls that he broke into song. Most days at around 2:00 P.M., he called Fred McBee. At 3:30 or so, he called Dan Hill. Hill also wrote copious letters; Susan was impressed by the thirty-page handwritten missives that arrived each month. In the late afternoon, Rescorla caught the six o'clock train and was usually home by seven-fifteen. Susan and Buddy would be waiting at the door.

The pond behind their new town house was a constant source of inspiration and renewal. It was lined with cattails, wild iris, and meadow grasses and attracted waterfowl and migrating birds. Together, Rick and Susan kept a nature log of life on the pond, recording the births of geese and ducks. Encouraged by Susan, Rescorla illustrated the log with sketches of the wildlife, his first attempts at drawing. Though hardly professional, they were charming and evocative, and he was delighted by the success of his efforts. Later, he bought paints and a folding easel. As soon as he retired, he told Susan, they would take up painting together.

They attended all the plays at the Shakespeare festival at Drew University, and every Friday night they ate at their favorite Italian restaurant. Rescorla befriended a waiter there, who was from Iran, and mentioned that his best friend, Dan Hill, was also a Muslim. The restaurant employed a pianist who played "To Each His Own," one of their favorite songs, whenever Rick and Susan walked in. Since the pianist was blind, it seemed to be magic that he knew it was they, until they learned the waiter was discreetly tipping him to their arrival.

Rick sometimes accompanied Susan to St. Peter's Episcopal Church, where, as he put it, he studied the architecture and read the hymnal. He, in turn, introduced Susan to Zen meditation, and sometimes they meditated together. While not a practicing Buddhist, he often quoted the Buddha and Buddhist writings, such as *The Tibetan Book of Living and Dying*. They also began attending yoga classes. Susan noticed that Rick stopped carrying the knife in his cowboy boot.

Rescorla thanked Susan constantly for bringing into his life the peace and tranquillity he had longed for. Susan had always prayed on a daily basis, asking for the strength to get through her marriages, to care for her mother, to educate her children. She had never prayed explicitly to meet the right man. It had seemed too selfish. But now she prayed every day to thank God she had met Rick.

Rescorla loved to drive with Susan on weekends in his green Lincoln, and he had stocked the car with his favorite tapes. Rescorla often sang along with the lyrics. One of his favorite performers was Garth Brooks, and one day Rescorla was singing along to "The Dance."

"Listen to the words," he told Susan.

"For a moment all the world was right. How could I have known that you'd ever say good-bye?"

Another time they were driving in silence while Rick held Susan's hand. He seemed thoughtful, then said he'd composed a poem for her. "You'll remember me in the petal of a flower, in the leaf of a tree, and in the ripple of the water," he recited.

"You're making me sad," Susan said. "Why would you say that? You'll remember me, too."

But he insisted: "I don't want you to ever forget that we'll be together forever."

As their relationship deepened, Susan naturally thought from time to time about marriage, but she never brought up the subject. She didn't want Rick to feel any pressure, and in any event, it didn't seem as important as it had when she was younger. She was trying to live in the present and enjoy it, and Rick's comments and poetry made it clear that they had already forged a lifetime commitment. But one day at a crafts fair in Morristown, they were admiring a display of rings. "Why don't you pick one out?" he suggested. Susan felt a little thrill of anticipation. He'd bought her jewelry before, but not a ring. She sensed this was significant. She looked more closely at the display and tried several on, but none seemed quite right. Once the subject of a ring was broached, they both threw themselves into a search for the perfect ring, stopping at jewelry stores wherever they traveled. Finally, one day when they were at a jewelry store in Millburn, New Jersey, Rescorla exclaimed, "That's the one!" It had a wide gold band, with thirty small cathedral-cut diamonds, a total of three carats. It sparkled brilliantly.

Susan put the ring on her finger. It looked beautiful. Then she looked up and said, "You've never asked me to marry you."

Rescorla seemed surprised. "Will you?" he asked.

Rescorla may have overlooked the proposal, but he had given considerable thought to the wedding itself. He wanted Dan Hill as his best man, as he had been at his first wedding, and he wanted to be married in St. Augustine, where Hill lived. He wanted the ceremony to be near the ocean, to remind him of his childhood home in Cornwall and his seafaring Celtic roots. Hill had found the perfect spot: a giant old oak tree that stood on a sweeping lawn just outside the Castillo de San Marcos, a fortress built by the Spanish in the seventeenth century and a national historic site. The fortress appealed to Rescorla's love of history, and the oak, the principal sacred tree of the Druids, symbolizes the human soul in Celtic lore.

Rick Rescorla and Susan Greer were married on February 20, 1999. The bride wore a dark brown Versace suit that the groom had chosen for her. She carried a single calla lily. He wore a dark pin-striped suit, white shirt, and gold tie. Hill asked a friend of his, a local judge who was a retired brigadier general, to preside at the brief ceremony. Fred McBee and his wife drove up from their home in South Florida, but otherwise there were no guests. They pointedly excluded their children from prior marriages; this was for them alone, not their families, and they didn't mind being selfish about it. After the ceremony, Dan and Patricia hosted a reception for the newlyweds at a French restaurant in St. Augustine.

In his toast, Hill called the marriage of Rick and Susan "a union of perfection." Then he presented Susan with his wedding gift to her, one of his most prized possessions: the nickel-plated .32 Smith & Wesson revolver that Juju had given him.

Susan didn't quite know what to make of it and handled the weapon somewhat gingerly. Hill gave her an explanatory letter with the gun:

"This particular weapon was owned by one Judith Jones, Madame [*sic*] of the finest house of ill repute on 12th Street in Chicago during the 30s and 40s. As a special bonus she would take me out into the alley behind her establishment and let me shoot this pistol, which went unnoticed along with the other gunfire on Saturday nights along 12th Street." After a detailed and graphic description of Juju's career, Hill concluded, "It is a real lady's weapon with a lady's look and style and a colorful history. It protected Miss Judith for decades and will, I am certain, do the same for you.

"With deepest regards and respect . . .

"Dan."

★

SUSAN'S COWORKERS at the bank had sent a beautiful flower arrangement, which Susan carefully dried and preserved. Soon after the ceremony, Susan announced that she was retiring. Though she was responding well to the holistic treatments and yoga and Rick massaged her back nearly every night, sitting at a desk all day seemed to aggravate her lower back pain. She and Rick had been talking about retiring together anyway, and now that they were married, the time seemed right. The bank held a farewell luncheon for her, and her boss said she could return to work anytime she felt like it.

Susan was eager for Rick to retire as well, so they could spend more time together, he pursuing the writing career he talked so much about, Susan helping with the research and typing. The den in their new town house would be perfect for their work together. And they'd have much more time for their other hobbies and for travel. Best of all, Rick could give up the commute to the World Trade Center, which took several hours out of his life each weekday. Rescorla had thought Morgan Stanley might offer him a buyout at the end of the year, but nothing had materialized.

Without such a package, Rescorla worried about having enough money for retirement. He was still making support payments to his ex-wife, and Kim, his daughter, was planning on attending law school. Trevor hadn't finished college and might need financial help if, as Rescorla hoped, he eventually returned. His Morgan Stanley stock was doing well, but he felt he didn't have enough of it. Hill, too, urged Rescorla to retire, arguing that he could make ends meet, but Rick resisted.

On one of Hill's visits to New Jersey, they were riding in Rescorla's car when he confided that despite the fact that he was a vice president at one of the biggest investment banks, he didn't make that much money. "I have a hard time saving a dime," he told Hill. "There's no money in security, not like at the top." He told Hill that the chief executive at Morgan Stanley had made more than $10 million the previous year, and some investment bankers were making even more.

"No, you're bullshitting me," Hill said.

"Their houses alone cost six million," Rescorla continued. "As good at construction as you are, if you had to be in Vietnam, you should have been there with Morrison Knudson. You would have made more in one year than you made in your whole army career." (Morrison Knudson, the large American construction company based in Boise, Idaho, fulfilled major government construction contracts during the Vietnam War.)

They were driving through the exclusive suburb of Bernardsville, and Hill spotted a large English Tudor house for sale. "I'd like that place," Hill said.

"Well, that's six million."

"Shit, Rick," Hill replied. "If I had six million I'd put it in the bank, live off the interest, and travel the world."

In May, Rick and Susan took a delayed honeymoon to his boyhood home of Hayle. He'd told Susan early in their relationship how his grandparents had raised him as their own child and how he'd thought his mother was his sister. Susan hadn't been the least bit concerned. "That's a beautiful love story," she told him, pointing out that the family had gone to such lengths in order to keep him as their child, and no one in the village had ever told him otherwise. "They must have loved you very much." Still, Rescorla and his mother had never had a frank discussion about his birth.

When they drove into town, Rescorla took her to the small stone cottage where his mother now lived alone. Little in Hayle had changed. The cottage had a view of the mill pond. His mother had never been on an airplane and never learned to drive. But behind the house was a new stone garage Rescorla had had built for her, and on the roof was a Celtic cross. His mother had told him she didn't need or want a garage, but he had insisted it would enhance the value of the property.

Annie Rescorla answered the door and gestured for them to come inside. At age eighty, she was a small woman, at least as short as Susan, with short curly hair, and she wore slacks and a blouse. There were no hugs or kisses. She seemed shy and reserved. She looked at them briefly, then said, "Okay, me 'andsome."

Rick introduced Susan. "Sis, she waits on me hand and foot, foot and hand."

Throughout the visit, Rick's mother took pains to see that Susan was comfortable, her tea hot. She seemed unimpressed with her son's career on Wall Street, a world she knew nothing about, and reminded him not to put on airs. "Oh, the 'how great I am,' " she said, rolling her eyes, when he said anything that could be interpreted as boastful.

The next day, Rescorla's schoolmate Mervyn Sullivan and his wife, Jan, came over, entering through the back door. They found Annie, Rick, and Susan sitting in the front parlor. Over the years, Rescorla had never said much about women to Sullivan, who, like most people in Hayle, was naturally reticent about such things. So Sullivan was surprised to learn of his marriage and curious to meet Susan. Since retiring as a meter reader for the electricity board, Sullivan had taken up painting full-time, and he unveiled an abstract landscape of the river Hayle at low tide that he'd painted for them as a wedding gift. Susan exclaimed with delight over the painting.

When Sullivan told him how much he liked Susan, Rescorla replied, "This is the best thing that ever happened to me." Despite his cancer, he told Sullivan that he was feeling better than he had in years. "No one's got me yet," he said, referring to his many brushes with death, "and this cancer is not going to get me."

Annie Rescorla stayed behind when they later left for the Cornish Arms, the pub owned by Rescorla's cousin John Daniels. "Tammy!" someone called out as Rick and Susan entered holding hands. Sullivan was delighted by the transformation in Rescorla. He'd never seen him like this before. Growing up, they'd always been in all-boys schools, and then he'd moved away. Now he seemed like a teenager in love, eager to show Susan off. There were more cries of "Tammy!" and everyone raised their glasses.

Every visit from Rescorla was an occasion in the small town. Residents had a vague idea that Rescorla had been decorated for heroism in Vietnam, but he never talked about it. It was more that Rescorla cherished his Cornish heritage, that it meant so much to him, even though he'd gone off and become a success in America, earning a law degree and working for a wealthy investment bank. In some ways, Rescorla seemed more Cornish than his friends who had stayed in Hayle. He knew all the old Cornish songs and the local history. He would invite everyone to the pub, throw open the bar, and have everyone singing. A few years earlier, he had arrived at the pub and called out, "It's drinks for everybody on Rick Rescorla." A young man wearing a knapsack started to leave, but Rescorla grabbed him by the collar.

"I really can't stay," he'd protested, but then he had. Just as in the old days, no one could say no to Rescorla.

Rescorla never seemed to forget anyone in the village. Before leaving one year, Rescorla had asked if there was anything he could do for an old friend, John Couch. Couch thought about it, then said that one thing he'd always wanted was an American silver dollar. A year later, Rescorla brought him one. It wasn't that the silver dollar was so valuable, but that "Tammy" had remembered him that made such an impression.

Rescorla also made a point of visiting old friends, some of them now confined to nursing homes. One evening Susan stayed behind with Jan Sullivan while Rick and Mervyn went to the Bonaer nursing home to call on Stanley Sullivan (no relation to Mervyn), who was now in his eighties and blind. Sullivan loved the old British military songs and Cornish folk songs as much as Rescorla. That year, Rescorla sat on the bed with his arm around Stanley, and together they sang "Men of Harlech," "Going up Camborne Hill," and "Trelawny." Rescorla waited until the announcement that visiting hours were over to sing their favorite, "The White Rose."

"The first time I met you, my darling, / Your face was as red as the rose . . ."

Stanley's singing faltered as tears streamed down his face. Rescorla continued alone: "But now your dear face has grown paler, / As pale as the lily white rose."

During the next few days, Rick and Susan toured Cornish villages, staying in seaside hotels, stopping in at practically every historic church. Though no longer a churchgoer himself, Rescorla loved the spiritual aura of such places. Rescorla filled Susan in on the history of the area. They traveled to the coast of Devon and stayed at bed-and-breakfasts along the sea before returning to Hayle and drinks at his cousin's pub.

A year later, in May 2000, they returned. They had planned to visit Rick's mother every spring and even briefly considered moving there to be near her. Susan had told Rick she would follow him anywhere, but they felt they needed to be near their children and friends in America. About a month before they left, Rick suddenly said, "When we get there, I'd like to renew our wedding vows." Susan was surprised, since they'd been married only just over a year. "What a wonderful idea," she said. "I love it."

In England, they spent a few days at a romantic cottage in Ludlow, a village near Wales, then went to Hayle. The morning they arrived, Susan got out at the cottage while Rick maneuvered the rental car through the narrow driveway by the house. Annie Rescorla watched from the window, then called to Susan, "He's going to snap that mirror off!" The outside rearview mirror was precariously close to the house, and moments later, it scraped the wall and broke off. "I told you so," she said as soon as Rick was out of the car.

Susan had learned that that was Annie's way. She asked her to accompany them to the renewal of their vows, but Annie didn't want to travel in a motorcar. "Oh no, you go on," she said. They drove along the coast to St. Uny Lelant Church, a particular favorite of Rescorla's, a Norman church completed in 1424, perched on a cliff above the sea. When they arrived, the church and coastline were shrouded in mist. Next to the church stood an ancient hawthorn tree, its branches swept inland by the constant offshore winds. Rescorla's great-grandparents were buried there. He and Susan searched but weren't able to locate their names on the wind- and rain-worn headstones. Still, Rescorla said he felt rooted to that location.

Some women were cleaning inside the church, so Susan removed her rain hat and she and Rick stood under the hawthorn tree, a symbol of everlasting life in Celtic lore. They held hands, and Rick began to recite from memory something he'd composed for the occasion:

"We, Rick and Susan Rescorla, husband and wife, lovers and companions, travelers from across the sea, have been blown by a sacred wind to this old Norman church. Standing in this holy garden, we affirm our wedding vows in the presence of our Celtic ancestors who sleep in peace in the graveyard on the sand dunes nearby.

"We perform this ceremony with all humility, knowing that we do not stand an inch higher than the lowliest of God's creatures. As we confirm our love for each other, we also unite two divine rivers of thought: the faith in the great Creator is bonded to the belief in the natural harmony of the spheres.

"May our love be renewed each day, shining as bright as the beautiful stained-glass windows of this church. . . ."

Susan could see tears in Rick's eyes, and then she began to weep. He wiped his eyes and struggled to continue.

"At this moment we feel the wonder of nature, a sense of unity with the earth, the sky, the sea, the lichen-covered rocks. Songbirds sit on the branches above us. We hear the music of a robin calling for her mate.

"The blossoming hawthorn tree nearby reminds us of a natural and orderly course of time. We are aware that our time on earth is brief: the footprints we make in the sandy soil will one day be washed away by an eternal tide. Our souls will then go forth on an everlasting journey.

"As the mist rises above the river, we hold hands and count our blessings. We ask the pink-and-white wildflowers that surround us, and every leaf of grass, to witness our vows and celebrate our happiness.

"We give ourselves to each other for all eternity, for better or worse, in sickness or in health, and in this instant seek the blessing of a merciful God."

When he was finished, they said nothing. Susan wiped the tears from her eyes and gazed at the ancient building in the mist. She felt a sense of love, peace, and security that she'd never known.

When they returned to the cottage in Hayle, Rescorla's mother asked Susan how it had gone. Susan began to describe the experience but had to stop. Overcome by the beauty and emotion of the ceremony and of Rick's words, she again began to cry. Rick's mother came to her and wrapped her arms around her. "I understand," she said as Susan sobbed. "I understand."

WE WERE SOLDIERS

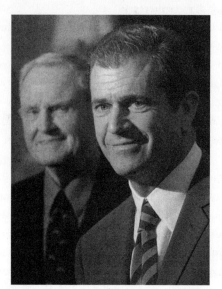

Mel Gibson with Lieutenant General Hal Moore (ret.), whom the star portrayed in *We Were Soldiers.* Some of Gibson's lines were actually Rescorla's.
(Reuters NewMedia Inc. / Corbis)

AROUND THANKSGIVING IN 1999, Dan Hill experienced some chest pains and numbness on his left side and went to the doctor. "I feel like I'm having a series of small heart attacks," he said, "and a big one is on the way." The doctor did some tests and told him he had indigestion. Then, on the morning of December 1, he was getting ready to come downstairs when he felt a sudden intense pain, as though someone had driven a bayonet through his chest. He collapsed to his knees. He called Patricia and told her to drive him to the hospital. She was too panicked to drive. "Call an ambulance," he said, and she dialed 911.

By the time the ambulance arrived and the paramedics started their procedures, precious time had been lost. "I'm having a heart attack!" he yelled. "Get me in that ambulance and drive!"

At the hospital, a shot of tPA, an anticoagulant, broke up the clot, but not before Hill had permanently lost the use of 60 percent of his heart muscle. He was moved into the cardiac emergency area and scheduled for surgery to receive some stents in his constricted blood vessels.

As soon as Patricia was allowed to visit him, he asked her to pick up the phone and dial Rick's number. "I just had a heart attack," he said when Rescorla answered.

"Oh, shit. Do I need to come down?"

"No," Hill said. He said he was about to have surgery. "If I come out of it, I'll call you. If not, come for the funeral," he said.

The next day, he called to report that he had survived. "You might not beat me to the barn after all," he told Rescorla. "I could drop at any time. Don't be shocked."

Having faced death so many times, having buried his son, Hill felt odd, really, to be facing it again, so much later in life. He and Rescorla had always described death as the last great adventure. After all, it was a mystery. Despite firsthand accounts of near-death experiences, of descriptions of a bright light glowing at the end of a tunnel, no one really knew what lay on the other side. Hill was in no hurry to get there, but he was also curious. He wanted to ask Adam: What was it like in the Garden of Eden? Or Moses: Did God make those tablets, or did you have a hammer and chisel? And as a Muslim, of course, he wanted to talk to Mohammed and ask if the angel Gabriel had really given him the Koran. He was just enough of a religious skeptic to wonder. Hill mentioned all this to Rescorla, who told him not to be too impatient. "It's not going to be long before we find out," Rescorla cautioned.

"Whoever goes first," Hill said, "can do the reconnaissance. Then he can come back and help the other one across."

The sense that he might not have much longer to live lent a new urgency to Hill's plan to capture Osama bin Laden. About a year after he had broached the subject of bin Laden with FBI agent Morris, Hill got a phone call from another agent named Ellen Glasser in the Jacksonville, Florida, office. "I've just read your file," she said, "and I'm interested." She suggested they meet in person and asked if she could meet Nader Zori, as well. Hill said that was fine, but he would ask Nader to join them at his house to avoid the risk of a fellow Muslim seeing Nader in public with a woman.

Glasser, an attractive woman with dark hair, arrived in the late spring of 2000, accompanied by her husband, Donald J. Glasser, a tall, ex–navy SEAL who also worked for the Bureau in the Jacksonville office. Hill assumed his function was to act as a kind of bodyguard. He didn't participate much in the discussion, but he certainly seemed interested in the details.

The four sat at Hill's kitchen table, and Hill outlined his and Nader's plan, which had progressed since he'd last discussed it with Agent Morris. Nader stressed that he wasn't doing this for the money. "The United States helped me and I want to help the United States," he said. Nader had just returned from a visit to Pakistan and had lined up a group of former Mujahedeen fighters willing to assist them. He and Hill had to work through individual couriers; the Taliban had bugged the phone lines and routinely opened mail. But the plan, in essence, was simple.

Their contacts in Afghanistan reported that bin Laden traveled frequently between meetings with Mullah Omar and other high-ranking Taliban officials in the southern city of Kandahar, and Kabul, the capital, near Farmihedda, where bin Laden kept his headquarters. He traveled with only light security: a convoy of three vehicles, bin Laden in the middle with eight armed guards—four in the front and four in the rear. The mountainous terrain provided several ambush sites. Their armed force would attack the convoy, kill the guards, and kill bin Laden.

She seemed a bit taken aback. "Oh," she said, "we don't do things like that."

"I know you don't," Hill said. "That's why we'll do it. You don't have to."

"Our idea was that you'd capture him, bring him back," she said.

"How would we do that?" Hill asked, incredulous. "What would we do with the bodyguards? How would we get him out alive?"

She seemed to ponder that. "How would you prove you'd killed bin Laden?" she asked.

Hill said they'd pack the head and hands in an iced cooler. But here was where they needed U.S. military assistance. A C-130 aircraft equipped with a skyhook would fly over their position, hook the cooler, and reel it into the cargo bay. There was no way that Hill and his Afghan partners could get it out over land. Once the United States had bin Laden's remains, they could verify his identity. The United States could surely obtain a DNA sample from one of bin Laden's many relatives.

Glasser looked skeptical. "Money's tight," she said, but Hill said they'd finance the entire operation except for the aircraft, as long as they knew that they'd get the $15 million bounty if they delivered him.

"How do we know you're telling the truth?" she asked. "How do we know you have the contacts in Afghanistan?"

Hill said they could bring a few of the key participants to the United States if she'd arrange for tourist visas. And he and Nader offered to take Pentathol and submit to questioning. Whatever it took, they were willing to do it.

Hill thought they were making some progress. Glasser's husband looked positively enthusiastic, though she still looked somewhat dubious. "Well," she said, "this would all have to be approved." She promised to refer his proposal to the counterterrorism center at FBI headquarters in Washington. But before she and her husband left, Hill made an impassioned plea. He pointed out that nuclear weapons had allegedly disappeared from the former Soviet arsenal in Uzbekistan and that all evidence suggested bin Laden was steadily growing more powerful and sophisticated. "Someone has got to take him out," Hill said. He quoted John F. Kennedy: "One man can make a difference, and every man should try."

*

IN FEBRUARY 2001, Rescorla finished a phone conversation with his mother in Hayle and came to Susan with tears in his eyes. "I can't get through to her," he said. "I say things and she doesn't even answer." Ever since the visit when he and Susan had renewed their vows, Mervyn Sullivan had reported that Annie Rescorla's health seemed to be declining; she was leaving the cottage less and less, her appetite was weak, and she seemed to be losing some of her mental agility. Perhaps it was the onset of senility. This worried Rescorla, because she'd never directly acknowledged being his mother. They had never discussed the subject, and he still called her Sis.

Susan suggested he visit her in person. She remembered her own mother's death and how important it had been that she was there and had been able to speak openly with her. "Don't hold anything back," she urged him. "Tell her your feelings, that you love her."

Rescorla left immediately for England and went from London to Hayle by train. He spent that evening with his mother at the cottage, but, as in the past, he found it impossible to broach the subject of his birth. Long after they went to bed, he was tossing and turning, and then he heard his mother in the kitchen. He got up and found her making a pot of tea. There, in the middle of the night, he told her he was grateful that she had kept him, and that he loved her. And he asked about his father. "What was he like?"

His mother smiled enigmatically. "He was a big one, wasn't he?" Rescorla waited, but that was all she said. He didn't know if she was simply evading the subject, as she had for so long, or if that was all she remembered, given her weakening health. In any event, he had tried.

232

He had been open with her, and he hadn't held back. It was all he could do.

The next day, Rescorla went for a walk along the beach with Sullivan and his dog. Rescorla was in high spirits, as if the talk with his mother had lifted a burden from his shoulders. He charged up the side of a large dune. "Once more unto the breach, dear friends, once more; / Or close the wall up with our English dead," he shouted, quoting from Shakespeare's *Henry V.* Later, on the cliffs overlooking the sea, he paid tribute to Susan, quoting T. E. Lawrence (Lawrence of Arabia), whom Rescorla much admired: "I loved you so, so I drew these tides of men into my hands and wrote my will across the sky in stars."

Rescorla stayed for ten days, and then Sullivan drove him to the station at Penzance to catch the 5:30 A.M. train to London. They sat together in the carriage, reminiscing that they had done the same as schoolboys fifty years earlier. Then the train whistle blew, signaling the train's departure. Sullivan stepped onto the platform and shook Rescorla's hand through the open window. He watched as the train began to pull out of the station. Rescorla made a fist, thrust it through the window, and shouted, *"Kernow bys vykken!"*—"Cornwall forever!"

★

BACK IN NEW JERSEY, Rescorla found himself brooding over the Officer Candidate School Hall of Fame, which is housed in Weigle Hall at Fort Benning. Hill and Rescorla had spent hours there as officer candidates, looking at the portraits of distinguished recipients, such as former Senator Robert Dole, Secretary of Defense Casper Weinberger, and Michael Healey, known to his men as "Iron Mike," a Congressional Medal of Honor winner for heroism in Korea. Healey had once invited Hill and Rescorla to the officers club for drinks and afterward taken them home for breakfast. They had considered the Hall of Fame an almost sacred shrine to honor, integrity, and heroism, and to gain admission was the Holy Grail of a military career. To be considered, army officers had to have retired with the rank of colonel, have rendered distinguished service in combat, or have received the Congressional Medal of Honor. Ever since Rescorla reached the rank of colonel in the reserves, Hill had been badgering Rescorla to let him submit an application on his behalf. "Let me put you in," Hill had suggested. "It inspires the younger guys, and it's a part of American history. Think of what it might mean to your kids. Your picture would be hanging up there with Iron Mike." When Rick mentioned the idea to Susan, she agreed with Hill that such an honor was important.

But Rescorla resisted the idea. He found distasteful the campaigns for military honors that persisted decades after the battles were over. He didn't care about any more military honors for himself, or for any other survivors, for that matter. As he told Susan repeatedly, "The real heroes are dead."

Even though Rescorla had renewed his friendships with some of the men who served with him in Vietnam, he avoided discussing their combat experiences. Sometimes other veterans tracked him down and phoned or e-mailed him. Susan didn't know what they talked about, but Rick always had trouble sleeping afterward, tossing and turning during the night. He had their phone number and e-mail address changed to make it more difficult for army colleagues to reach him. It wasn't that he didn't care, he told Susan, but that he didn't want to live in the past.

Still, in the fall of 2000, Rescorla had cautiously agreed to visit West Point, where Hal Moore was speaking to cadets about his book. Rescorla had never visited the historic military academy that he'd heard so much about, the place where, he often wryly noted, Generals George Patton and George Custer had graduated last in their class. He had sometimes resented the elite education and advantages West Point conferred on its graduates, opportunities he had never had, yet at the same time he was in awe of its place in military history and the uncompromising military values it stood for.

Rick and Susan toured the campus, then had dinner with Moore, faculty members, and some senior cadets in a beautiful private dining room overlooking the parade ground and the Hudson River. At the speech afterward, Moore introduced Rescorla and had him come to the stage. There was a murmur of surprise and recognition from the audience and then a huge round of applause. Afterward, cadets swarmed around him, asking him to autograph copies of their books. Rescorla seemed startled by the attention and recognition from the cream of American youth, the army's future leaders. Susan could tell he was flattered and pleased.

Bob Bateman, an army captain and professor of history at the academy, approached him "almost as a religious supplicant," as he later wrote in a newspaper account of the occasion. Bateman asked him to sign his copy. Rescorla excused himself for a moment, then got a drink from the bar. He quickly composed a poem for the occasion:

> To: Captain Bob Bateman:
>
> ### Old Dogs and Wild Geese are Fighting
>
> Head for the Storm
> As you faced it before
> For where there is the Seventh
> There's bound to be fighting
> And where there's no fighting
> It's the Seventh no more.
>
> Best,
> Rick Rescorla,
> Hard Corps One-Six

Given his interest in movies, Rescorla was excited to learn from Dennis Deal, the lieutenant he'd fought with at Ia Drang, that *We Were Soldiers Once* was being made into a movie starring Mel Gibson, with a script by Randall Wallace, the creative team behind the Academy Award–winning *Braveheart*. However reluctant he was to call attention to his own war exploits, a movie was something else altogether, something Rescorla had dreamed about since he was a child. Rescorla eagerly scanned a Web site for the film, watching for the latest news about where it would be filmed and, especially, who was being cast. He kept watching to see who would play him. "Surely it will be someone British," he suggested to Susan. "They've got to get the accent right." As time passed, various cast members and the parts they would be playing were announced, but there was no mention of Rescorla. Still, he held out hope, even if it was obvious that his would not be a major role. "They've got to have the scene with the bugle," he told Susan, "or one of the scenes where I was singing."

But then he got a copy of the script, which he read with mounting disbelief. He read it aloud to Susan to get her reaction. The scene of Rescorla discovering the French bugle on the dying Vietnamese soldier was there all right. Yet in the script it was not Rescorla, but an otherwise unidentified "platoon leader from Wales." Wales—not Cornwall. That was adding insult to injury. The movie also depicted the incident where Rescorla and Fantino had been sweeping through the field of dead bodies when suddenly a machine gunner had opened fire on them and Rescorla had silenced the attack with a grenade. But in the script, someone else conducts the sweep and throws the grenade. Some of the lines attributed to Colonel Hal Moore in the film had actually been spoken by Rescorla. Rescorla had waited in vain to see who would play him, since he wasn't even mentioned by name in the script. He had simply been eliminated from the battle of Ia Drang, along with all of his platoon and the entire Second Battalion.

Susan could tell he was extremely upset. He talked about the script all the time. Then he learned that that year's Ia Drang reunion, to be held in Washington, D.C., in November, was going to feature a preview of the film, with Randall Wallace and some of the cast members, maybe even Mel Gibson, as the featured guests. Rescorla was indignant. "I'm not going," he told Susan. He agonized over what to say, whether to make some kind of protest.

"Say nothing," Susan advised. "Silence is your best statement."

Hill, too, could tell that Rescorla was hurt and upset, even though he tried to minimize his disappointment. "What did you expect?" Hill asked. He was skeptical of anything Hollywood turned out. "They're not going to pay Mel Gibson twenty million to have him sit next to an anthill."

"I guess you're right," Rescorla conceded. "This isn't a documentary. It's entertainment."

Rescorla expressed similar feelings in an e-mail to his old friend Jim Kelly, the fellow lieutenant he'd bested at beer walking at An Khe:

"Jim, me boy.

"Hope all is well with you. This is a bootleg copy of the script. Do not say where you got it. As you can see, every effort has been made to cut out the second battalion entirely.

"Check out the dialogue. Real corny. Reminded me of some bad Westerns. Laughable. I especially liked the part where Mel Gibson says, 'The NVA are trying to kill us all.' What about Colonel Ahn saying at the end, about Moore, 'He was brilliant.' Ah, Hollywood. It looks like a five-hanky movie, with childish dialogue, and the action bears no resemblance to the real thing.

"It remains to be seen if Gibson and company can redeem this script. Randall Wallace is going to conduct a show and tell in November. I am sure it will be a good dog and pony show, with hats and T-shirts, photos, etc. Jim, do not ask me if I am going to attend.

"Here's the funny twist about truth being stranger than fiction. The Beleaguered Bastards from Benning, the 2/7 otherwise known as the Gray Ghosts (their bodies do not appear in movies), saw three times as much action as the First Battalion, Hollywood's finest, using any criteria: number of firefights, KIAs [killed in action], WIAs [wounded in action], confirmed body count, before during and after Ia Drang."

He signed his e-mail "From a fellow member of the Ghost Battalion," a reference to the Second Battalion's nickname.

Rescorla also wrote Bill Shucart, now a respected neurosurgeon in

Boston, that he wouldn't be there. "I came away from the reunions with a strange sense of unease," he said. But "I really would like to meet you under different circumstances. Now and then I recall our conversations, heating up our C-rats, musing about the human condition. Bill, another time, another place, we'll get together. Garry Owen."

Even though he claimed to have accepted the idea that the movie was just entertainment, the idea that it was rewriting history, and that for the possibly millions of people who saw it, it would be history, continued to bother him. Finally he told Hill that he was having second thoughts about the Hall of Fame. Hill jumped at the opening, saying he'd handle all the paperwork, gather the necessary testimonials and records, and submit the application. They had only a few weeks before the deadline, so Rescorla hurried to gather the materials. He was especially keen to get a photograph of himself in uniform that he'd left behind with his daughter, and when she was slow to produce it, he drove over to his ex-wife's house to get it himself. Susan helped him comb through his records. She was surprised by his change of heart, but all he said was that he thought it would be good for his children to see their father in the Hall of Fame.

On March 1, Hill received a letter from Fort Benning, mistakenly mailed to him, which announced that Rescorla had been accepted for induction into the Hall of Fame. Hill called him, and he could tell how pleased Rescorla was. He forwarded the letter, which congratulated him and explained that the Hall of Fame is "the single highest honor bestowed upon an OCS graduate," intended to honor those who "have left an indelible mark on the Army" through "exceptional leadership and dedication to public service."

The induction ceremony was scheduled for April 5, 2001, at Fort Benning, and as the date neared, Susan found herself looking forward to the trip with mounting excitement. She felt she knew so little about his military experience, but she had seen at West Point the awe with which young soldiers viewed her husband. Though she had read *We Were Soldiers Once,* his trip might help her fill in the gaps. Yet when she mentioned this to Rick, she sensed that he didn't share her enthusiasm. Finally he said, "I hope you don't mind, but I think I'd rather go to the ceremony alone." He mentioned Hill's recent heart attack and stroke and said he was worried about his old friend's health. "This may be the last time Dan and I will be together."

Susan gave the matter some thought and decided she could see his point. Dan was his lifelong friend, and they needed this time to be together.

But then Hill's wife, Patricia, called. "What are you going to wear?" she asked Susan.

"I'm not invited," Susan said. Patricia said that both she and her daughter would be accompanying Dan, and this bothered Susan.

"This is ridiculous," Susan said to Rick as soon as she got off the phone. "Dan is bringing his wife and daughter and I'm not going?"

"I didn't know you really wanted to go," he replied, somewhat disingenuously, she thought.

"Of course I want to go," she said.

He thought about it briefly and then agreed. "Okay, you're going to go. That's the end of it."

The next day, in his afternoon call to Hill, Rescorla mentioned that Susan wanted to come, and Hill conceded that Patricia felt the same way. "We might not be able to get out of this," he said.

But Susan had been giving the matter some further thought. Rick's first reaction had been that he didn't want her to go, and perhaps she should honor that. She strongly suspected that if she didn't go, Patricia wouldn't, either. So finally she backed out. "Sweetheart, I'm not going to go. You need to be with Dan and say good-bye." Rescorla seemed relieved. Hill promised Patricia that he and Rescorla would arrange another trip that would include their wives. She understood. She'd always joked that if Dan ever left her, it would be to run off with Rescorla to some exotic place.

The day before the ceremony, Hill left early and drove to Fort Benning, arriving before Rescorla. He checked into the transit hotel on the post, and at registration, which was manned by some of the current officer candidates, he mentioned that he was there for Colonel Rescorla. "Yes, sir!" they exclaimed. Hill went straight to the base liquor store and stocked a full bar: gin and brandy for Rescorla, of course, as well as Scotch, bourbon, vodka. Since his heart attack Hill had resumed drinking, even though it violated the strictures of his Muslim faith. He'd started smoking again, too. He didn't see the point of abstaining from two of life's pleasures if he was just going to have another heart attack anyway.

Hill was back in his room, setting up the bar, when there was a knock. It was several of the young officer candidates. "Sir, we'd just like to shake your hand," they said. While he was out, they had checked his service records and had seen all the decorations and combat experience, as well as the fact that he'd been the top honor graduate in his class at Officer Candidate School. Hill was touched and pleased. "We were hoping to shake Colonel Rescorla's hand, too," they said. Some of them had brought their copies of *We Were Soldiers Once*. Hill invited them in and threw open the bar.

By the time Rescorla arrived, the party was in full swing, with Hill regaling them with stories of his own officer training, including how he'd spirited Rescorla off the base for steak and beer, then made him double-time it back to the barracks. Hill had a drink in his hand and was smoking a cigarette. Rescorla had had several drinks himself en route. Jim Kelly had insisted on picking him up at the Atlanta airport and driving him to Fort Benning. He'd put a cooler of British ale in the car as a surprise for Rick, but when Rescorla opened the cooler, Kelly realized he'd forgotten to pack an opener. "Stop right over there," Rescorla ordered, pointing to a sign along the road. Rescorla jumped out of the car, grabbed the bottles, and popped them using the metal edge of the sign. Most of the ale had been drunk by the time they arrived.

At one point, Rescorla leaned over to Hill and asked discreetly, "Should you be smoking and drinking?"

"Hell, no," Hill responded. "But I intend to live like I always lived. And who knows, I could still go out in a firefight."

"Yeah," Rescorla said. "Then you could go out in a blaze of glory."

Like Hill, Rescorla seemed pleased and touched by the candidates' interest. After two decades of feeling as though the army wanted to expunge memories of the Vietnam conflict, he was celebrating with a new generation of soldiers who actually seemed interested, even fascinated, by their accounts. Hill recounted several of Rescorla's exploits in Ia Drang and told them that "Rick was a hero of that battle," not that they needed any persuading. Rescorla was modest, insisting that Hill, too, was a hero, as was Kelly. But Rescorla remained the center of attention. That evening there was a cocktail party and dinner for the inductees, hosted by three-star General John M. LeMoyne. Hill wore his full dress uniform with medals and decorations; Rescorla and Kelly wore dark business suits. Wherever Hill and Rescorla paused, a group of ten to fifteen young officer candidates quickly gathered. Before his welcoming speech General LeMoyne came over to Rescorla and saluted him. "Candidate LeMoyne, sir," he said, and then smiled. Rescorla, he reminded him, had been his senior tactical officer when he was an officer candidate at Fort Benning.

After dinner, Rescorla, Hill, and Kelly returned to Rescorla's room, where the three downed a bottle of Maker's Mark bourbon. They talked about their time at Fort Benning, Vietnam, the years that had intervened, the strange turns that life had taken. "Time is running short," Hill said.

"Yeah," Rescorla agreed. "Who would have guessed we'd run out of time before we ran out of money?" They grew pensive, and then Rescorla broke the silence. "Christ," he said. "Look at us. Hill with a heart attack. Me with cancer. Kelly—he's tall, dumb, and ugly. We're going to die as old men, with people spoon-feeding us and changing our diapers." They nodded in agreement. "Men like us shouldn't go out like this," Rescorla said. "We're supposed to die in some desperate battle performing great deeds."

"Hear, hear," Kelly said, and they raised their glasses.

"You can't tell," Hill added. "It might happen yet."

Later, Hill and Rescorla mused about their lives. "Could we have been more than we became?" Rescorla asked. Back in Africa, sitting out under the stars, they had had such grand plans. Now Hill was working in construction, Rescorla in security, waiting to retire.

"But look at you," Hill protested. "You're a lawyer, an author, a vice president of a big financial firm."

"Yeah," Rescorla conceded. "But none of that matters very much." He looked into his drink. "In my heart, I've always been a soldier."

Rescorla was formally inducted into the Officer Candidate School Hall of Fame in a ceremony the next day. Hill noticed that Rescorla was doing his best to suck in his stomach to look thin. Afterward, there was a reception under a big tent set up near the parade ground. Then Kelly pulled up to drive Rescorla back to the airport in Atlanta.

Hill didn't want to say good-bye. He didn't know when, or if, he would see his closest friend again. Before he could say anything, Rescorla faced him and grabbed him by both of his ears. He pulled Hill close and kissed him on the forehead. "Don't die before we see each other again, Danny," he said. Then he got into the car, and Hill watched them drive away until they disappeared.

*

LATER THAT MONTH, Rick and Susan took a vacation to New Mexico. Though they'd separately traveled all over the world, neither had seen much of the United States. Rick had been fascinated with the American West and the frontier culture of rugged individualism ever since he watched the Hollywood westerns at the Palace cinema in Hayle. And increasingly, he had come to revere the culture of the Native American Indians and the unsung heroism they had displayed in the U.S. military's frontier campaigns. After the Hall of Fame ceremony, when Jim Kelly asked Rescorla to attend the dedication of a memorial to General Custer and the Seventh Cavalry, he had refused, noting that

Custer had lost the battle of Little Big Horn as well as most of his men. "If they ever establish a memorial to Sitting Bull and Two Moons, I'll go," he'd said. He was eager to experience the spiritual aspects of Indian culture, which, like Buddhism, was deeply rooted in nature. Susan had booked them into a spa and signed up for massages using warm stones.

After leaving the spa, they drove to Santa Fe, where they stayed at a small hotel, the Inn of the Governors, built in the traditional Spanish adobe style. It had a rooftop garden and a fireplace to take the chill off the evenings. They loved the art galleries and shops, and in one boutique, Rick bought Susan a silk blouse with hand-painted eagle feathers on it. Rescorla revered the eagle as a symbol of both American freedom and Native American mysticism. Then they drove to Taos. The pueblo-studded desert landscape was breathtaking, and they pictured it as it must have been before the Spanish and then the Americans arrived, with herds of buffalo and Indian tribes roaming on horseback. Rescorla could feel the old westerns come alive. In Taos, he and Susan fantasized about retiring there and living in an adobe hacienda.

Susan was pleased by the effect of the trip on Rick, because even with a regimen of yoga and meditation, he often had trouble relaxing. But one afternoon when they returned to their hotel, a barrage of urgent messages awaited them from Ihab Dana and others on Rescorla's staff. With the stock market in a continuing slump, Morgan Stanley was about to lay off 1,500 people, and it was the job of Rescorla's security staff to escort people out of the building the day they got the news they had been fired. Rescorla felt he needed to be there. He wanted to make sure that his staff treated every dismissed employee with the dignity he felt each deserved. And he wanted to personally escort some of the longtime employees from the building. Some of them had worked for the firm for twenty-five years or more. They were expected to pack their belongings and leave by the end of the day. Though this was standard practice on Wall Street, Rescorla knew how hard it would be.

They cut the trip short and flew back to New York. Susan wasn't happy about it and would have liked to stay, but she didn't complain. She knew Rick felt this was his duty and he was too responsible to ignore it. But it made her more determined that they find a way for him to retire.

Morgan Stanley announced the layoffs on April 24, and when Rescorla got home that evening, he said the experience had been almost as hard on him as it was on the employees let go. Some of them had broken down and cried as he stood beside them. Rescorla didn't understand why the firm didn't offer him a buyout package, since it was trying to reduce staff and overhead. Because of the plunging stock market, the value of his 401(k) retirement savings and his Morgan Stanley stock was declining, and he felt financial security receding ever further into the future. He should have sold his Morgan Stanley stock when Hill had told him to. Even so, he told Susan, he was going to quit at the end of the year, December 31, 2001, buyout or no buyout.

Then he would write full-time. He was percolating with ideas for screenplays and even had Susan begin some research for him. Many ideas came to him while they were driving, and Susan began keeping a tape recorder in the car so she could record them. He also talked of writing a memoir, focusing not on his military career but on life with Susan. "I want people to see that as you get older, you don't have to give up on life, even if you have cancer," he told her. "You can find peace. You can have love in your life at a time you thought it would never happen." But other than recording the ideas and jotting down some notes and outlines, he made little progress. Working full-time and commuting to Wall Street didn't leave him the time he needed for sustained concentration.

★

HILL, MEANWHILE, was pressing the FBI office in Jacksonville for a response to his plan to kill bin Laden but felt he was getting nowhere. He felt a growing sense of urgency because Nader told him his sources in Afghanistan were reporting that something big was going to happen, probably timed to coincide with the holy month of Ramadan, which would begin in October. But finally, nearly a year after their initial meeting, Agent Glasser got on the phone and told him the plan had been rejected. "Nothing can be done," she said.

Hill was upset. "This guy is not screwing around," he said of bin Laden. He mentioned Rescorla's report warning of a cargo plane attack. "It's going to strike New York, Philadelphia, or Washington, D.C.," he insisted. "Or maybe all three." And he warned that it was likely to happen around Ramadan, which was just over three months away. If their plan was going to succeed, they had to begin now.

"I'm sorry," Glasser repeated. "Nothing can be done."

Hill called Rescorla to report that the plans had been dashed and he wouldn't be able to give him the $1 million. Rescorla said he wasn't surprised. "The FBI is a bunch of incompetent duds," he said. "And don't bother going to the CIA. It's just as bad."

Hill was disappointed, but after spies Robert Hanssen and Harold Nicholson were unmasked in both agencies, he felt Rescorla's judgment was vindicated. It made him angry, but also sad, that two agencies he had once so respected had been compromised.

★

UNDER SUSAN'S GUIDANCE, Rick had adhered religiously to Brad Snyder's holistic treatments, and he felt better, had more energy, and was losing some of the weight that so embarrassed him. In July, he stopped taking the pills that made him so thirsty and threw them away, though he continued to receive the interferon shots in his stomach. He had a CAT scan that showed the cancer in his bone marrow hadn't spread and seemed to be in remission. His PSA count was stable. Susan felt that her love for him was slowly but surely pulling the cancer out of his body. His doctor was so impressed by his latest round of test results that he had his nurse call Rescorla, asking him to come in so he could interview him to determine why he was doing so well. Before meeting Susan, Rescorla thought he might have only a few years to live. Now, "I'm going to make it to seventy," he predicted confidently.

Soon after they were married, Rescorla and Susan had rewritten their wills, and Rescorla had said explicitly that in the event of his death, he wanted no memorials, no military tributes, no burial in Arlington National Cemetery. He wanted to be cremated and his ashes scattered in Hayle. But during the summer, he and Susan visited a wild-bird sanctuary in Millington, New Jersey, the Raptor Trust, located on sixteen acres of marshland, meadows, and woods adjacent to a national wildlife refuge. The goal of the sanctuary was to rescue and rehabilitate injured eagles, falcons, hawks, owls, and other raptors, then release them back into the wild. If they couldn't be cured, the sanctuary kept them in cages and cared for them for life.

Rescorla was moved by the plight of the proud birds, struggling to heal and to return to the freedom of the wild, especially the two eagles. Their names were Treader and Uno. Both had been rescued after the *Valdez* oil spill in Alaska; Uno had one eye, and it was unlikely either could fly again. And he admired the trust's guiding philosophy: "A belief that all living things are important and if, because of humans and human activities, injuries and injustices befall wild creatures, then humans have a responsibility to help heal the injuries and attempt to correct the injustices." Some of the cages had plaques memorializing donors to the trust's endowment, but the eagle cage had none. When he and Susan left, he mentioned that when he died, he wanted her to make a donation. Susan was inspired by the idea. She knew how much her husband loved the eagles. As soon as they were home, she wrote something that she planned to have engraved on a plaque for the eagle cage at the preserve:

"Just like the eagle, you have spread your wings, and soared into eternity."

A few weeks later, in mid-August, Rescorla said he wanted to visit the preserve again. He greeted the eagles Treader and Uno like old friends, encouraging them not to give up. As they were driving home, he mentioned again that he wanted her to make a donation.

"Sweetheart, I know what you want me to do," she assured him. But Susan never showed him what she had written for the plaque.

★

AS THE SUMMER DREW TO A CLOSE, Susan was busy with wedding plans for her daughter Alexandra, who was marrying an Italian living in New York. The wedding was going to be in Tuscany, and she and Rick would be staying in a beautiful castle owned by friends of the groom's family. After the wedding, Susan had mapped out a trip through Tuscany, staying at Siena, San Gimignano, and then Florence. She'd booked a car and driver so Rick could relax and enjoy the scenery. Then they planned to visit Hayle to see Rick's mother.

But Rick's cousin in Hayle called to say that his mother's health was failing rapidly and she wasn't eating. He didn't know how long she might survive. Rescorla didn't know whether to leave immediately to see his mother or whether to attend the wedding, try to enjoy the trip, and hope his mother would survive until he arrived. He knew the trip meant a lot to Susan. Adding to his worries were depositions related to the 1993 bombing of the World Trade Center. Rescorla was a key witness, and he was scheduled to testify during the first week of September.

Susan felt the stress, too. The wedding was scheduled for September 22, and she had wanted to leave the week before so they could relax and adjust to the time change. But Ihab Dana, Rick's deputy, had already reserved that week to visit his family in Lebanon and wouldn't be returning until September 11. Rick didn't feel he could leave until Dana was back, so he and Susan had tickets for a flight to Florence on September 17. Her daughters and their children were traveling on the same flight, which made both Rick and Susan nervous; if something terrible happened, the whole family would be extinguished. Susan was having her dress made for the wedding, and when they drove to New

Hope, Pennsylvania, where it was being made, she discovered it wasn't ready. Susan became visibly upset. "Calm down," Rick told her. "Give them a break. We've got another week." He was right, of course; Susan realized it wasn't like her to get so upset over something so insignificant.

Susan couldn't shake a mounting sense of tension and dread. Something just seemed to be in the air. And she could tell that all of this was weighing on Rick. He wasn't sleeping well, tossing and turning, sometimes waking her up as well. Often he got up and went downstairs. When she asked what he did during these interludes in the night, he said he read or wrote his thoughts in a notebook. He was jotting down ideas for the book he wanted to write. Sometimes, he said, he just lay awake and watched her sleep. One afternoon he e-mailed her from the office a poem he'd composed:

> *Subject: Soul mate just before dawn.*
> *Awakening in the dark*
> *When the geese are silent on the pond*
> *Your steady breathing helps me*
> *Face the daybreak with a smile.*

Susan finally decided the trip through Tuscany was too much; she suggested they attend her daughter's wedding, leaving as scheduled on September 17, then have an open return ticket via London, so Rick could leave to see his mother at any time. He seemed relieved, and Susan concluded her instinct had been correct. Rick told Ihab Dana that "I just want to stay home in bed with Susan."

14

A DAY TO BE PROUD

Rescorla directing the evacuation of Morgan Stanley's offices on September 11, 2001. Godwin Forde is on the right, Jorge Velazquez in the middle.
(Courtesy of Eileen Maher Hillock)

O N Tuesday morning, September 11, 2001, the alarm went off as usual at 4:30 A.M. Susan stirred sleepily, barely opening her eyes, as Rick rose and headed into the bathroom. Buddy was still asleep. He had developed a tumor on his back, and not only was Rick walking him frequently, he had insisted that Buddy share their bedroom. Susan heard the water in the shower and, over it, Rick's voice. He was singing one of the countless English music hall ditties he seemed to know.

Susan got out of bed, donned her robe, and looked in Rick's closet. She knew he wanted to look his best for the luncheon that day. She chose a navy pin-striped suit, a light blue shirt, and a red silk tie. She was laying the suit out on the bed when Rick emerged naked from the bathroom, his hair still uncombed and wet. "Tiptoe through the tulips," he sang, "Through the tulips, through the tulips." As he sang he danced a soft-shoe routine in his bare feet. Susan started laughing and couldn't stop. Then he did an imitation of Anthony Hopkins as a ventriloquist in the 1978 thriller *Magic,* a movie they'd watched on video the night before. "I've never felt better in my life," he said. He grabbed her and whirled her into a ballroom dance routine.

Susan walked with him to the head of the stairs, where he kissed her and said, "I love you so." She stayed behind, waiting for Buddy to awaken. She heard Rick in the kitchen, where he took the pills she'd laid out for him the night before. Then the front door opened and closed, and she heard him pull out of the driveway for the ten-minute trip to the station. It was just before 6:00.

By then the sun was up, and Susan could tell it was going to be a spectacularly beautiful day. She helped Buddy down the stairs and took him out for his morning walk. The sky was a clear blue, there was very little humidity, and there was a pleasant coolness in the morning air. Already, some of the geese and ducks had begun migrating.

★

IT WAS SUCH A beautiful morning that John Olson, a friend of Rescorla's who was a regional director at Morgan Stanley and also lived in Morris County, decided to take the ferry that crossed the Hudson from Hoboken to the World Trade Center, rather than the PATH train. He and Rescorla shared an interest in Native Americans and had attended a weekend gathering of Indian tribes together in New Jersey. Olson was of Scandinavian descent, and when he mentioned this, Rescorla gave Olson a hunting knife in a leather sheath that had been handmade in Norway. As he rode the ferry, Olson looked at the twin towers gleaming in the brilliant morning light, the downtown skyline rising from the water, and, farther out in the harbor, the Statue of Liberty. They had never looked more beautiful. After he disembarked, he walked across the plaza and noticed a large stage with a blue canopy over it. Perhaps there was going to be a concert at lunchtime. It would be a beautiful day for lunch outdoors with some live music. Olson glanced at his watch and saw that it was just 7:00 A.M. He had breakfast at the cafeteria on the forty-third floor, then went to his office on sixty-nine.

At eight, Barbara Williams arrived on the forty-fourth floor of 2 World Trade Center and took up her position at the large console of video screens located just outside Rescorla's office. "Good morning," she called in the soft Jamaican accent that Rescorla liked so much. Rescorla was on the phone, checking to make sure all of his deputies were at their posts, but he waved to her and smiled.

At 8:15, Susan called Rick at his office, and he answered the phone. They laughed about his morning song-and-dance routine. "I don't need the movies or the theater, because I have you," Susan said.

"I love you so," he replied.

Susan resumed packing for their trip to Italy, then called her daughter Cristina to discuss plans for the wedding.

★

ON THE SEVENTIETH FLOOR, Kathy Comerford convened a staff meeting at 8:30 A.M. in the conference room in the southeast corner of the building. It had magnificent views from the floor-to-ceiling windows, and she always enjoyed meetings in that room. Lolita Jackson had come down from Morgan Stanley's headquarters in midtown, and Tom Swift, an assistant vice president with blond hair and an Irish complexion, had joined them. Comerford loved working with Swift, the oldest of six children and the first in his family to graduate from college. Though he had recently married, he always called Comerford "Mom."

At 8:46 the group heard a loud noise. "Was that a firecracker?" someone asked. Comerford wondered if it might have been one of the window washers, who worked from small cabs that moved on tracks up and down the outside of the building. But they never made any noise that she could recall. Then the building shook and swayed, as though it were in an earthquake.

Seconds later, they saw a sea of paper passing by the window. They looked at one another, wide-eyed. "Grab your purses," Comerford said. "We're out of here." Instinctively, they moved to the staging area by the elevators, as they had drilled. As they gathered, they heard an announcement from a Port Authority official carried over the loudspeaker: "The building is secure. Please remain at your desks. There is no cause for alarm. The building is secure."

John Olson's office looked north, toward midtown and 1 World Trade Center. He looked up abruptly when he heard a terrific explosion. From his window, it looked like a snowstorm, there was so much paper flying in the air. Then he saw that some of it was on fire. Other debris whirled through the air. He saw his colleagues moving toward the corridor leading to the stairwell, as instructed, and he got up to join them. But then a colleague gestured to come to the window, and he and several others gathered for a commanding view of the adjacent tower. Much of the debris had cleared, and he now had a clear view. Smoke was billowing from Tower One, carried to the east by the morning breeze. On the upper floors, he could see people standing where the explosion had blown the glass from the windows. He could see the flames of the fire behind them. It registered that some of the people were on fire. Then he watched, horrified, as one of them jumped. Others followed. All he could think about was the blue canopy he'd seen on the plaza that morning. He knew it didn't make any sense, but he hoped their bodies would land in the canopy and their lives would be spared.

Shaken, Olson grabbed a phone and called his son, who also worked at Morgan Stanley on the sixty-first floor. Other phones were ringing, and he put his son on hold. When he returned, his son was frantic. "Dad, don't ever put me on hold." Just then, they heard an announcement from the Port Authority: "A plane has hit Tower One.

Our building is secure. Go back to your desks." Olson told his son to stay where he was and to answer his phone. "See you later," he said. "Maybe we'll do lunch." As instructed over the loudspeaker, he returned to his office.

Four floors up, on seventy-three, in the exclusive private banking area, Lindsay Herkness III came rushing out of his office. As usual, he was wearing suspenders and a bespoke suit. His secretary, Macie Stratton, had thought the initial explosion might be thunder, though it seemed odd on such a sunny day. Then the debris had started flying around the windows, some of it on fire, and she and several others went to take a closer look. "Get back from the windows," Herkness ordered. "What's happened?" he asked. No one knew, but the floor's deputy fire marshal said she thought they were being ordered to evacuate. Herkness said that made no sense. "This is the safest building in the world," he insisted. "Look at all that debris downstairs, look at all the commotion." Then they heard the announcement that they should remain at their desks.

Stratton had to concede that what Herkness said made sense, but she didn't like the idea of staying up there. Everyone else seemed to be evacuating. She didn't want to abandon Herkness, but he told her to go ahead if she felt like it. Herkness went back into his office. Stratton changed her shoes, gathered some belongings, and, with a temporary secretary in tow, joined the throng in the stairwell.

Herkness's phone rang. It was Ted Hamilton, a close friend and a fellow member of the Union Club. Hamilton was coming down to discuss his career with Herkness, and then they were going to have lunch. Hamilton was in his car, motoring down the East River Drive, when he heard on the radio that a plane had hit the World Trade Center. "It looks like it's off," Hamilton said.

"No, no, no," Herkness insisted. He wasn't about to let anything interfere with lunch. "Let's do it. It's the other building. They've been telling us to stay at our desks." Hamilton agreed and continued to head south in his car.

On the forty-fourth floor, Barbara Williams heard the explosion; the building shook, and then her phone rang. It was a friend, an ex–Morgan Stanley employee who lived in New Jersey. "Barbara, a plane just flew into the building!" She turned to tell Rescorla, but he was already on his way out. He put on his suit jacket, grabbed his bullhorn, walkie-talkie, and cell phone, and left the office. He was followed by Wesley Mercer, who had been promoted to be Rescorla's deputy in 1997. Williams could see them on one of her monitors, huddling with Titus Davidson, another security deputy, just outside of human resources. Then Rescorla moved to one of the stairwells, Mercer to the other.

In New Jersey, Susan was still talking with Cristina when the phone beeped, indicating another call. Susan put her daughter on hold. It was Alexandra, the bride-to-be, calling from Manhattan. She sounded frantic. "Turn on the TV." Susan went to the set. When the picture came on, she felt her heart skip a beat. There was the World Trade Center, smoke pouring from the tower. Susan screamed. She told her daughters she had to hang up. She instinctively dialed Rick's number.

Williams's phone rang, as it did whenever Rescorla failed to pick up. "Are you all okay?" Susan asked. "Where's Rick?"

"Don't worry," Williams assured her. "It's fine, it's contained. Mr. Rescorla and Mr. Mercer are out on the forty-fourth floor now, helping get everyone out."

Susan felt a little better but still wasn't entirely reassured. She hung up.

Then Williams's phone rang again. "Mommy, are you all right?"

"Relax, it's not our building," she assured her daughter.

In St. Augustine, Dan Hill was upstairs, laying new tile in the bathroom, a task he'd been promising Patricia for months that he would complete. Suddenly he heard his wife call him from the floor below, where she was watching TV. "Dan, get down here! A plane just flew into the World Trade Center. It's a terrible accident."

Hill rushed to the television and saw the familiar towers, one with a gash through it, with flames and smoke pouring out. He had barely absorbed the shocking image when the phone rang. "Hill here," he said. It was Rescorla, calling on his cell phone from the forty-fourth floor.

"Are you watching TV?" he asked. "What do you think?"

"Hard to tell. It could have been an accident, but I can't see a commercial airliner getting that far off."

"I'm evacuating right now," Rescorla said. Rescorla broke off, and Hill could hear him giving orders through the bullhorn. He spoke calmly but firmly, assuring people that they'd be fine, directing them toward the stairwells. Then Hill heard Rescorla break into the familiar refrain of "Men of Harlech," the theme from *Zulu*, substituting "Cornwall" for the Welsh "Harlech":

> *Men of Cornwall, stop your dreaming;*
> *Can't you see their spear points gleaming?*
> *See their warriors' pennants streaming*
> *To this battlefield.*
>
> *Men of Cornwall, stand ye ready;*
> *It cannot be ever said ye*
> *For the battle were not ready;*
> *Stand and never yield!*

Rescorla came back on the line. "Pack a bag and get up here," he said. "You can be my consultant again."

"You bet," Hill said.

Rescorla added that the Port Authority was telling him not to evacuate and to send people back to their desks. The agency had said it was like in 1945, when a B-25 bomber had accidentally hit the seventy-ninth floor of the Empire State Building.

"What did you say?" Hill asked.

"I said, 'Piss off, you son of a bitch,' " Rescorla replied. "Everything above where that plane hit is going to collapse, and it's going to take the whole building with it. I'm getting my people the fuck out of here." Then he said, "I've got to go. Get your shit in one basket and get ready to come up."

Hill went upstairs, got down his suitcase, and began packing.

★

ON SEVENTY, Comerford and her staff had gathered at the staging area by the elevators. Though there were nearly seventy people there, it was oddly quiet. People looked scared. The public address system continued to exhort them to return to their desks. Finally someone said, "What are we waiting for?"

"Instructions," someone answered. But no one from security appeared, so Comerford, as a deputy fire marshal, took charge. Rescorla had told them not to use the elevators in an emergency, so she felt the door to the stairwell. It was cool to the touch, so she opened it. People were moving downstairs from higher floors in a quiet, orderly fashion. "Grab a partner," she said, as Rescorla had instructed. "Let's go." She held the door open as her colleagues began to file out. But then one persuaded her to give up her post and leave herself. "You have three children," she reminded her. She grabbed on to Yucinda Vallejo, a meeting planner whose husband worked on the other side of Tower One, in 7 World Trade Center. As they started down the stairs, Comerford wished she'd worn sneakers rather than the stylish, thin-soled sandals now on her feet.

The stairs were well lit, and each tread was clearly marked with fluorescent tape. They moved at a steady pace, though Comerford had to stop each time Vallejo tried to call her husband on her cell phone. "Put that away," she finally commanded. Comerford heard someone say that a plane had hit the north tower.

"It was a small commuter plane," someone else volunteered.

"No, it was an American Airlines jet," corrected another.

Comerford and the people around her speculated about what

might have caused such an accident. Had the plane's navigational equipment failed? Had the pilot had a heart attack? It just seemed too bizarre.

When their group reached the fifty-ninth floor, a door was open and they came out into the lobby. The elevators were working, and people were using them to descend to the sky lobby on forty-four. Tom Swift said he was going to find a phone, and he told Comerford he'd meet her on forty-four. He reached his mother, said he was okay, and asked her to call Jill, his wife, to tell her they were evacuating. When he finished, he returned to the lobby and noticed that there was still room in one of the elevators that seemed to be functioning normally. He got in, and the door closed.

When Comerford and Vallejo reached the forty-fourth floor, hundreds of people were milling in the lobby. Comerford was relieved to see Rescorla in the middle of the elevator bank, using his bullhorn to direct traffic in a calm, reassuring voice. "Keep moving, stay calm. Move towards the stairwells," he said, pointing them toward the southeast corner of the floor. He had blocked off access to the elevators and insisted that people walk down in pairs. Comerford fell into line with Vallejo and was only a few feet from Rescorla. She wanted to thank him for their preparation and for being so reassuring. Just seeing him made her feel safer.

Suddenly a huge blast shook the building. Bulbs in the chandeliers exploded, all lights went out, and the floor was plunged into darkness. Comerford was blown out of her sandals and thrown hard against the marble surface that surrounded the elevator doors. She heard a tremendous rush of air in the elevator shaft, as if an enormous vacuum had been released. She staggered to her feet, her shoulder throbbing, and noticed Rescorla trying to regain his footing next to her. But it was hard to stand. She couldn't find her shoes. The floor was undulating in huge waves, as if she were on a roller coaster. She felt the entire tower lean precariously. Suddenly it snapped back to vertical, again throwing people to the floor. People started running for the stairwell, pushing and trampling one another. But that stairwell had filled with smoke. People were beginning to panic. Comerford felt her heart pounding.

Then Comerford heard Rescorla's voice. "Stop!" he commanded. "Stay calm. There's another staircase. " His tone was measured, but there was an element of steel in it that made people obey. The crowd fell silent. "The lights are going to come back on momentarily," he assured them. Then, as if by a miracle, the emergency generator began to function, and lights did appear. People looked around, dazed. Rescorla spoke continuously through the bullhorn in soothing, repetitive tones. "Be still," he said quietly. "Be silent. Be calm." No one spoke or moved. It was as if Rescorla had cast a spell. One of Rescorla's staff appeared. "Is it clear?" Rescorla asked.

"Yes," he answered.

"Okay, everyone," Rescorla said. "The northeast staircase is clear." He pointed in that direction. "Let's move. Stay calm. Watch your partner." A line formed quickly, and people began streaming into the stairwell. As Comerford and Vallejo passed through the door, they could hear Rescorla in the background. He was singing into his bullhorn. Comerford had heard Rescorla singing and humming on many other occasions and had thought it was a little odd. Now she found it strangely reassuring. She and Vallejo took a deep breath and headed down the stairs. There was no smoke, but it was growing hot. Everyone was perspiring.

In the security office, Barbara Williams was rocked by the blast, and the windows blew out. The security monitors went dark. She heard shouting: "Get out, get out!" She grabbed her handbag, her glasses, some workbooks. But then she started crying, and she dropped everything. Someone came to her rescue, helping her gather things, steering her toward the stairwell. In the background she could hear the phone ringing, but there was no turning back. In the lobby area she heard Rescorla singing into his bullhorn, and when she reached the stairs, she, too, inspired by his example, began to sing: "Guide Me, O Thou Great Jehovah" and "I Need Thee Every Hour, Every Hour."

★

SUSAN WAS WATCHING THE TELEVISION in the den upstairs when she saw the second passenger plane make a sharp left turn and plunge into the second tower. She screamed and ran out of the room. Frantically she called Rick's office, hoping that she could at least reach Barbara Williams. But the phone rang and rang. There was no answer.

Susan felt her anxiety mount. She felt helpless, which only made it worse. She called Rick's number over and over. The phone just kept ringing. She didn't know whom to call. An endless fifteen minutes went by, and then the phone rang. It was Rick. She burst into tears and couldn't talk. She sobbed uncontrollably.

"Stop crying," he told her. "I have to get these people out safely. If something should happen to me, I want you to know I've never been happier. You made my life."

Susan cried even harder, gasping for breath. "And you made mine," she managed to get out between sobs.

But then she felt a terrible stab of fear, because his words sounded like those of someone who wasn't coming back. "No!" she cried, but then Rick said he had to go. He'd been asked to limit cell phone use so as not to interfere with emergency communications. The line went dead.

The phone rang, and Susan grabbed it, hoping Rick might have called back. It was Sam Fantino, in Chicago. He'd just seen the footage on TV and had tried to call Rick, but the phone rang and rang. Susan sobbed. "He just called. He told me he loved me, and if he didn't get out . . ." She couldn't go on.

"He's going to make it," Fantino insisted. "He's been through the worst, and he always made it."

Susan did her best to calm herself. Desperate to connect with someone close to Rick, she called his boyhood friend Mervyn Sullivan in Cornwall. Sullivan had been watching TV that afternoon when a news flash interrupted the program. "Do you know what's happening here?" she asked. He told her he'd been watching CNN for the last twenty minutes. "Rick is in there," she said. "He just phoned me and said he had to stay in there and do what he can. It's so dangerous."

Susan started to cry, and Sullivan tried to comfort her, saying that Rick was doing what he had to do, and then he'd return safely. But then Sullivan's Cornish reserve failed him, and he started crying, too.

★

ON THE SIXTY-NINTH FLOOR, John Olson thought a missile had hit the building. Was someone attacking them from a ship in the harbor? It made no sense, but he wasn't staying behind to find out. He and three others gathered at the emergency stairway, but the door was jammed shut. The lobby ceiling had collapsed, and through frosted glass doors on the other side, Olson could see flames. Someone said there was another stairwell, and they rushed to the other side of the building.

On the sixty-third floor, Macie Stratton had stopped to call her husband, who told her that a plane had crashed into the north tower. She was still worried about leaving Herkness behind, but when she heard the news, she thought she'd better continue down the stairs. As soon as she hung up, she felt the building rock from the impact of the second plane. Several people were knocked to the floor, but she managed to stay standing. As soon as the building stopped leaning, she raced to the stairwell, but it had filled with smoke. So had the other, but she felt she had no choice but to go in. She covered her mouth and joined the throng moving downstairs. Five floors later, the smoke cleared, and she saw two brokers from her floor, Rick Greenstein and Josh Frankel. "Lindsay wouldn't leave," they reported.

"What?" she said, incredulous.

They said he'd been pacing the floor after the building was hit only ten stories above them. "Lindsay, we've got to go," they insisted.

"Can I take the elevator? Is it working?" he asked. Finally they'd gone into the stairs without him.

On the East River Drive, Ted Hamilton heard on his car radio that the second tower had been hit. The towers were visible from the highway, and he could see that smoke was now pouring from both. He called Herkness again on his cell phone, but the circuits were busy and he couldn't get through. This time he turned around. He called Herkness at home and left a message on his answering machine saying he was sorry he couldn't make lunch and he hoped he was okay.

As soon as the lobby on forty-four was clear, Rescorla moved into the stairwell, using his bullhorn to encourage people, to tell them to stay calm and orderly and to fill the stairwell with song. Though the heat was growing intense, Rescorla kept his suit jacket on. At one point, he was nearly overcome and had to sit down. But he kept speaking into the bullhorn and was soon back on his feet. At first, he moved farther up into the tower to make sure that no one had remained behind in the Morgan Stanley offices. Macie Stratton passed him at about the fiftieth floor.

"Slow down, pace yourself," he said. "Today is a day to be proud to be an American."

When Kathy Comerford reached the twenty-third floor, she felt the building shudder. "We've got to get the hell out of here," she said to Yucinda Vallejo. She felt a surge of adrenaline. "I will not die in this building."

A few floors later, an older woman was sitting on the steps. "I can't go anymore," she said. "I've got arthritis and bad knees."

"Well, I've got bad knees, too," Comerford said. "We are going to make it out of here together." She and Vallejo helped lift the woman to her feet, and together they resumed their descent.

Olson was among the last to leave his floor and was near the end of the stream of people descending the stairs. When he reached Rescorla, he had worked his way down to the tenth floor. Olson spoke to him:

"Rick, you've got to get out, too." Rescorla was calm but had that intense look that meant nothing would stand in his way.

"I will, as soon as I've got everybody else out," he said.

Soon after Olson moved on, the stream of evacuees came to an end, and firemen laden with gear were now moving up the stairs. Rescorla could easily have left the building. Instead, he called Hill on his cell phone and somehow got through.

The moment Hill saw the second plane make a sharp turn and plunge into the tower, he knew it was a terrorist attack. It was almost exactly what he and Rescorla had predicted, though he'd thought the hit would come during Ramadan, as he had warned Ellen Glasser, the FBI agent. "This is a hit!" Hill said as soon as he heard Rescorla's voice. "Get the fuck out of there."

"I've got people to take care of," Rescorla said.

"Are they out yet?" Hill asked.

"Most of them are out. They'll all be out in a few minutes."

"Then get the fuck out!" Hill yelled. He was starting to feel panic himself.

Rescorla said he was taking some of his men and would make a final sweep, to make sure no one was left behind, injured, or lost. (Rescorla didn't mention Herkness, but it's possible someone on the staircase had mentioned that he had stayed on the seventy-third floor.) Then he would evacuate himself. Rescorla said he thought the other tower, since it was the first hit, would collapse first, giving them time to get out.

"Don't assume that!" Hill yelled. "They got a better hit on you. The top of that SOB is about to come down, and it's going to take everything with it."

"I don't have time to screw with you anymore," Rescorla said. "Get up here. Charge your tickets on your American Express card, and I'll reimburse you." Then he added, "Call Susan and calm her down. She's panicking."

The line went dead.

★

When Barbara Williams reached the plaza level, flaming debris was falling to the streets and walkways outside the towers. Police directed her down into the shopping concourse, past the PATH train escalators. A long line stretched toward an exit at the northeast corner of the complex, near the Borders bookstore. She closed her eyes and began to pray, "Lord, you didn't take us this far to leave us behind."

A man touched her on the shoulder and pointed out that the line was moving. "You're going to be okay," he said, then took her hand and guided her outside to the street. There, people were screaming. She saw bodies lying in pools of blood. She began to cry. She looked back and saw that the towers were on fire, and she felt a pang of fear for Rescorla and Wesley Mercer. Two other women joined hands with her, and they began to pray out loud: "Lord, take my bosses and coworkers out of there."

Then a National Guardsman came up. "Ladies, you have to move."

Comerford exited the stairwell on a balcony above the lobby. As she passed the elevators, she could hear screams. "Help us, help us!" people cried.

She saw a police officer. "There are people in the elevator! What can we do?" The police officer told her to keep moving.

Dazed, she found her way through a corridor and down a stairway she'd never noticed to the ground level. Just outside the broken windows, she saw bodies, some burned beyond recognition; pools of blood, water, broken glass, and debris. She and Vallejo moved through the lobby, down into the concourse, and through the line to the exit by Borders. When they reached the street, they sat on a curb, exhausted. A triage unit was working just behind them.

"I'm going to find my husband," Vallejo said.

"The hell you are," Comerford replied. Then, for the first time, she looked back at the towers and was stunned by the sight. She still had no idea what had happened. "Don't look up," she told Vallejo. "We have to get out of here, as far away as we can."

They struggled to their feet and joined people moving east. But they had moved only a block and a half when Vallejo was overcome by shock. She lay down on the pavement, hyperventilating, unable to move. Comerford knelt next to her. Suddenly she heard screams and the sound of a jet plane. She saw people panicking and running for cover. My God, she thought, we're under attack. She instinctively threw her body over Vallejo. But then the plane passed.

Comerford heard a voice. "I'm a police detective." He got an oxygen tank and administered it to Vallejo. Then they flagged down a passing ambulance. They had just gotten Vallejo into it when Comerford heard an ominous rumble, which quickly grew to a roar. She looked back and saw a whitish gray cloud, like a dense fog, racing toward them. Terrified, she jumped in and slammed the door. Then they were engulfed by dust and debris and could see nothing.

At that moment, Dan Hill was on the phone speaking to Susan, who had just finished talking to Sullivan. She was crying again. He tried to reassure her. "Take it easy," Hill said as she continued to sob. "He's been through tight spots a million times."

Suddenly Susan screamed. Hill turned to look at his own television and saw the south tower implode from the top, just as he had feared. Then, as the collapse rapidly gained momentum, the base of the tower crashed in a great cascade of dust and debris. All he could think of were the words Rescorla had so often used to comfort his dying soldiers. "Susan, he'll be okay," he said gently. "Take deep breaths. Take it easy. If anyone will survive, Rick will survive."

When Hill hung up, he turned to his wife. Her face was ashen. "Shit," he said. "Rescorla is dead."

They sat for a moment in stunned silence, staring at the images on the television. Finally Patricia said, "You'd better finish packing."

"It's no use," Hill said sadly. "There's no reason to go. It's all over."

15

THE COURAGE TO HEAL

Tower Two collapses, 9:59 A.M., September 11, 2001.
(Steve McCurry/Magnum Photos)

S USAN RAN SCREAMING from the town house into her front
yard. There was no one in sight; she ran to a neighbor's house two
houses down. The neighbor was at home and put her arms around
Susan as she sobbed and gasped for breath. People tried to comfort her,
but she felt nothing but despair. "I know he's not coming back," she
said, his last words echoing in her mind. Now other neighbors were
emerging. Some of them, too, were screaming and sobbing. Three
other people who lived on the street had been in the building.

Susan felt she had to return home. She called her daughters. Phones
in Manhattan weren't working, and the bridges and tunnels were
closed. She reached Cristina in New Jersey. "You've got to come over,"

she gasped. But Cristina had to wait for her two young children to return from school. They both started crying. Susan hung up and called Trevor. There was no answer. She reached Kim.

"Dad's going to be okay," Kim insisted. She said she was sure Rick had gotten out and was probably helping with rescue efforts. He would surely call once he got out of the chaos and reached a phone, just as he had after the 1993 bombing.

"But this is different," Susan cried.

In Manhattan, Kathy Comerford stared in shock as debris from the fallen tower rained around them. It was dark as night. Then the air cleared somewhat, and the ambulance began to move. She saw two colleagues from Morgan Stanley, covered in soot and dust. She asked the driver to stop for them, but they passed by. When they arrived at Beekman Downtown Hospital, the wounded were everywhere. The most serious cases, many people with severe burns, were rushed into the emergency area. Comerford pitched in, administering the Heimlich maneuver to one woman who was choking, helping another who was vomiting. Yucinda Vallejo had been revived by the oxygen, and when she felt able to walk, they moved to the cafeteria. Minutes later, they heard another roar in the distance, and then it again grew dark.

When they stepped out, wearing surgical masks given to them by the hospital, there was a blanket of dust covering the ground, like a new-fallen snow, only it was pale gray. Vallejo headed west, to make her way back to New Jersey. Comerford had relatives in Brooklyn and walked southeast, joining the throngs crossing the Brooklyn Bridge on foot. On the other side, a man had opened his small grocery store and offered water, food, and use of his phone. She reached her relatives and found a gypsy cab to take her to Park Slope. Her husband arranged for a car to pick her up there, and she reached her home in Long Island at 7:00 P.M.

When she arrived, her family and neighbors had all gathered in the driveway. Her husband came toward her, and she rushed into his arms. She started to cry with relief. Then she went limp, slumping to the pavement. She was too drained and exhausted to move.

Later, she called her boss at Morgan Stanley to report that she had made it out. Her shoulder throbbed, her feet were blistered, and her knees ached. Who else had she seen? She told him what she knew of the others and mentioned she'd been standing next to Rescorla when the second plane hit. "What about Tom Swift?" he asked. Yes, she'd seen him on the fifty-ninth floor; he was going to call his wife and mother. "No one has seen him," he said. She felt a spasm of anxiety.

John Olson was walking north along Broadway when Tower Two collapsed. He hoped to God his son hadn't taken his advice and stayed at his desk or, worse, tried to go upstairs to find him. He reached 34th Street, next to the Empire State Building. People were fleeing that area, too, because they feared the Empire State Building, once again the city's tallest, would be the next target. All the Hudson River crossings from the city were closed, so Olson and several others persuaded a cab to take them to Morgan Stanley's office in White Plains, twenty-five miles north of the city. From there he was able to reach his wife, and he learned that his son was safe. Finally, he learned from the television what had happened: Terrorists had hijacked two commercial airplanes and flown them into the towers. Something so horrible had never crossed his mind.

Barbara Williams, too, found a gypsy cab and reached her apartment in the Bronx at about 4:00 P.M. She had another woman with her, a stranger she'd met while running up Broadway, fleeing the ash and debris. The woman had stopped and was crying. "I don't know where to go," she had said when Williams paused beside her.

"Just come with me," Williams said, taking her by the hand. "You can call your family at my house."

They kept running until they were too exhausted to continue. Then a cab had appeared. As soon as she arrived at home, she turned on the television and saw the footage of the towers collapsing.

"Lord, you took me out of that," she marveled. "Let them find my bosses and coworkers."

Macie Stratton made it over the Brooklyn Bridge, and when she got to a phone, she called Lindsay Herkness at home. His answering machine picked up. She called again at five; his message machine was full. She was getting worried. Herkness's friend Ted Hamilton called and also got the message that the machine was full. At 5:30 P.M. he went to the Union Club; he knew Herkness played squash every night at six. Other members showed up there, too, looking for him. But there was no sign of him. Hamilton called him again the next morning at 6:45. There was still no answer. Later in the day, a housekeeper answered. She said something in Spanish, which Hamilton couldn't understand. Finally, she said, "Lindsay no come home."

"Are you telling me Lindsay is dead?" he asked.

There was silence.

★

BILL RANDOLPH, Wesley Mercer's companion, had been at the doctor's when he saw the television footage of the attack. He had immediately tried to call Wesley but hadn't gotten through. He went home, hoping desperately for a call. He wished Wesley had a cell phone. His phone rang often, but it was friends, asking if Wesley had come home. Each time, he had to say no. He asked every coworker who called if they'd seen him that day. Some had seen him in the ground-floor concourse, so they assumed he had gotten out. But another security person, Waldo Waterman, reported that Mercer and Rescorla "went back upstairs."

Randolph remembered 1993, when he had heard the sound of the key in the door and Wesley had come in dirty and exhausted but safe. They had hugged while their Akita dog jumped up and down. This time Randolph stayed up late, crying, watching television, hoping for the sound of the key in the door. But finally he collapsed across the bed. The TV and radio were still on when he awoke the next morning. Wesley had not come home.

★

IN ST. AUGUSTINE, Dan Hill angrily drafted a letter to Glasser, the FBI agent who had rebuffed his plan to kill Osama bin Laden. It was dripping in irony. "It looks like the big hit by Osama Bin Laden was about sixteen days off my predicted schedule," he wrote. That was all he said. Glasser later interviewed Nader Zori, asking about possible terrorists. "I'm sorry," she said, adding that the bureau didn't feel it could pursue his and Hill's plan. "It's too late to be sorry," Nader replied.

Susan spent the rest of the morning and afternoon alone, watching TV as it carried the increasingly grim news into her home. Every time the phone rang, her heart leaped, only to be disappointed when it wasn't Rick. Later in the afternoon, her daughter Cristina arrived, and then Rick's daughter, Kim. Others began to filter in: Brad Snyder, the holistic practitioner; Joe Holloway, Rick's medic in Vietnam; other friends and neighbors. Hill called her every hour to see how she was doing. McBee called often; so did Fantino. They offered hope and encouragement, but Susan was too dazed to respond. She couldn't bear to see the terrible day come to an end. She didn't want Rick to return to a darkened home. She turned on all the lights and lit candles. As darkness fell, she and her visitors began a twenty-four-hour prayer vigil.

Anne Robinson, her childhood friend, spoke to Susan the next day. "I haven't heard from him," Susan reported. "I just haven't heard. . . ." Her voice trailed off, and she started to cry. "He's going to come home, isn't he?"

"All we can do is pray," Robinson said. As a former nun and a nurse, she knew there was nothing more anyone could say. Suddenly Susan said she had to get to the train station. She didn't want the parking meter to have expired when Rick returned for his car. She was leaving his Mark VIII exactly where he'd parked it.

Later that night, her friends finally persuaded Susan to try to get some sleep. She took the suit Rick had worn on Monday and carefully laid it in his place in their bed. She could still smell Rick in the fabric. She lay down next to it and clutched the suit close to her. But she couldn't sleep. She found herself feverishly speculating that Rick was trapped in an air pocket under the rubble. She understood that a person might survive several days without water or food; she'd heard someone on TV say it could be as long as ten days. Susan held the suit fabric to her face and breathed deeply into it, as though by doing so she could give him mouth-to-mouth resuscitation.

Susan had no official word on Rick's fate, and as time passed with no word from him, she didn't want any. Finally, on Friday, Philip Purcell, chairman of Morgan Stanley, called. She didn't answer the phone. He left a message saying he was saddened that Rescorla was still missing. She kept the lights on and the candles lit. After all, New York City mayor Rudolph Giuliani had stressed repeatedly that a rescue mission was still under way and there might be more survivors.

On Sunday, Purcell called again, and Susan answered. She felt a chill as he said that Morgan Stanley had concluded it was "unlikely" any more survivors would be found. The firm was holding a memorial service for the victims on September 20, at St. Patrick's Cathedral, and he offered her a limousine for the trip from Morristown. Susan said she would take the train. A human resources counselor from Morgan Stanley met her at the station and escorted her to the cathedral. She sat with the families of the other victims, though not, she discovered, with Bill Randolph, Wesley Mercer's companion. Morgan Stanley offered to send a car to pick him up, but after Mercer's family members objected to the presence of Wesley's same-sex companion, the firm suggested he sit elsewhere in the cathedral. So Randolph stayed away.

As the strains of the organ echoed in the vast nave of the cathedral, Purcell stepped up to the pulpit. "It has been nine days since our country was struck in a horrible terrorist attack. In our immense sorrow and anger it is still almost impossible to comprehend these awful events . . . but we know we will continue, and we take solace in faith and prayers. Today we gather together as our own special community to join in prayers of sorrow and thanksgiving. We are joined by the families of Morgan Stanley people who have not been found: Jennifer de Jesus,

Titus Davidson, Joseph Di Pilato, Godwin Forde, Lindsay Herkness, Charles A. Laurencin, Wesley Mercer, Rick Rescorla, Nolbert Salomon, Steven Strauss, Tom Swift, and Jorge Velazquez. Our thoughts and our prayers are with these families and all of us will do everything we can to help them in their time of need. We give prayers of thanksgiving for the lives of all who were spared, including three thousand seven hundred in our firm who were able to get safely out.

"We know that some of those unaccounted for stayed behind or went back. They were like the Good Shepherd in the Bible, looking for the one sheep missing from a flock of a hundred.

"It is appropriate that that parable of the Good Shepherd was shared in churches across America this Sunday. As Cardinal Egan said here on Sunday, the demolished World Trade Center should be renamed 'Ground Hero.' Heroes like Louis Torres, who is with us, and Rick Rescorla, who is not."

John Olson, one of the last to leave, shared his recollection of meeting Rescorla on the tenth floor and recalled his pledge that he would leave only when everyone else had been safely evacuated. He was a "reassuring voice for everyone in that stairwell," he said. Then his voice faltered, and he had trouble continuing. "We miss you, Rick," he said, tears welling in his eyes.

Of the names Purcell mentioned, Morgan Stanley had lost just six employees: Rescorla; Mercer; Velazquez; Herkness; Swift, who apparently was in the elevator when the second plane struck; and de Jesus, a data clerk who worked on the fifty-ninth floor. Forde, Davidson, Salomon, and Laurencin were security guards who reported to Rescorla but worked for an outside contractor. Strauss and Di Pilato were outside electricians, working on a job that day for Morgan Stanley.

"May God bless you and give us strength," Purcell concluded. Then the congregation rose and began to sing, as the organ swelled with the familiar strains of "God Bless America."

★

AFTER THE CEREMONY, survivors of the attack pressed themselves on Susan to offer their thanks, to insist that Rick had saved their lives. Many others called after the ceremony. Susan felt compelled to try to piece together what had happened that day and asked everyone if they had seen Rick. She heard many accounts in which Rick, always wearing his suit jacket and tie despite sweating profusely, had kept people marching down the staircase, talking soothingly and singing into his bullhorn, getting them to move to the right side so firemen could make their way up. She heard how the heat had nearly overcome him and he'd had to sit down on the stairs. But he'd kept using the bullhorn.

Susan called Comerford when she heard that she had been with Rick when the second plane hit their tower. "He was calm," Comerford told her. "It was like he was the commander in chief and we were his troops."

Susan was struck by the military analogy. "Do you know that he fought in Vietnam?"

"No," Comerford said. She'd had no idea. "He was so calm," she continued. "His singing was so reassuring. He was like an angel, a heavenly voice, saying, 'Everybody's going to get out.' "

Someone told Susan that Rescorla had used his cell phone to report that all Morgan Stanley employees were out of the building. But both John Olson and another executive told her that just ten minutes before the building collapsed, they had seen him on the tenth floor—climbing back up into the building.

That was as far as she could get. She tossed at night, trying to imagine what had happened next. Had Rick heard and felt the beginning of the building's collapse? Had he known what was coming? What was it like in those final moments? The horror of it was almost more than she could bear. It kept her awake, night after night.

In Hayle, no one had told Annie Rescorla, Rick's mother, that her son had perished. Relatives cared for her, and she almost never left her home. But on September 23, Susan sent an e-mail for Rick's cousin to read to her:

"Grieve with me at the loss of our beloved Rick (your Cyril, your

Tammy, your Rick). But feel joy and happiness that Rick died, as he lived, a true hero. . . . We have kept vigil for the last two weeks, praying there would be a miracle and the thousands of firemen and police would be able to find him alive among the rubble. This has not happened.

"Rick never forgot his roots as a Cornishman. He was very proud. He loved you so. He loved your mother and father. There was not a day that went by that we did not think of you, hoping that you would be well."

Susan herself still clung to some faint hope that Rick was still alive, but she was quickly swept into the bureaucracy of the investigation and relief efforts. Two Morristown policemen came to the house and questioned her extensively. Then Morgan Stanley arranged for her to go to Pier 94, to which she took a hairbrush of Rick's for a DNA sample. There was confusion at the site, because Rick's daughter and one of Susan's daughters had already begun separate folders, which meant Rick had been counted as a victim twice. Then she was told the hairbrush wasn't enough; could she find some more DNA samples? When she called Dan Hill, she was frantic; she desperately wanted them to find Rick's body, or at least a part of it. "Susan, you don't need his body," Hill said. He remembered what Rick had told him after Danny died. "It's just the container he came in."

Three weeks after her visit to Pier 94, Susan received a certified envelope. When she opened it, she found a death certificate. She wasn't prepared for what she read: "Cause of death: homicide." She hadn't thought of it as murder, but of course it was. She started sobbing.

Susan was an emotional wreck. She stopped exercising and paid no attention to what she ate. In October, her mortgage payment came due. Though her husband had earned a good salary at Morgan Stanley, he wasn't paid like an investment banker, as he'd told Hill. Their town house was attractive but hardly ostentatious; the mortgage and maintenance payments combined would barely rent a studio apartment in a Manhattan high-rise. She read that contributions were pouring into the national Red Cross, but when she called, she was asked, "Off the top of your head, what are your monthly expenses?" When she couldn't immediately answer, she was told she'd have to submit copies of all her bills. She couldn't face the paperwork.

Susan had also read that Morgan Stanley had started a fund for victims and had made a $10 million contribution. As the widow of a Morgan Stanley employee, Susan was entitled to certain defined benefits, but that, too, required extensive paperwork, and none of the forms had arrived. Susan hated to ask for more immediate help, but she called Morgan Stanley and was referred to someone in personnel. "What is this victims fund?" she asked.

"It's strictly voluntary," she was told, and nothing was yet being disbursed. "Are you in dire need?" the woman asked. Susan burst into tears. It was humiliating. She was in dire need of the husband she'd never see again.

Susan felt she was all but reduced to begging. She appealed to the United Way of Morristown, which came to her assistance. The national Red Cross sent a check. And Morgan Stanley eventually came through with what Susan felt was a generous payment. Still, though the payments meant she wouldn't have to go back to work, the money brought her scant comfort.

On October 11, the one-month anniversary of the attack, Susan decided that she wanted to see the site. Her daughter Alexandra and the Morgan Stanley human resources counselor met her in Manhattan, and they were taken to ground zero. It was a beautiful autumn day. If you looked away from the site, at the buildings gleaming in the sunlight, it was almost as if nothing had happened. Susan made herself stare at the ashes and rubble in the vast pit where the Trade Center had once stood. The stench was awful. Smoke still wafted from the debris. She noticed that something as seemingly fragile as office papers was still visible, but she couldn't make out anything else.

Susan concluded at that moment that they would never find her husband's body, not even a piece of it. As she looked at the wreckage, she realized that his spirit was gone.

★

AT HOME, Susan at first moved nothing that had been Rick's. His comfortable old shoes, the ones he changed into when he got home, stayed by the front door. His clothes remained in the closet. She displayed their photographs—the ones of their wedding, of the two of them in a horse-drawn carriage in Chicago, and in a sculpture garden—on the dining room table. She filled the vases with white roses.

Here and there around the house, she found scraps of paper on which Rick had written notes to himself. Then, tucked into a kitchen cabinet, she found a bound notebook with a black cover. She turned the pages, looking at the entries. She read with mounting fascination and deepening concern:

"The problem of war is that the great force of energy is devoted to destructive ends, that most memories of war are fragmented, not holistic.

"The problem in the aftermath of war is to transcend the fragments of memory and emerge as a whole, complete man.

"Broken mind patterns, broken bodies. . . ."

This, she realized, must be the notebook in which Rick had been writing when he couldn't sleep during those last weeks before September 11. Some of it seemed fragmentary, but clearly he was grappling with his past—the part he had never wanted to talk about.

The courage to heal and to help others take the healing path.
War is an extreme form of separation from the healing path.
It is difficult to come back to the path after fighting a war.

An entry titled "Sacred Places" sounded so like Rick that Susan could almost hear his voice.

Find sacred places near to you. These can be little
rock gardens, or trees. You can touch the bark. Don't

tell anyone about your sacred places, or they will spoil it for you.

Meditate, go with yourself, find your essence, develop your belief system.

Honoring by developing your sense of touch.

Listen to your heartbeat, body, spirit, mind, soul and physical capability together, dancing to the music of song-birds, the honking of geese. Center yourself.

Walk barefoot over wet grass.

Touch the petals of a flower.

Visualize—Puddles of water are important bodies of water, important in the scheme of life.

But all the other passages dealt with war, in one way or another. An entry titled "Heal Soldier, Yourself" read:

There is no such thing as a hero, and yet heroic acts flare up everywhere. You can find heroic acts in the eyes of the sick and the dying, the will to hang on to the bitter end, through the knife edge of pain, coughing up the blood and phlegm and trying to hold on to the gray light of dawn drifting up to bring in yet another day.

[The] terrible, awful beauty that is surviving a battle—elation. Elation does not last.

Distorted minds.

Distorted bodies.

Grotesque.

Heroic acts tend to gather around soldiers, perhaps stirred up by the cries for patriotic duty, and encouraged by pretty ribbons and medals. The plain facts are that awards of medals for heroism are political acts, notions of general approval usually requiring surviving witnesses.

Think for a moment about a luckless platoon cut off and annihilated fighting for survival with every ounce of guts they can muster. All the heroic acts of these soldiers go unnoticed, with no one to sign the affidavits witnessing their heroism.

The same is true of the lone acts of soldiers.

Awards are political, no doubt about that, and you only have to look at the statistics. More awards (purportedly) go to officers than to enlisted men, even though enlisted men walk the point and engage in more close quarter fighting, catch more injuries and make the ultimate sacrifices, dying in greater proportion than the officers. This remains true in all armies.

In the next entry, he offered a definition of "Bravery":

Acts of energy in a certain direction at a definite moment in time. The urge to sacrifice yourself for your fellow soldiers, to be strong and part of the effort, is strong—much stronger than the urge to kill the enemy (strangers against whom you have no specific grudge).

Freedom . . . is the first step to healing. Cut the umbilical cord from the army, from the cause, from the politics of war. . . . Join the community of men in the power of time.

You have the energy and the will to face adversity

The sweating man next to you—

Understand him.

Leadership—

Keep them alive.

On the last page on which anything was written, Rescorla appears to have been experimenting with the title of the book he had told

Susan he wanted to write. He seems to have tried and discarded several ideas: *Immigrant Soldier, American Son; Redemption of a Soldier; A Time to Fight, a Time to Heal.*

At the top of the list was the one Susan knew he would have wanted: *The Heart of a Soldier.*

★

ON OCTOBER 27, Susan held a memorial service for her husband at the raptor preserve. She knew Rick wanted no elaborate memorial, so she invited only a small group of people: Dan Hill and Fred McBee; her three daughters; Rick's two children and their mother; Brad Snyder, the holistic practitioner; Joe Holloway, Rick's medic; and her friend Anne Robinson. Hill drove up with Patricia. McBee and his wife, Kathy, were on their way when they learned their daughter was ill. The group of mourners filed into the preserve followed by a single bagpiper.

"As most of you know," Susan told the group, "it was Rick's wish to have no memorial or grave service. Cremation and a simple urn. He wanted me to scatter his ashes. Then, about four months ago, as we returned from our second outing at the Raptor Trust, he told me of his desire to give a donation to the trust and have a simple plaque on one of the cages. He specifically wanted the cage to house the American eagles. And so it is fitting to do this today. To have a place where one can go and reflect."

Then Susan unveiled the plaque and read the words she had composed: "In loving memory of my sweetheart, my soulmate forever, my Celtic hero in life and our hero in death. Richard C. Rescorla, May 27, 1939–September 11, 2001. Just like the eagle, you have spread your wings, and soared into eternity."

As the bagpiper played softly in the background, Susan read the words to the Cornish song Rick had loved so much, "The White Rose":

> *The first time I met you, my darling*
> *Your face was as red as the rose,*

But now your dear face has grown paler
As pale as the lily white rose.

So fair as the spring, oh my darling
Your face shines so bright, so divine
The fairest of blooms in my garden
Oh lily white rose, you are mine.

Now I am alone, my sweet darling,
I walk though the garden and weep,
But spring will return with your presence
Oh lily white rose, mine to keep.

Then a hawk, recently restored to health, was released into freedom.

Dan Hill wished he could have covered his hands in Rescorla's blood, as Rescorla had done in Vietnam. But that, of course, was impossible. Hill was as certain as Susan that no trace of Rescorla would ever be found.

★

ON VETERANS DAY WEEKEND, Susan traveled to Washington for the reunion of veterans of the battles of Ia Drang, which was going to feature film clips from the forthcoming *We Were Soldiers.* Even though this was the very event Rescorla had planned to boycott to protest the movie, Susan was persuaded to go by Sam Fantino, who planned to offer a tribute to Rescorla. She didn't want to disappoint the men who had fought with her husband and now mourned him. And after reading Rick's notebook, she wanted to learn more from them about his experiences in Vietnam.

Though the event had been billed as a chance to meet the Hollywood stars featured in the film, especially Mel Gibson, only one, Sam Elliot, showed up, and he had a secondary role. Perhaps this was just as

well, since the tributes to Rescorla overshadowed the film that so con-
spicuously failed to mention him.

Larry Gwin reminded the audience of how Rescorla had rescued
so many of them at Albany. "To those of you who knew Rescorla, we
lost a brother," he said. "We lost one of the best men we've ever
known. For those of you who don't know Rick Rescorla, he was a
warrior, a leader, and a friend. He was the bravest man I ever saw.
Everything he did was bigger than life. Rick inspired us to be the best."

General Hal Moore went to the podium and said he hadn't seen
Rescorla since Vietnam until they met each other at the 1992 Ia Drang
reunion. He said he hadn't recognized Rescorla until he walked up and
made the quip about the book title, *We Were Soldiers Once . . . and
Thin*. The audience laughed appreciatively, but then Moore grew
somber. "He talked about one of his men who died at X-ray: If a man
is dying, you hold him in your arms. You say, 'You're not alone, son.
You're going to be okay. . . .'"

"Most of us know how he died: how he ignored orders to stay put
and ordered a complete evacuation; how he was gasping on the stairwells; how he broke into song to help them, as he did in Vietnam; how
he insisted on going back up. The last words he was quoted as saying:
'Today is a day to be proud to be an American.'"

Moore paused. "He went out a hero. I felt truly grateful to have
known him."

Then Fantino rose to read a poem written by David Prowse, an ad-
mirer of Rick's in Cornwall.

> *The veterans recalled him in the killing fields of war
> As a man whose potent presence would inspire and reassure . . .*
>
> *And on that evil morning, so deceptively serene,
> Amid another carnage, just as callous and obscene
> Again he took the mantle of the sainted and the strong
> To save the lives of others with a blessing and a song.*

Between the Hudson river and the sandy shores of Hayle,
Though eyes encompass differences of latitude and scale,
All hands are linked together in the testimony they bear,
They are but Rick Rescorla's friends, united by a prayer.

There was a moment of silence.

★

IN THE WEEKS AND MONTHS AFTER SEPTEMBER 11, there were many tributes to Rick Rescorla, large and small. The University of Oklahoma gave him a posthumous award, its first, as Alumnus of the Year. His daughter, Kim, accepted the award, and the dean of the university read a letter from Susan, saying that Rick referred to Norman as "the Paris of the Southwest" and felt his "golden years" there "had nourished his passion for writing and love of learning."

There was a memorial service in Hayle, where Mervyn Sullivan eulogized Rescorla as a "beautiful man" with a "hug for everyone." He spoke of his kindnesses to Stanley Sullivan and to John Couch. It was these small but important gestures, not his heroism, that made him beloved in Hayle. Queen Elizabeth II attended a ceremony at Westminster Abbey for Rescorla and other British victims, and Rescorla's mother received a letter of condolence from Prince Charles. Susan invited Bill Randolph, Wesley Mercer's companion, to accompany her to one of the dinners in honor of victims of the attack. "I'm so sorry I never contacted you," she said. "I know you loved him and you're hurting. I want to embrace you."

In February 2002, Susan visited Hayle. Mervyn Sullivan met her at the station. About two months after the attack, Sullivan had sent her an e-mail: "Tammy never stopped telling me how happy you both were and how he was so lucky to have met such a beautiful gal as you. These were the happiest of years of his life and he loved being with you. I know how much he meant it, because men don't usually say things like this to each other." They visited Rick's mother, who wept and told

Susan she didn't want her to leave. In gratitude to many of Rick's friends in Cornwall, Susan hosted a roast beef dinner at the Cornish Arms, where John Daniels arranged for the Hayle men's choir to perform. There she had a surprise, at first jarring but later strangely comforting. She met a man named Clive Durrant who identified himself as Rick's younger half brother. He was an adopted child, but he had seen his birth records. His mother's name had been Rescorla. When he read of Rick's death and saw the name, he contacted people in Hayle, who had referred him to Sullivan. Annie Rescorla had indeed had another child, though Rick had never been aware of her pregnancy.

Susan needed no proof. She was amazed by how much Clive looked like Rick and how much they had in common. It was as if a small part of Rick had miraculously survived.

★

HILL AND SUSAN SPOKE COUNTLESS TIMES AFTER SEPTEMBER 11, first every hour, then several times a day, then every day, even months after Rescorla's death. To have waited so long to meet her "soul mate," and then to have had him taken from her so soon, was almost more than Susan could bear. She felt the loss of her husband constantly, especially at unexpected moments that reminded her of him and sometimes took her breath away: the geese migrating over the pond, the sight of the first snow, the puddles of water left by a spring rain. But even beyond that, something haunted Susan that no number of condolences, tributes, or memorial services could erase: Rick had left her behind to face life without him. Unlike many of the other victims, Rick could have come out alive with the other Morgan Stanley survivors.

"What's really difficult for me is that I know he had a choice," Susan said repeatedly. "He chose to go back in there." She knew that he would never have left until everyone was safe, until his mission was accomplished. That was his nature, and that was the man she loved. "I can understand why he went back," she said. "What I can't understand is why I was left behind."

Hill understood. He knew how much Susan had loved Rick, and he her, for the last three and a half years of his life. But Hill had also known Rick in his twenties, when he was "a hundred-and-eighty-pound, six-foot-one piece of human machinery that would not quit, did not know defeat, and would not back off one inch," as he put it. Hill had known and admired Rick his entire adult life. He felt he knew him better than his wife, children, or parents. And he knew that if Rescorla had come out of that building and someone died whom he hadn't tried to save, he would have had to commit suicide.

Hill waited some months to press this view on Susan, until he felt she was ready to absorb it. He had wanted to take her for a long walk along St. Augustine beach, but he ended up flying to New Jersey, to be with her in the home that she and Rick had loved so much. When they were together, she agonized again over the decisive moment when, faced with an irreconcilable choice between love and duty, Rick had chosen to stay in the doomed tower. "I'm afraid he didn't love me," she sobbed.

Hill was glad she had gotten it out in the open. "Are you nuts?" he replied. "He talked so much about you, it was sickening. With practically his last breath, he called you and said, 'You made my life.'" Then Hill quoted from the Bible: "Why are ye fearful, O ye of little faith?"

Hill wanted Susan to understand that Rick had died a natural death. "People like Rick, they don't die old men," he said. "They aren't destined for that, and it isn't right for them to do so. It just isn't right, by God, for them to become feeble, old, and helpless sons of bitches. There are certain men born in this world, and they're supposed to die setting an example for the rest of the weak bastards we're surrounded with."

★

WITH HIS LAST WORDS, Rescorla had asked Hill to take care of Susan. There was no one, really, to console Hill. As he had so often, he put his thoughts in a letter, written in longhand. But this time, he couldn't mail it to Rick.

> One of my life's biggest regrets is that I couldn't have been with Rick at the moment of the last great challenge and crisis of his life. Then again, maybe it was so destined, because if I didn't survive, there would be nobody left to tell his full story.
>
> Kipling wrote that "all men should count with you, but none too much."
>
> I failed there. Rick counted as the world to me.
>
> Somebody cautioned that if a person or thing means the world to you, and you lose that person or thing, then you have lost the world.
>
> I lost the world when Rick died.

Dan and Rick at Fort Benning, April 2001.
"Don't die before we see each other again, Danny," Rescorla said.
(Courtesy of Patrick J. Kelly)

EPILOGUE

YOU'LL REMEMBER ME

by Susan Rescorla

I WASN'T CONSCIOUSLY LOOKING, but I never gave up hope that someday I would meet my soul mate.

I can't say I regret any part of my life—even the bad and scary times—because if it weren't for those experiences I would not have understood what was really important or have been able to listen to myself quite clearly and know I would have to take the risk of my life if someone came into my life. I honestly knew if this happened this man would truly be my soul mate.

My thoughts and prayers told me this.

When we met, Rick and I never looked at each other's faces. We simply heard each other's voices. We both knew this was forever. How does one know? I don't know if I can describe it. It has to happen to you. It had to have been spiritually orchestrated. You would have to have been on the journey of your life. You would have to have been to hell and back to know that now you had the very best. And from that moment I thanked God and the universe and chanted and visualized that this time on Earth would be frozen in time. Just as if the Earth had stopped rotating. This time was for Rick and Susan. Yes, of course we let our children in and some friends, but this precious moment was for us. We couldn't believe our love, our happiness—that feeling of divine comfort, safety, sexual attraction, acknowledging and understanding each other as if we had known each other from another time, another place.

I have given a lot of thought not only to why we were soul mates but also to what a soul mate is and what Rick and I felt for each other that validates this. We allowed each other to be ourselves. We didn't have to speak of our needs. We just knew. That is what soul mates do— they listen to each other with a third ear. From the moment we met, Rick would engage me in many conversations in which he assumed I knew the people, places, and things he was talking about. It was apparent that we would be together forever. Rick gave me unconditional love, complete trust in every way. He gave me an enormous amount of respect. He liked my head—my philosophies and my spirit. He made me feel wonderful every day. He was always considerate and understanding. He opened his love up not only for his two adult children but for my three daughters, their partners, and my two granddaughters, who also became his. He was totally concerned for them.

We needed to love ourselves in order to really love each other. I hadn't really loved myself in a great many years. This was a totally intimate, truly loving experience for both of us. We talked about it often. We said that we knew most couples could never experience the kind of love we had. We were always thankful for this time and for each other.

On the morning of September 11th, my life and those of others who lost loved ones in the World Trade Center, the Pentagon, and Pennsylvania shook to hell and back. Our entire world felt this shock. Unless we join hands across this earth in peace and strive to eliminate terrorists and evil, our world will never be the same. We have no choice but to go on. We who are victims of war have to deal with this in our own way.

For me, I wondered "Why was I left?" But I know why Rick died. I know this was the way of the warrior—to help others and leave himself last. This was my sweetheart, my soul mate, the love of my life. I knew when Rick called me on his cell phone on that fateful day that I would never see him again. I knew by the words and the quiet firm way he said them: "You made my life." I will take that message with me for the rest of my life.

I wrote this in my diary after the first snowfall arrived: "I can't bear the first snowfall without you. The coziness of the day, the quiet envelopment of the house with a whisper of snow, the extreme silence—nothing will ever be the same. The pond is covered with ice and even the geese and ducks seem different. I long for your words, to touch your hair, rub your neck—nothing will ever be the same. Moments tick away and I try to fill up the day. My energy is depleted—nothing will ever be the same. I miss you so."

I didn't want to live. I couldn't sleep. I didn't care if I ate or drank, took vitamins or exercised. My family wanted desperately to comfort me, but nothing helped. I was completely overwhelmed by the media coverage, the outpouring of people talking about Rick's heroism, his military career, the bombing of the World Trade Center in 1993. Each day and night I tried to remember every conversation Rick and I had had. Of course, I couldn't remember them all, because we talked and talked and talked. One can have such intimacy with special conversations. After September 11th I wanted Rick to come back, even for only a moment, to tell me that he loved me. I wanted us to touch each other, to look, just to reinforce everything that had happened. As I agonized over this each day and night, it finally became apparent to me that Rick had already told me everything he wanted me to know. He had prepared the way for me. I had to pick out the really important pieces: that he would love me forever, that he had never loved anyone as much as he had loved me. He had even told me where to look for him. He as much as told me he would be waiting for me and that we would be together for an even longer time.

And then I found his notebook, and other things he had written, tucked in places all over the house. I wanted to be involved in his book, the book he wanted to write. I wanted to tell people more about his passions: his love of words, singing, dancing, and his love of life. I wanted to honor him, to keep his spirit alive, and to let no one forget what happened on September 11th. Now I knew my mission.

Rick made me feel important; he gave me the confidence I needed be able to do anything. And he gave it to his family, his dearest friends, and his hometown of Hayle. He gave us all a reason to go on—to make the world a better place, to be proud of who we are. He gave us a modern-day hero to learn from and to have forever.

Even though time has passed, I can never get through a day without something reminding me of my sweetheart. Last spring, I drove out to the Raptors and placed a bouquet of flowers at the bottom of his memorial plaque. I chatted with the owners, discussing the spring plantings and what else we would do for his memorial. I came home and I wrote:

> *Six months have passed since that fateful day*
> *When evil took you away.*
> *I asked over and over why couldn't you stay,*
> *But God and the Universe had their way.*
> *A new mission you had to take in the course of the horrible wake.*
> *I honor your life and your death*
> *To the end of time and with each breath.*
> *Together, our love is forever.*

Heroic acts tend
to gather around
soldiers, ~~and~~ perhaps
stirred up on the
~~cries~~ cries for patriotic
duty, and encouraged
by pretty ribbons
and medals. The
plain facts are that
~~the~~ awards of medals
for heroism ~~is~~ are
~~mere~~ political acts,
~~the~~ motions of
general approval
usually requiring ~~serving~~
witnesses. Think for
a moment about

A page from Rescorla's notebook, written during his last weeks.

NOTES AND SOURCES

I WAS AT HOME in Manhattan the morning of September 11, 2001. My parents called me from the Midwest. I turned on the television; I went downstairs and watched from Sixth Avenue, where hundreds of my neighbors had instinctively gathered. Like most Americans, I will never forget where I was that morning, or the sense that my life would never be the same.

That first week I did some reporting on the attack for *The New Yorker,* but the immediacy and the enormity of the event and its aftermath were overwhelming. I wasn't sure I could write about it until several weeks later, when my friend James Cramer, founder of TheStreet.com, mentioned Rick Rescorla to me. I knew immediately that I wanted to tell his story, that of a man who gave his life for his fellow man.

My account first appeared as "The Real Heroes Are Dead" in the February 11, 2002, issue of *The New Yorker.* But my early reporting only hinted at the richness and depth to be found in the fuller story of Rescorla's life and relationships.

I wasn't the only journalist to be attracted to the remarkable story of Rick Rescorla. His heroism has now been mentioned many times, but among the earliest and best articles were those by Michael Grunwald in *The Washington Post,* "A Tower of Courage," October 28, 2001; Lawrence Ingrassia in *The Wall Street Journal,* "The Human Toll—One Month Later, Reflections on the Victims of Sept. 11," October 11, 2001 (reporting by Randall Smith); and Emilie Lounsberry in *The Philadelphia Inquirer,* "Firm Credits a Hero, and Not for First Time," September 15, 2001.

Rescorla was also the subject of "Unsung Hero" a moving, three-part segment on *Dateline NBC,* March 20, 2002, Colleen Halpin, producer; Jane Pauley, correspondent.

This book would not exist without the extraordinary cooperation and enthusiastic participation of Susan Rescorla, Rescorla's widow, and Daniel J. Hill, his close friend. I first met Susan in early November, at the home she shared with Rick. Still shocked and grief stricken, she was nonetheless able to convey the depth of their relationship and a sense of Rick's many dimensions. We met on many subsequent occasions and spoke often by phone. Susan encouraged others to speak and shared Rick's work, including the notebook he was keeping during the last weeks of his life. Susan imposed no conditions on my work. All of the statements and thoughts attributed to her, as well as her conversations with Rick, came from our interviews. Susan reviewed and made corrections to the chapters that relied heavily on her as a source.

Dan Hill was a true friend to Rick and possesses a remarkable memory. He provided a detailed recollection of their lifelong friendship. I first met Dan for dinner in Manhattan and then spent a weekend in February as a guest in his home in St. Augustine, Florida. I visited the mosque he helped build and met many of his Muslim friends, including Nader, with whom he had hoped to assassinate bin Laden. I was impressed by his fluent Arabic. We had numerous long phone conversations, and I also benefitted from a stream of lengthy, well-written letters further responding to my questions. Dan shared his diaries, letters, and a book of Kipling verse given him by Rick. He showed me the lion's tooth necklace Rick gave him and the bowie knife that still bears the bloodstain of the Vietnamese sentry. All thoughts and statements attributed to Dan, as well as many conversations with Rick, are taken from our interviews and contemporaneous written accounts. Dan imposed no conditions on my work. As with Susan, he reviewed and made corrections to those chapters for which he was the major source.

Where possible, I relied on Rescorla's own writings. In other instances, his statements and descriptions of his states of mind come from people who were close to him, primarily Susan and Dan, but also others, as indicated.

All interviews for this book were on the record. Where I have attributed a state of mind to someone, that person either expressed it directly, in an interview or in contemporaneous notes, or revealed it to someone else.

I did not discover any material differences in the accounts of the many people I interviewed for this book. Nonetheless, readers should bear in mind that no one's memory is perfect. Remembered conversations rarely reproduce the exact words used. Still, I was impressed at how careful sources were and how hard they tried to be accurate.

1: PEACHEY AND DRAVOT

Hill's detailed memories of the battles of the Katanga Secession and his time in Northern Rhodesia are drawn from letters, personal diaries, and interviews.

For background on the history of Africa and the struggle for independence in the Congo, as well as the attempted Katanga secession, I relied on John Reader, *Africa: A Biography of the Continent* (New York: Alfred A. Knopf, 1998), especially the chapter "First Dance of Freedom," pages 655–59. The role of the CIA in Katanga is also discussed in Madeleine G. Kalb, *The Congo Cables: The Cold War in Africa— from Eisenhower to Kennedy* (New York: Macmillan, 1982).

A history of the Belgian colonization of the Congo is Adam Hochschild, *King Leopold's Ghost: A Story of Greed, Terror, and Heroism in Colonial Africa* (New York: Houghton Mifflin, 1999).

For background on the British colonization of Northern Rhodesia I relied on Anthony Thomas, *Rhodes* (New York: St. Martin's Press, 1997).

p. 8 There has never been any official recognition that the United States played any military role in the 1956 Hungarian uprising. But a spokesman for the Special Forces acknowledged that the army did engage in top secret logistical support for the Hungarians against the Soviets.

pp. 12–13 The material on Kitwe and the Northern Rhodesia Police is from Tim Wright, *The History of the Northern Rhodesia Police* (London: British Empire and Commonwealth Museum Press, 2001), especially Chapter 16, "Retreat from Federation." The quotation from the report of the Monckton Commission appears on page 319. Other material, especially on life in Kitwe and the colonial police force, is from interviews with Rescorla's colleagues in Northern Rhodesia: Allan Young, assistant inspector, Northern Rhodesia Police, Luanshya, 1960–62; Neil Ashton, assistant inspector, Northern Rhodesia Police, Kitwe, 1960–63; Marcus Ward, assistant inspector, Northern Rhodesia Police, Kitwe, 1961–62. Further background is from John Coates, assistant superintendent, 1962, chairman of the Northern Rhodesia Police Association.

p. 19 For background on Kipling, I relied on David Gilmour, *The Long Recessional: The Imperial Life of Rudyard Kipling* (New York: Farrar, Straus, Giroux, 2002).

pp. 19–20 The quotations from "The Man Who Would Be King" and other works by Rudyard Kipling are from *Collected Works of Rudyard Kipling* (New York and London: Everyman Library, Knopf, 1994).

2: WINDS OF WAR

For descriptions of Rescorla's youth and events in Hayle I relied on interviews with Mervyn Sullivan, Shirley Hubbard, David Gee, Colin Philp, Terry Mungles, Norman Woodcock, Maurice Rothero, Elisabeth Honess, Anthony "Titchy" Bawden, Peter Hosking, and Trevor Lawrence.

pp. 24–25 For historical information on Hayle I relied on interviews with Mervyn Sullivan's brother and local historian Brian Sullivan, and Marlene and Martin Rew, *Images of England: Hayle* (Stroud, U.K.: Tempus Publishing, 1998).

p. 24 For background on American troops in Cornwall, see also Michael Charleston, "How the 29th Prepared in the West to Go off to War," *Western Morning News,* Plymouth, U.K., April 27, 1994.

p. 27 The text of Churchill's address to the Commons on June 6, 1944, "The Invasion of France," is from the Churchill Society, London.

pp. 28–29 The account of the boxing match between Mauriello and Woodcock is from www.secondsout.com, "British Heavyweight Flops," by Joe Queijo.

pp. 29–34 The account of Hill's upbringing is from interviews with and letters of Dan Hill.

pp. 42–43 Rescorla's tenure in Cyprus was the subject of interviews with Adrian Walker, NCO, a national serviceman in the Intelligence Corps at the same time as Rescorla. For background on national servicemen in Cyprus, I relied on a monograph by Adrian Walker, "Labyrinth: Cyprus 1957–1959," Brockley Press, London, 1996, as well as interviews with Lt. Col. John Woolmore, British Army, Intelligence Corps; Alan Edwards, British Army, Intelligence Corps, archivist; and Terry Mungles, NCO, British Military Police, Cyprus.

3: HEART OF A LION

p. 50 The quotation from "If" comes from *Kipling's Ballads,* a collection of poems by Rudyard Kipling presented to Hill from Rescorla. The volume is undated, published by Hurst & Co.

4: AMERICAN DREAM

The account of Susan's early years is from interviews with Susan Rescorla and Susan's friends Anne Robinson and Marilyn Rollins.

5: HARD CORPS

pp. 69–70 Information on Rescorla's arrival in America is from interviews with Kim and Trevor Rescorla, and Dan Hill.

p. 71 Kipling, "If," as above.

pp. 74–77 The account of Rescorla's time at Fort Benning is from interviews with Sam Fantino, Patrick "Jim" Kelly, and Dan Hill.

p. 77 The quotation is from Stanley Karnow, *Vietnam: A History* (New York: Viking Press, 1983, p. 426).

6: IN THE VALLEY OF DEATH

Rescorla described his experiences in Vietnam many times, in great detail, to Dan Hill. Additional details of Rescorla's experiences at An Khe and in the battles of X-ray and Albany are drawn from interviews with his surviving colleagues: Sergeant Pete Thompson, Second Lieutenant Dennis Deal, radio operator Sam Fantino, First Lieutenant Bud Alley, medic Bill Shucart, and medic Joe Holloway.

The battles of X-ray and Albany are the subject of Lieutenant General Harold G. Moore (Ret.) and Joseph L. Galloway, *We Were Soldiers Once . . . and Young* (New York: Harper Perennial, 1992). Rescorla submitted a nineteen-page account of his experiences to the authors in late 1991 and was interviewed by them. Therefore, I have relied on their account for many of Rescorla's statements and thoughts, as noted below.

The battle of Albany is also covered in detail in Larry Gwin, *Baptism: A Vietnam Memoir* (New York: Ballantine, 1999). Rescorla's statements appearing in *Baptism* are indicated below.

p. 79 Reference to the journey to Vietnam is from *We Were Soldiers,* p. 29.

pp. 79–80 The description of the ocean crossing is from interviews with Dennis Deal, David Patricelli, and Patrick "Jim" Kelly.

pp. 82–83 The description of building the camp is from *We Were Soldiers,* p. 30, as well as from an interview with Bill Shucart.

pp. 86–87 Gen. Kinnard's speech is quoted in *Baptism,* p. 108, and also from an interview with Larry Gwin.

p. 87 The account of the platoon's journey to Pleiku is in *We Were Soldiers,* p. 49.

p. 88 The description of the "hot LZ" is in *We Were Soldiers,* p. 148.

p. 90 Rescorla's thoughts on the death of Burlile are as reflected in a letter he wrote to Burlile's sister, Delores Call, on July 4, 1994.

pp. 92–95 The night account is from *We Were Soldiers,* p. 163, and also from interviews with Fantino, Thompson, and Deal.

p. 100 "No stragglers, sir" is from *We Were Soldiers,* p. 313.

p. 101 The jump from the helicopter is from an interview with Sam Fantino, cf. also *We Were Soldiers*, p. 326.

p. 101 An account of Rescorla's arrival is in *Baptism*, p. 151.

p. 105 The account of Mullarkey is in *Baptism*, pp. 154–55.

p. 105 Jack P. Smith's comments are from *We Were Soldiers*, p. 337.

p. 107 The discovery of the bugle is described in *We Were Soldiers*, p. 338.

p. 108 The quotation by an unidentified soldier, "The Little Big Horn," is from *We Were Soldiers*, p. 365.

p. 109 Kinnard's quotation is from *We Were Soldiers*, p. 402.

7: CHARGE OF THE LIGHT BRIGADE

p. 114 The account of Hill's arrival in Vietnam and the quotations on this and the following pages are from Dan Hill's handwritten diary of his time in Vietnam.

pp. 119–23 The accounts of the recon platoon are from interviews with Dennis Deal and Larry Gwin.

pp. 120–21 The description of the recon platoon is from *Baptism* (p. 191); Gwin's impressions of Rescorla are in *Baptism*, p. 197.

p. 126 Rescorla's reference to the "rosy red hue" is from John Milton, *Paradise Lost*, Book viii, line 618: "With a smile that glow'd Celestial / rosy red, love's proper hue."

pp. 128–29 The account of "beer walking" is from interviews with Larry Gwin and Jim Kelly. It is also described in detail in *Baptism*, pp. 217–19. Trevor Rescorla also demonstrated the technique, as taught by his father, in the Cornish Arms in March 2002.

pp. 129–33 The battle of Trung Luong is the subject of S. L. A. Marshall, *The Fields of Bamboo* (New York: Dial Press, 1971). Dan Hill's role is described on pages 92–93, 100–101, and 106.

p. 130 Hill's encounter with Captain Furgeson is described in *Fields of Bamboo*, pp. 92–93, and based on interviews with Dan Hill.

8: HOME FRONT

The accounts of Susan's divorce and second marriage are drawn from interviews with Susan Rescorla.

9: NOT TO REASON WHY

pp. 141–47 The accounts of the sentry and the dinner with North Vietnamese officers are from interviews with Dan Hill.

p. 141 Rescorla's citation for the Silver Star reads: "Second Lieutenant Rescorla distinguished himself by exceptionally valorous actions from 15 November 1965 to 17 November 1965. . . . Rescorla exposed himself to the heavy volume of Viet Cong automatic weapons fire while moving from foxhole to foxhole to personally direct the retaliatory fire of his platoon and urge them to battle. . . . On two occasions Second Lieutenant Rescorla with complete disregard for his personal safety assaulted well-fortified Viet Cong machine-gun positions and neutralized them with hand grenades. He was most instrumental in the defense of the landing zone and the defeat of the Viet Cong battalion."

p. 143 The reference to Rescorla's degree is from an interview with Bill Shucart.

p. 143 The Tet Offensive is described in *Vietnam*, p. 543.

pp. 148–51 The account of Rescorla at the University of Oklahoma is from interviews with Fred McBee and Dan Hill.

p. 149 The quotation is from Raymond Chandler, *The Simple Art of Murder* (New York: Vintage Books, 1988).

pp. 156–57 Dan Hill and others in similar circumstances sued the army for wrongful discharge, and prevailed on the grounds that the review boards that denied them promotion were improperly constituted. Hill was awarded back pay and retirement benefits, but was not reinstated in the army. The decisions in the case, *Major Joe L. Adams et al.* vs *United States,* are reported at 220 Ct. Cl. 285 (1979) and 226 Ct. Cl. 720 (1980).

p. 157 The description of the fall of Saigon is from *Vietnam,* pp. 667–68.

p. 162 Rescorla's role in the investigation of Continental Bank is from interviews with Joe Barrett, his deputy.

pp. 162–63 Information on the collapse of Penn Square is from Mark Singer, *Funny Money* (New York: Dell, 1986, p. 68). Penn Square is also the subject of Phillip L. Zweig, *Belly Up: The Collapse of the Penn Square Bank* (New York: Crown, 1985).

p. 163 Lytle's conviction and sentencing were reported in "An Oklahoma Bank That Wasn't OK," *The Wall Street Journal*, December 4, 1989.

pp. 166–70 The account of Hill's experiences with the Mujahedeen in Afghanistan is from interviews with Hill and Nader Zori. Other participants knew Hill only by his Muslim name, Abdullah.

10: TOWERS IN THE SKY

pp. 171–72 The description of the architecture and engineering of the World Trade Center is from John Seabrook, "The Tower Builder," *The New Yorker*, November 19, 2001.

p. 177 The quotations from the Port Authority reports are from Peter Caram, *The 1993 World Trade Center Bombing: Foresight and Warning* (London: Janus Publishing Co., 2001, pp. 97 and 103). Asked to comment on this and other references to the Port Authority, its reaction to Recorla's concerns, and its response to the 1993 bombing, a spokesman for the Port Authority said that security at the World Trade Center "took into account all known threats at that time" and "was better than in most office buildings in New York."

p. 180 The account of the visit to Chicago is from Sam Fantino.

pp. 181–82 The text quoted is from a letter to Delores Call from Rick Rescorla, July 4, 1994.

11: THE TARGET

p. 185 The account of the death of his son is from Dan Hill.

pp. 189–90 Accounts of the bombing of February 26, 1993, are from Barbara Williams, George Golub, and Kathy Comerford. Bill Randolph described Wesley Mercer's role on that day.

p. 193 The reference to "lofty towers" is from Chapter IV of the Koran, "The Women." The translation is by M. H. Shakir from the Holy Qur'an published by Tahrioke Tarsile Qur'an Inc.

p. 198 Morgan Stanley's lawsuits against the Port Authority were discussed in interviews with Blair Fensterstock and Steven Herzog, attorneys for the class action plaintiffs and Morgan Stanley, respectively.

p. 198 The confidential memo is a twenty-page memorandum from Christine A. Edwards to Anthony Basile et al., dated October 27, 1993.

p. 200 Background on Lindsay Herkness is from interviews with Frank "Ted" Hamilton, Doug Braff, Isabel Carden, Bunny Whiteley, and Twig Mowatt, "Foundation Member Killed in World Trade Center Attack," *Life Extension,* January 2002.

p. 201 Rescorla's thoughts on the future of war and the nature of terrorism are taken from Robert Edwards's documentary film, *The Voice of the Prophet,* 1998.

p. 202 The friendship of Ernest Hemingway and Gary Cooper made a great impression on Rescorla and Hill. When Cooper and Hemingway met for the first time in 1940, a mutual friend described their meeting: "They were like strange schoolboys sizing each other up. . . . then they were like old buddies from that moment on." The account is from John Mulholland, "Cooper & Hemingway: A 20-Year Friendship," *The Idaho Press,* May 13, 2000.

12: SOUL MATES

The romance of Rick and Susan was the subject of interviews with Susan Rescorla, Dan Hill, Fred McBee, Sam Fantino, Anne Robinson, and Ihab Dana.

p. 214 The account of the visit to the holistic practioner is from an interview with Brad Snyder.

p. 219 The quotation is from the song "The Dance," written by Anthony M. Arata, EMI April Music Inc., ASCAP 340301613.

pp. 223–25 The account of the visit to Cornwall is from interviews with Mervyn and Jan Sullivan and John Daniels.

pp. 225–26 The account of Rescorla's visit to Hayle is based on interviews with Mervyn Sullivan.

13: WE WERE SOLDIERS

pp. 228–29 The account of Hill's heart attack is from Dan Hill and Patricia Hill.

pp. 230–31 The account of the plot to kill bin Laden is from interviews with Dan Hill and Nader Zori. Ellen and Donald J. Glasser did not return numerous phone calls to the Jacksonville office of the FBI, though the office did confirm they work there. Leo Morris, the agent with whom Hill first discussed the plan, has retired and couldn't be located. The National Press Office of the FBI in Washington declined to comment.

p. 234–35 The account of the reunion at OCS is from interviews with Dan Hill and Jim Kelly.

p. 235 The poem by Rescorla and an account of his meeting with Bateman appear in an article by Bateman, "Memorial to Rescorla," *The Veteran's Observer,* May 2002.

p. 236 References to the script are from Randall Wallace, *We Were Soldiers: The Screenplay* (Los Angeles: Wheelhouse Books, 2002). The reference to a "Welsh" platoon leader that upset Rescorla doesn't appear in the final script; the bugle was discovered by another character.

p. 237 E-mails quoted were provided by Jim Kelly and Bill Shucart.

p. 242 The account of the ceremony at OCS is from interviews with Dan Hill and Jim Kelly. A program of the induction ceremony was provided by the public affairs office at Fort Benning.

14: A DAY TO BE PROUD

Accounts of their experiences in the World Trade Center on September 11 were provided by John Olson, a regional director of sales at Morgan Stanley; Barbara Williams, security specialist; Kathy Comerford, event planner; Macie Stratton, personal assistant to Lindsay Herkness; Doug Brown, associate director of sales; and George Golub, comptroller of corporate services. Doug Braff, a broker and friend of Herkness; Frank "Ted" Hamilton, an investment banker and friend of Herkness. Bill Randolph, Mercer's companion, also provided accounts of their experiences that day.

15: THE COURAGE TO HEAL

p. 269 The text of the letter to Glasser is from Dan Hill. Her visit and interview were described by Nader Zori.

pp. 270–71 The text of Purcell's speech at the St. Patrick's Memorial is from a tape recording provided by Morgan Stanley.

pp. 275–78 Quotations from Rescorla's notebook are taken directly from the notebook, with minor punctuation and spelling corrections.

pp. 280–81 The poem by David Prowse was published in the *Western Morning News,* Cornwall, October 8, 2001.

p. 283 The quotation is from the King James version of the Bible, Matthew, 8:260.

p. 284 The quotations from Dan Hill's letter were contained in a letter from Hill to the author.

ACKNOWLEDGMENTS

A S A JOURNALIST AND WRITER, it has been an honor and privilege for me to work on a story of such breadth, culminating in what will surely rank as one of the defining events of my lifetime. I am grateful to everyone who made this possible, and, above all, to the many people who lived this story, including those who sacrificed their lives.

Damian Fowler served as my research assistant and rendered dedicated and invaluable service. He traveled to Rescorla's boyhood home of Hayle, where his Yorkshire accent proved no obstacle in penetrating the famous Cornish reserve. His knowledge of British educational and military institutions, not to mention the contents of the Harvard Classics, no doubt saved me from many slips. He also tracked down in London the remarkable photograph of the lion in Northern Rhodesia that appears before Chapter 3. I am proud of his work and will miss working together.

My assistant, Julie Allen, stepped in on countless occasions to help keep this project moving forward, always with tact and good cheer.

Alice Mayhew, my longtime editor at Simon & Schuster, guided this project from its inception and was, as always, a brilliant critic and enthusiastic supporter. Thanks also to Carolyn Reidy, president of the Adult Publishing Group, and David Rosenthal, Simon & Schuster's publisher; to Roger Labrie and Jonathan Jao; to Emily Remes, who rendered legal advice; to Victoria Meyer, executive director of publicity; and to Aileen Boyle.

Amanda Urban, my agent, and Ron Bernstein, her colleague at International Creative Management, strongly encouraged me to pursue this story and worked tenaciously to make it possible.

At *The New Yorker,* John Bennet encouraged me to persist in this story and to reach in new directions. I can never repay him for all he has taught me. David Remnick, editor of *The New Yorker,* is a writer's dream of an editor in chief, perhaps because he's such a fine writer himself. He published my story on Rescorla and provided encouragement at just the right moments. Thanks also to Dorothy Wickenden, Lauren Porcaro, and Jesse Lichtenstein.

I am grateful to *SmartMoney* magazine and the Hearst magazines division for providing a professional home for this project. Editor Pete Finch offered encouragement and suggestions. Kate Sullivan generously provided photo research. Computer expert Mark Dunmire grappled with innumerable technical problems. My good friend Steve Swartz, executive vice president, Hearst Newspapers, read the manuscript and offered valuable suggestions.

Writing and reporting this story over such a short time span was unusually intense and draining emotionally. I am grateful to my friend and colleague Marie Brenner, who came to my rescue many times, and to my students at Columbia School of Journalism for their understanding.

At such times the support and understanding of often-neglected friends and family is even more important. Thanks to my remarkable parents, Ben and Mary Jane Stewart; my brother Michael; his wife, Anna; and my nephew, James Aidan Stewart, who was born during this project; my sister Jane Holden; her husband, John, and my nieces and nephew Lindsey, Laura, Jack, and Maggie. And I am grateful for the special young people in my life: Kate McNamara, Langley Grace Wallace, and James Swartz.

Among my friends, a special thanks to Jane Berentson, Jeannine Burky, Rob Coburn, James Cramer, Erica Feidner, Edward Flanagan, Jim Gauer, Joel Goldsmith, David Kratz, Monica Langley, Arthur Lubow, Bari Mort, Dave Nogaki, Gene Stone, Roger Wallace, Neil Westreich, and Daphne and Richard Weil.

I have saved the most important for last: Benjamin Weil, who provided both emotional and editorial support at every critical juncture. I will always be grateful, since this book would not exist without him.

INDEX

NOTE: Italicized page numbers refer to picture captions.

Bon Song (Vietnam), 120–22

"Bravery" (Rescorla notebook), 277

Bravo Company: as best, 77, 78; Diduryk as commander of, 84; at Fort Benning, 77–78; as getting dangerous missions, 84–86; as "Hard Corps," 78, 84, 100, 108, 110, 120; morale of, 84, 92, 108; Rescorla as platoon leader of, 77–78; Rescorla leaves, 119–20; Rescorla's training of, 77–78; sea journey to Vietnam of, 79–82; in Vietnam, 82–111. *See also specific person or battle*

British: Hill's views about, 52

British Army: Rescorla in, 14, 39–40, 42–43, 80, 120; in Rhodesia, 52–53; social class in, 42–43. *See also* Cyprus

British Colonial Police Force. *See* Northern Rhodesia Police Force

British Post Office: Rescorla as apprentice in, 39

British South Africa Company, 12

Brown, Eddie, 127

Brown, Tom, 99, 100

Buchanan, Lorna, 35

Buddhism, 166, 197, 216, 218, 243

Buddy (Rescorla golden retriever), 1, 3, 196, 197, 205, 206, 208, 210–11, 215, 218, 249, 250

bugle: Rescorla discovers French, 107, 108, 109, 110, 236

Burlile, Delores, 84, 111, 181–82

Burlile, Tom: childhood and youth of, 84; death of, 90–91, 98, 111; as medic in Vietnam, 83, 85, 88, 89; Rescorla recounts death of, 181–82; Rescorla's memories of, 110, 127, 178, 179, 182; and Rescorla's wound, 85; Vietnam views of, 84

Camp Alpha base (Vietnam), 114

Camp Holloway (Vietnam), 87, 99–100, 108–10

Capitol building (Washington, D.C.): Hill's plan for attack on, 153

Caprio, Terry, 64, 197

Carley, John, 152

Carnehan, Peachey (fictional character), 19–21, 53, 161, 166, 204

Central Highlands (Vietnam), 82–111, *112. See also specific battle*

Central Intelligence Agency (CIA), 6, 11, 13, 16, 167, 245

Chandler, Raymond, 149

"The Charge of the Light Brigade" (Tennyson), 133

Charles (prince of Wales), 281

Charlie Company: in Vietnam, 89, 91–92, 103–4, 105–6

Chicago, Illinois: Hill family in, 8, 24, 188; Rescorla and Susan visit Fantino in, 214; Rescorla works in, 158–63

Chu Pong massif, 95, 99, 103

Churchill, Winston, 27, 50

Comerford, Kathy, 198–99, 201, 251–52, 256–58, 261, 263–64, 266–67, 272

communism: Rescorla and Hill's views about, 22, 41, 50, 53

Congo, 6, 8–10, 167

Conrad, Joseph, 36

Constitution, U.S.: Hill and Rescorla's views about, 19, 22, 126, 155

construction business: of Hill, 154, 157, 159, 163

Continental Illinois National Bank and Trust Company: Rescorla works for, 158–63

Cooper, Gary, 202

ABOUT THE AUTHOR

JAMES B. STEWART is the author of the bestselling *Blind Eye, Blood Sport,* and the blockbuster *Den of Thieves.* Former Page One editor of *The Wall Street Journal,* Stewart won a Pulitzer Prize in 1988 for his reporting on the stock market crash and insider trading. He is a regular contributor to *The New Yorker* and *Smart-Money.* He lives in New York.